RAGBAG
OF LEGAL QUOTATIONS

compiled by

M. FRANCES MCNAMARA

Member of the New York Bar
Librarian, New York State Department of Law

The Lawbook Exchange, Ltd.
New York, NY
1992

Library of Congress Catalogue Card Number 92-074141
ISBN 0-9630106-3-8

**Printed in the United States of America
on Acid-Free Paper**

The Lawbook Exchange, Ltd.
New York, NY
1992

RAGBAG

OF LEGAL QUOTATIONS

compiled by

M. Frances McNamara

Member of the New York Bar

Librarian, New York State Department of Law

1960

Matthew Bender & Company, Incorporated

Albany 1,
New York

205 East 42nd Street
New York 17, New York

Printed in U. S. A.

SUBJECT HEADINGS

Subject Headings

Subject Headings

Acknowledgments

Grateful acknowledgment is made to the publishers, authors and authors' representatives for permission to use selections from the publications as indicated below.

Appleton-Century-Crofts, Inc.
in respect to: Frederick Trevor Hill, *Lincoln, the Lawyer,* 1906.

Butterworths, Lond.
in respect to: *All England Law Reports* and *Law Times Reports.*

Callaghan & Co.
in respect to: Rudolph von Jhering, *Struggle for Law,* 2nd ed. (trans. Lalor) 1915.

Cambridge University Press
in respect to: Lord Macmillan, *Law and Other Things,* 1937, and Frederic Wm. Maitland, *Collected Papers* (ed. by H. A. L. Fisher) 1911.

Cassell & Co., Ltd.
in respect to: Frederick E. S. Birkenhead, *Fourteen English Judges* [1926].

Henry Cecil
in respect to: Henry Cecil, *Friends at Court,* published by Michael Joseph Ltd., 1956.

Columbia University Press
in respect to: Charles Evans Hughes, *Supreme Court of the United States,* 1928; Frederick Pollock, *Genius of the Common Law,* 1912; and Woodrow Wilson, *Constitutional Government in the United States,* 1908.

Coward-McCann, Inc.
In respect to: Jerome Frank, *Law and the Modern Mind,* 1949.

Erle Stanley Gardner
in respect to: A. A. Fair (pseud.) *Some Women Won't Wait.*

K. Frederick Gross
in respect to: Fred L. Gross, *What is the Verdict?* Macmillan Co., 1944.

Harcourt, Brace & Co.
in respect to excerpts from *Law and Literature and Other Essays* by Benjamin Cardozo, copyright, 1931 by Harcourt, Brace and Company, Inc. and reprinted with their permission and from *Collected Legal Papers* by Oliver Wendell Holmes, copyright, 1920, by Harcourt, Brace and Company, Inc.

Harper & Brothers
in respect to: Finley Peter Dunne, *Dissertations by Mr. Dooley,* 1906, and Dorothy L. Sayers, *Unnatural Death,* 1927.

Harvard University Press, The President and Fellows of Harvard College
in respect to: Eugen Ehrlich, *Fundamental Principles of the Sociology of Law,* c. 1936; Felix Frankfurter, *Mr. Justict Holmes and the Supreme Court,* c. 1938; *Holmes-Laski Letters,* ed. by Mark DeWolfe Howe, c. 1953, and *Holmes-Pollock Letters,* ed. by Mark DeWolf Howe, c. 1941.

Acknowledgments

Sir Alan Herbert, The Proprietors of Punch and Methuen & Co. Ltd.
in respect to: A. P. Herbert, *Uncommon Law,* 1935.

B. Herder Book Co.
in respect to: Heinrich Rommen, *Natural Law* (trans. Hanley) 1947.

Mrs. Reginald Hine
in respect to: Reginald L. Hine, *Confessions of an Un-Common Attorney,* Macmillan Co., 1945.

Houghton Mifflin Co.
in respect to: Albert J. Beveridge, *Life of John Marshall,* 4v., 1916-19.

Hutchinson & Co., Ltd.
in respect to: Lord Hewart, *Not Without Prejudice.*

Incorporated Council of Law Reporting for England and Wales
in respect to: *The Law Reports*

Alfred A. Knopf, Inc.
in respect to: Curtis Bok, *I Too, Nicodemus,* 1946; Learned Hand, *Spirit of Liberty,* ed. by Irving Dilliard, 1952, and Robert H. Jackson, *Struggle for Judicial Supremacy,* 1941.

Little, Brown & Co.
in respect to: Oliver Wendell Holmes, *Speeches,* 1913, and Charles Warren, *Supreme Court in United States History,* 3v., 1922.

Little, Brown & Co. and Atlantic Monthly Press
in respect to: Catherine Drinker Bowen, *Yankee From Olympus,* 1944.

Longmans, Green & Co., Inc.
in respect to: George M. Trevelyan, *Lord Grey of the Reform Bill,* 1920.

Macmillan Co., New York
in respect to: John Chipman Gray, *Nature and Sources of the Law,* 2nd ed., 1921; Edward Marjoribanks, *For the Defence,* 1929, and Merlo J. Pusey, *Charles Evans Hughes,* 1952.

Macmillan & Co., Ltd. and St. Martin's Press
in respect to: Lord Macmillan, *A Man of Law's Tale,* 1952.

Hon. Miles F. McDonald, in respect to his *Prayer for Lawyers.*

New York University Press
in respect to: Arthur T. Vanderbilt, *Cases and Other Materials on Modern Procedure,* 1952.

Princeton University Press
in respect to: Piero Calamandrei, *Eulogy of Judges* (trans. Adams and Phillips) 1942; Alpheus T. Mason, *Brandeis, Lawyer and Judge in Modern State,* 1933, and Jerome Frank, *Courts on Trial,* 1949.

Charles Scribner's Sons
in respect to: Finley Peter Dunne, *Mr. Dooley on Making a Will,* 1919; Finley Peter Dunne, *Mr. Dooley Says,* 1910; John Galsworthy, *In Chancery,* 1920, and John Galsworthy, *Justice* and *Windows* from *Plays,* 1929.

William Seagle
in respect to: William Seagle, *Quest for Law,* Knopf, 1941.

Session Cases Committee of the Faculty of Advocates, Scotland
in respect to: *Session Cases.*

Sheed & Ward, Inc., New York
in respect to: G. K. Chesterton, *Tremendous Trifles*, c. 1909.

Simon & Schuster, Inc.
in respect to: Charles P. Curtis, *A Commonplace Book*, 1957.

Stevens & Sons, Ltd.
in respect to: JPC, *Poetic Justice*, 1947.

University of Kansas Press
in respect to: Lord Evershed, *Practical and Academic Characteristics of English Law*, 1956.

University of North Carolina Press
in respect to: Felix Frankfurter, *The Commerce Clause Under Marshall, Taney and Waite*, 1937.

Viking Press Inc.
in respect to: Louis D. Brandeis, *Curse of Bigness*, ed. by Osmond K. Fraenkel, 1934, and Alpheus T. Mason, *Brandeis, A Free Man's Life*, 1946.

Yale University Press
in respect to Benjamin N. Cardozo, *Growth of the Law*, 1924; Benjamin N. Cardozo, *Nature of the Judicial Process*, 1921, and Felix Frankfurter, ed., *Mr. Justice Brandeis*, 1932.

Credit is also given for brief quotations from the following publications:

John F. Blair, Winston-Salem
in respect to: George W. Dalzell, *Benefit of Clergy in America*, 1955.

Boston Book Co.
in respect to: James Bradley Thayer, *Legal Essays*, 1908; Eugen Ehrlich, *Freedom of Decision* in Science of Legal Method, v. 9 Modern Legal Philosophy Series (trans. Bruncken), and Rudolph von Jhering, *Law as a Means to an End* (trans. Husik) 1913.

Cambridge University Press
in respect to: Roscoe Pound, *Interpretations of Legal History*, 1923,

Doubleday & Co., Inc.
in respect to: H. G. Wells, *Work, Wealth and Happiness of Mankind*, 1931.

Houghton Mifflin Co.
in respect to: John Buchan, *Homilies and Recreations*, 1926.

I also wish to express my appreciation of the facilities of the New York State Library and the courtesies extended to me by the entire staff. I am the more particularly indebted to Mr. Ernest Breuer, the Law Librarian, and his staff.

RAGBAG
OF LEGAL QUOTATIONS

"When I began, the law presented itself as a ragbag of details."

OLIVER WENDELL HOLMES

Accord and Satisfaction

And it was resolved by the whole court, that payment of a lesser sum on the day in satisfaction of a greater, cannot be any satisfaction for the whole, because it appears to the judges that by no possibility a lesser sum can be a satisfaction to the plaintiff for a greater sum: but the gift of a horse, hawk, or robe, etc. in satisfaction is good. For it shall be intended that a horse, hawk or robe, etc., might be more beneficial to the plaintiff than the money, in respect of some circumstance, or otherwise the plaintiff would not have accepted of it in satisfaction.

COKE, *Pinnel's Case* (1602) 5 Rep. 117 a.

A creditor might accept anything in satisfaction of his debt except a less amount of money. He might take a horse, or a canary, or a tomtit if he chose, and that was accord and satisfaction; but, by a most extraordinary peculiarity of the English Common Law, he could not take 19s. 6d. in the pound; that was *nudum pactum*. . . . That was one of the mysteries of English Common Law.

JESSEL, M.R., *Couldery v. Bartrum* (1881) 19 Ch. D. 394, 399.

Accuracy

There is an accuracy that defeats itself by the over-emphasis of details. . . . The sentence may be so overloaded with all its possible qualifications that it will tumble down of its own weight.

BENJAMIN N. CARDOZO, *Law and Literature* 7 (1931).

Delusive exactness is a source of fallacy throughout the law.

HOLMES, J., *Truax v. Corrigan,* 257 U.S. 312, 342 (1921).

Achievement

One cannot be pulled up a great height. Only a short distance can you be lifted by your arms. But by climbing with your feet and stepping on the solid ground below, you can climb mountains.

LOUIS D. BRANDEIS, *Notebook, November 12, 1880.*
See, MASON, *Brandeis, — A Free Man's Life 61* (1946).

Actions

The forms of actions we have buried, but they still rule us from their graves.

FREDERIC WM. MAITLAND, *Forms of Actions at Common Law,* Lecture 1 (1909).

I am a great friend to the action for money had and received; and therefore I am not for stretching, lest I should endanger it.

LORD MANSFIELD, C.J., *Weston v. Downes* (1778) 1 Doug. 23, 24.

Administration of Justice

If I were to ask you, gentlemen of the jury, what is the choicest fruit that grows upon the tree of English liberty, you would answer, security under the law. If I were to ask the whole people of England, the return they looked for at the hands of government, for the burdens under which they bend to support it, I should still be answered, security under the law; or, in other words, an impartial administration of justice.

THOMAS ERSKINE, arguendo, *Trial of Thomas Paine* (1792) 22 How. St. Tr. 358, 417.

The sound of their voices arose, together with a scent as of neglected wells, which, mingling with the odour of the galleries, combind to form the savour, like nothing but the emanation of a refined cheese, so indissolubly connected with the administration of British justice.

JOHN GALSWORTHY, *Man of Property*, ch. 28.

Important as it was that people should get justice, it was even more important that they should be made to feel and see that they were getting it.

FARRER HERSCHELL, retort at Bar when Sir George Jessel attempted to cut him short in an argument. See, 2 Atlay, *Victorian Chancellors* 460 (1908).

It . . . is of fundamental importance that justice should not only be done, but should manifestly and undoubtedly be seen to be done.

LORD HEWART, C.J., *R. v. Sussex Justices, ex p. McCarthy* [1924] 1 K.B. 256, 259.

The most important and most constant cause of dissatisfaction with all law at all times is to be found in the necessarily mechanical operation of legal rules. This is one of the penalties of uniformity. Legal history shows an oscillation between wide judicial discretion on the one hand and strict confinement of the magistrate by minute and detailed rules upon the other hand. . . . The law has always ended in a compromise, in a middle course between wide discretion and over-minute legislation. In reaching this middle ground, some sacrifice of flexibility of application to particular cases is inevitable. In consequence, the adjustment of the relations of man and man according to these rules will of necessity appear more or less arbitrary and more or less in conflict with the ethical notions of individuals.

ROSCOE POUND, *The Causes of Popular Dissatisfaction with the Administration of Justice*, 29 A.B.A.R. 395, 397 (1906).

The sporting theory of justice, the "instinct of giving the game fair play," as Professor Wigmore[1] has put it, is so rooted in the profession in America that most of us take it for a fundamental legal tenet. But it is probably only a survival of the days when a lawsuit was a fight between two clans in which change of venue had been taken to the forum. So far from being a fundamental fact of jurisprudence, it is peculiar to Anglo-American law.

ROSCOE POUND. *The Causes of Popular Dissatisfaction with the Administration of Justice*, 29 A.B.A.R. 395, 404 (1906).

The fundamental premise of the federal rules is that a trial is an orderly search for the truth in the interest of justice rather than a contest between two gladiators with surprise and technicalities as their chief weapons, an outmoded point of view that unfortunately still lingers on in all too many states.

ARTHUR T. VANDERBILT, *Cases and Materials on Modern Procedure* 10 (1952).

Admissions

No admission of the party . . . can make that legal which is in its nature illegal.

ASHHURST, J., *Atherfold v. Beard* (1788) 2 T. R. 610, 615.

Admissions are mostly made by those who do not know their importance.

LORD DARLING, *Scintillae Juris: Of Witnesses.*

---

[1] 1 Wigmore, *Evidence* 127 (1904). See also, 20 J. Am. Jud. Soc. 176 (1937) where Wigmore refers to this classic speech of Pound as "The spark that kindled the white flame of progress."

Advertising

Johnson: Sir, it is wrong to stir up law-suits; but when once it is certain that a law-suit is to go on, there is nothing wrong in a lawyer's endeavoring that he shall have the benefit rather than another.

Boswell: You would not solicit employment, Sir, if you were a lawyer?

Johnson: No, Sir, but not because I should think it wrong, but because I should disdain it. However, I would not have a lawyer to be wanting to himself in using fair means. I would have him to inject a little hint now and then to prevent his being overlooked.

SAMUEL JOHNSON. Boswell, *Life of Johnson*: *1776.*

To get his name on the title page of a useful law book has always been recognized as one of the few legitimate methods of publicity open to an aspiring member of the Bar.

LORD MACMILLAN, *Man of Law's Tale* 55 (1952).

Advice

The greatest trust between man and man is the trust of giving counsel: for in other confidences men commit the parts of life, their lands, their goods, their children, their credit, some particular affair; but to such as they make their counsellors they commit the whole; by how much more they are obliged to all faith and integrity.

BACON, *Essays*: *Of Counsel.*

Your law may be perfect, your ability to apply it great, and yet you cannot be a successful adviser unless your advice is followed; it will not be followed unless you can satisfy your clients, unless you impress them with your superior knowledge, and that you cannot do unless you know their affairs better than they do because you see them from a fullness of knowledge. The ability to impress them grows with your own success in advising others, with the confidence which you yourself feel in your powers. That confidence can never come from books; it is gained by human intercourse.

LOUIS D. BRANDEIS, Letter to William H. Dunbar, 1893. Mason, *Brandeis, A Free Man's Life* 80 (1946).

The fact that a lawyer advised such foolish conduct, does not relieve it of its foolishness.

EMERY, J., *Hanscom v. Marston,* 82 Me. 288, 298 (1890).

When lawyers take, what they would give
And doctors give what they would take.

O. W. HOLMES, SR., *Latter-Day Warnings.*

A lawyer's advice is his stock in trade.

ABRAHAM LINCOLN—attributed to.

Go not for every grief to the physician, nor for every quarrel to the lawyer, nor for every thirst to the pot.

Proverb. HERBERT, *Jacula Prudentum (1651).*

Advocacy

He had a habit of refusing to appear in civil actions where he was not persuaded of the justice of the cause. This is not to be commended. The Bar as a profession offers its services to all litigants. Counsel supports his client's case within the limits prescribed by personal and professional honour. He is not the judge to decide the merits; his function is to present his client's case. If counsel usurps the duties of the judge, then two results follow. First, men are deprived of that legal assistance to which they are entitled. Secondly, the fact that counsel is known only to accept cases in which he personally believes may work injustice to those whom he refuses. . . . And so Hale (Sir Matthew) sometimes found that he had caused injustice in several instances where he had made up his mind on the merits and found afterwards that he had rejected the case on insufficient grounds.

LORD BIRKENHEAD, *Fourteen English Judges* 61 (1926).

A man's rights are to be determined by the Court, not by his attorney or counsel. It is for want of remembering this that foolish people object to lawyers that they will advocate a case against their own opinions. A client is entitled to say to his counsel, I want your advocacy, not your judgment; I prefer that of the Court.

BRAMWELL, B., *Johnson v. Emerson* (1871) L.R. 6 Ex. 329, 367.

An advocate, by the sacred duty which he owes his client, knows, in the discharge of that office, but one person in the world, that client and none other. To save that client by all expedient means— to protect that client at all hazards and costs to all others, and among others to himself,—is the highest and most unquestioned of his duties; and he must not regard the alarm, the suffering, the torment, the destruction which he may bring upon any other. Nay, separating even the duties of a patriot from those of an advocate, and casting them, if need be, to the wind, he must go on reckless of the consequences, if his fate it should unhappily be, to involve his country in confusion for his client's protection.[1]

HENRY BROUGHAM, arguendo, *Trial of Queen Caroline,* 1820.

It is a great mistake to consider the speeches we deliver before the courts as a faithful depository of our personal opinions. All these speeches emanate from the cause and the circumstances rather than the man and the orator, for if the cause could speak for itself there

[1] This speech has been severely criticized. Brougham in 1859 wrote to Forsyth that his statement was anything but a well considered opinion on the duties of an advocate. It was a "menace" directed to George IV to stop him from pressing the bill of divorcement beyond a certain point. It was a threat to impeach the King's own title by proving that he had forfeited the crown by marrying while heir apparent, a Roman Catholic, Mrs. Fitzherbert. See, Forsyth, *History of a Lawyer* 380 (1875).

"I never did commit adultery but once, and I have repented it ever since. It was with the husband of Mrs. Fitzherbert." Queen Caroline, in Grey family correspondence. See, Trevelyan, *Lord Grey of the Reform Bill* 191 (1920).

would be no need of counsel. We are therefore called upon not to utter our own maxims, but to bring out everything of significance that the cause can furnish.

CICERO, *Pro Cluentio,* L.

My noble and learned friend, Lord Brougham, whose words are the words of wisdom, said that an advocate should be fearless in carrying out the interest of his client; but I couple that with this qualification and this restriction—that the arms which he wields are to be the arms of the warrior and not of the assassin.

LORD COCKBURN, November 8, 1864, Middle Temple Banquet in honor of Mons. Berryer.

He [the advocate] is a representative, but not a delegate. He gives to his client the benefit of his learning, his talents, and his judgment; but all through he never forgets what he owes to himself and to others. He will not knowingly misstate the law—he will not wilfully misstate the facts, though it be to gain the cause for his client. He will ever bear in mind that if he be the Advocate of an individual, and retained and remunerated (often inadequately) for his valuable services, yet he has a prior and perpetual retainer on behalf of truth and justice; and there is no Crown or other license which in any case, or for any party or purpose, can discharge him from that primary and paramount retainer.

CRAMPTON, J., *R. v. O'Connell* (1844) 7 Ir. L.R. 261, 313.

He [the advocate] lends his exertions to all, himself to none. The result of the cause is to him a matter of indifference. It is for the Court to decide. It is for him to argue. He is, however he may be represented by those who understand not his true situation, merely an officer assisting in the administration of justice, and acting under the impression that truth is best discovered by powerful statements on both sides of the question.

LORD ELDON, *Ex parte Lloyd* (1822) Montagu Bankr. R., 70 n. 72.

If the advocate refuses to defend, from what he may think of the charge or of the defence, he assumes the character of the judge; nay, he assumes it before the hour of judgment; and in proportion to his rank and reputation, puts the heavy influence of perhaps a mistaken opinion into the scale against the accused.

THOMAS ERSKINE, arguendo, *Trial of Thomas Paine* (1792) 22 How. St. Tr. 358, 412.

It is a popular, but gross mistake, to suppose that a lawyer owes no fidelity to anyone except his client; and that the latter is the keeper of his professional conscience. He is expressly bound by his official oath to behave himself in his office of attorney with all due fidelity to the court as well as the client; and he violates it when he consciously presses for an unjust judgment. . . . The high and honorable office of a counsel would be degraded to that of a mercenary, were he compelled to do the biddings of his client against the dictates of his conscience.

GIBSON, C.J., *Rush v. Cavenaugh,* 2 Barr(Pa.) 187, 189, (1845).

He is an ingenious counsel, who has made the most of his cause: he is not obliged to gain it.

SAMUEL JOHNSON. Boswell, *Life of Johnson*: 1772.

No counsel supposes himself to be the mere advocate or agent of his client, to gain a victory, if he can, on a particular occasion. The zeal and the arguments of every counsel, knowing what is due to himself and his honourable profession, are qualified not only by considerations affecting his own character as a man of honour, experience, and learning, but also by considerations affecting the general interests of justice.

LORD LANGDALE, M.R., *Hutchinson v. Stephens* (1837) 1 Keen 659, 668.

Advocacy is an enthralling vocation but an exhausting one, and after many years of it one grows a little weary of throwing all one's energies into other people's disputes. It becomes increasingly difficult to keep up a head of steam in the boiler. The unique advantage of the Bar as a profession is that it offers in their later years to those who have succeeded in it the sanctuary of the Bench where they may continue to serve the law in a serener atmosphere and turn to useful account the garnered stores of their experience.

LORD MACMILLAN, *Man of Law's Tale* 142 (1952).

My profession and that of an actor are somewhat akin, except that I have no scenes to help me, and no words are written for me to say. There is no black-cloth to increase the illusion. There is no curtain. But, out of the vivid, living dream of somebody else's life, I have to create an atmosphere,—for that is advocacy.

SIR EDWARD MARSHALL HALL. Marjoribanks, *For the Defence* 1 (1929).

I always said, I will be my client's advocate, not his agent. To hire himself to any particular course, is a position in which no member of the profession ought to place himself.

POLLOCK, C.B., *Swinfen v. Lord Chelmsford* (1860) 2 L.T. (N.S.) 406, 413.

An advocate will not defend all persons indiscriminately, nor will he throw open the harbor of his eloquence as a port of refuge to pirates; and he will be influenced to advocate any cause chiefly by the good opinion which he forms of the nature of it.

QUINTILIAN, *Inst. of Oratory,* bk 12, 7, 4.

Age

Men of age object too much, consult too long, adventure too little, repent too soon, and seldom drive business home to the full period, but content themselves with a mediocrity of success.

BACON, *Essays: Of Youth and Age.*

There is not a man in England who can rightly adjudge her of age or under age. Some women who are thirty years old will seem eighteen.

CAVENDISH, C.J., 6 Y.B. 50 Edw. III (1375) 6, 12.

Agreement

That what is agreed to be done, must be considered as done.

LORD HARDWICKE, L.C., *Guidot v. Guidot* (1745) 3 Atk. 254, 256.

That is to be looked upon as done which ought to be done.

JEKYLL, M.R., *Banks v. Sutton* (1732) 2 P. Wms. 700, 715.

Be at agreement with thy adversary betimes, whilst thou are in the way with him.

Matthew 5:25.

Agree for the law is costly.

Proverb. CAMDEN, *Remains Concerning Britain: Proverbs* (1674).

An ill agreement is better than a good judgment.

Proverb. HERBERT, *Jacula Prudentum* (1651)

Aliens

I have never discovered that disregard of the Nation's liquor taxes excluded a citizen from our best society and I see no reason why it should banish an alien from our worst.

JACKSON, J., *Jordan v. DeGeorge*, 341 U.S. 223, 241 (1951).

Let there be equal judgment among you, whether he be a stranger, or a native.

Leviticus 24:22.

Hear them, and judge that which is just; whether he be one of your country or a stranger.

Deuteronomy 1:16.

Ambition

Ambition which ever rideth without reines.

COKE, *Second Institute: Proeme.*

Amendment

A state without the means of some change is without the means of its conservation. Without such means it might even risk the loss of that part of the constitution which it wished the most religiously to preserve.

EDMUND BURKE, *Reflections on the French Revolution.*

Blessed be the amending hand.

EDMUND PLOWDEN. See, Coke, *Fourth Institute: Epilogue.*

It is between the stirrup and the ground, Brother; but you may amend by replying.

TINDAL, C.J., *Spincer v. Spincer* (1841) 5 Jur. (O.S.) 100, 102. Alluding to the gentleman who fell from his horse and broke his neck—"Betwixt the stirrop and the ground, Mercy I askt, mercy I found." Camden, *Remains Concerning Britain: Epitaph* (1674).

Analogy

If any new and unwonted circumstances, hitherto unprecedented in the realm shall arise, then if anything analogous has happened before, let the case be adjudged in like manner, since it is a good opportunity for proceeding *a similibus ad similia.*

BRACTON, *De Legibus et Consuetudinibus Angliae,* f. 1b.

For like reason doth make like law.

COKE, *First Institute* 10.

Analysis

Dismemberment may be necessary in aid of the process of analysis, but in the end there must be a synthesis that will bring the severed parts together.

CARDOZO, C.J., *Marchant v. Mead-Morrison M. Co.*, 252 N.Y. 284, 299 (1929).

Animals

THE PLAINTIFF

O where, O where is my leetle hound's tail
    That you've made of no worth to be,
From a hound of fame, and Dutch Oven his name,
    To a dog of low degree?
Mit your negligent shove-car trundling around,
    You trod on his tail full sore;
Dutch Oven was worth to me sixty pound,
    And he never will course no more.

THE RAILWAY COMPANY

The tail and the claim they are both cut short,
    You paid us a common dog's fee;
Two pounds you may have, and they lie in Court,
    For the balance you signed us free.
And if more you meant, it was five per cent.
    You'd have paid on our special scale
('Twould make shillings threescore and other four)
    To insure that little hound's tail.

SIR FREDERICK POLLOCK, *Leading Cases Done Into English: The Hound's Tail's Case* 52 (1892). For reported case see, *Dickson v. Great Northern Ry. Co.*, 18 Q.B.D. 176.

THE COURT OF APPEAL

Now here, O here's an unanimous voice
    Against this proud Company;
They takes your money and gives no choice
    In reason, that we can see;
But will break, steal, kill at their servants' will,
    Or a monstrous rate will fix—
Eighteenth of the Queen,[1] it shall well be seen,
    Was made for to stop such tricks.

THE REPORTER

But where, O where is the tailless hound,
    And what shall be done with he?
Shall a place for him in the Court be found,
    The Lords Justices' dog to be?
With glory increased, a reported beast,
    Though he course no more on ground,
He shall hunt like a spectre the grasping Director,
    Dutch Oven the tailless hound.

SIR FREDERICK POLLOCK, *ibid.*

Anomaly

Anomalies in the law . . . sometimes arise from blindly following the hasty decision of a distinguished judge.

COWEN, J., *Waydell v. Luer,* 5 Hill (N.Y.) 448, 453 (1843).

Answer

In law also the right answer usually depends on putting the right question.

FRANKFURTER, J., *Rogers v. Commissioner,* 320 U.S. 410, 413 (1943).

---

[1] The Railway and Canal Traffic Act, 17 & 18 Vict. c. 31.

Appeal

The point appears here in its virgin state, wearing all its maiden blushes, and is therefore out of place.

BLECKLEY, J., *Cleveland v. Chambliss*, 64 Ga. 352, 359 (1879).

Supposing fishes had the gift of speech, who would listen to a fisherman's weary discourse on flycasting, the shape and color of the fly, the size of the tackle, the length of the line, the merit of different rod makers and all the other tiresome stuff that fishermen talk about, if the fish himself could be induced to give his views on the most effective methods of approach.

JOHN W. DAVIS, *The Argument of an Appeal.* Address October 1940, Assn Bar N.Y.C. In *Jurisprudence in Action.*

An appeal, Hinnissy, is where ye ask wan coort to show its contempt f'r another coort.

FINLEY PETER DUNNE, *Mr. Dooley Says: The Big Fine.*

We granted certiorari, and in this Court the parties changed positions as nimbly as if dancing a quadrille.

JACKSON, J., *Orloff v. Willoughby*, 345 U.S. 83, 87 (1953).

It had been publicly asserted that appeals in the House of Lords were nothing more than appeals from the Lord Chancellor in one place to the Lord Chancellor in another.

TWISS, 2 *Life of Lord Eldon* 477 (1844).

Arabiniana

The Court: If ever there was a case of clearer evidence than this of persons acting in concert together, this is that case.

ARABIN, J. The dicta and charges of Judge Wm. St. Julien Arabin were collected by H.B.C. (H. Blencowe Churchill) and privately printed in 1843. Arabin has been described as a "quaint little man who enunciated absurdities with the most perfect innocence." He was "not wanting in mother wit, but very much so in the faculty of expressing himself rationally."

The Court, in charge: I cannot suggest a doubt: she goes into a shop, and looks at several things, and purchases nothing: that always indicates some guilt.

ibid.

The Court, in charge (speaking of the inhabitants of Uxbridge): They will steal the very teeth out of your mouth as you walk through the streets. I know it from experience.

ibid.

The Court, to prisoner: I have no doubt of your guilt; you go into a public house, and break bulk, and drink beer; and that's what in the law is called embezzlement.

ibid.

Arbitration

The arbitrator looks to what is equitable, the judge to what is law; and it was for this purpose that arbitration was introduced, namely, that equity might prevail.

ARISTOTLE, *Rhetoric,* bk 1, ch. 13.

Argument

The distinguished counsel who argued this case before us have I think, drawn three red herrings across the path of the Court, in the hope that we should be drawn off the scent.

LORD BOWEN, *Re Blackburn & District Benefit Bldg. Soc.* (1883) 24 Ch.D. 421, 436.

Expediency may tip the scales when arguments are nicely balanced.

CARDOZO, J., *Woolford Realty Co. v. Rose,* 286 U.S. 319, 330 (1932).

"In my youth," said his father, "I took to the law,
And argued each case with my wife;
And the muscular strength which it gave to my jaw
Has lasted the rest of my life."

LEWIS CARROLL, *Alice in Wonderland,* ch. 5.

The Judge left the Court, looking deeply disgusted:
But the Snark, though a little aghast,
As the lawyer to whom the defence was intrusted,
Went bellowing on to the last.

LEWIS CARROLL, *The Hunting of the Snark: Barrister's Dream.* When sentence was imposed "the pig had been dead for some years".

When the defendants had failed in satisfying him that the plaintiff was wrong, the plaintiff's counsel often succeeded in doing so.

LORD ELDON. See, 129 Edinburgh Rev. 48, per Lord Kingsdown.

Much cry and little wool.

SIR JOHN FORTESCUE, *Governance of England,* ch. 10.

After all, advocates, including advocates for States, are like managers of pugilistic and election contestants in that they have a propensity for claiming everything.

FRANKFURTER, J., *First Iowa Hydro-Elec. Coop. v. Fed. Power Comm.,* 328 U.S. 152, 187 (1946).

Nay, Sir, argument is argument. You cannot help paying regard to their arguments if they are good.

SAMUEL JOHNSON. Boswell, *Life of Johnson: 1784.* Reply to Sir James Johnston's remark that he paid no regard to the arguments of counsel at the bar of the House of Commons, because they were paid for speaking.

It is unjust, Sir, to censure lawyers for multiplying words when they argue; it is often necessary for them to multiply words.

SAMUEL JOHNSON. Boswell, *Life of Johnson*: 1781.

This is not a case of murder nor assault nor poison. It's a case involving three goats. I claim that my neighbor stole them and the court wants the accusation proved. You keep telling us about the battle of Cannae, the war with Mithridates, the furious struggle with the perfidious Carthaginian, about Sulla, Marius and the like. And all with a roar and a waving of hands. Don't you think it's about time, Postumus, that you talked about those three goats.

MARTIAL, *Epigrams*, VI, 19.

The last point is perfectly new, and it is so startling that I do not apprehend it will ever become old.

MAULE, J., *Whitaker v. Wisbey* (1852) 12 C.B. 44, 58.

He was a bad lawyer, said O'Connell, but he was the most sensible looking man talking nonsense he ever saw.

DANIEL O'CONNELL, referring to Lord Manners. Burke, *History of Lord Chancellors of Ireland* (1879) 203.

He that has the worst cause makes the most noise.

Proverb. THOMAS FULLER, *Proverbs* (1732).

No case abuse the plaintiff's attorney.

Proverb.

Am I then to attack the man when there is no room for argument. *(In hominem dicendum est igitur, quum oratio argumentationem non habet.)*

CICERO, *Pro Flacco* 10. Actually Cicero was protesting that the witnesses were under the control of the prosecutor.

Then, if at any time you find you have the worst end of the staff, leave off your cause and fall upon the person of your adversary.

JOHN WILSON, *The Cheats*, I, 4 (1664).

I well remember that on one occasion, when he was speaking in the Basilica Julia before the first tribunal, and the four companies of judges, as is usual, were assembled, while the whole place resounded with noise, he was not only heard and understood, but was applauded from all the four tribunals, to the great prejudice of those who were speaking at the same time.

QUINTILIAN, *Inst. of Oratory,* bk 12, 5, 6 (trans. Watson). Referring to the stentorian voice of the advocate Trachalus.

Bluster, sputter, question, cavil; but be sure your argument be intricate enough to confound the court.

WILLIAM WYCHERLEY, *The Plain Dealer,* III, 1.

This argument has indeed a captivating sound; it strikes the passions with a winning address: but it will be found as fallacious as the rest, and equally begs the very question in dispute.

YATES, J., *Millar v. Taylor* (1769) 4 Burr. 2303, 2359.

Assumption the Risk of

If you cannot see where you are going, you must not go.

BARON BRAMWELL. See, Scrutton, L.J., in *Evans v. Downer & Co.* (1933) 102 L.J.K.B. 568 n.

The timorous may stay at home.

CARDOZO, C.J., *Murphy v. Steeplechase Amusement Co.,* 250 N.Y. 479, 483 (1929).

His poverty, not his will, consented to incur the danger.

HAWKINS, J., *Thrussell v. Handyside & Co.* (1888) 20 Q.B.D. 359, 364.

Attack

He has peculiar powers as an assailant, and almost always, even when attacked, gets himself into that attitude, by making war upon his accuser; and he has, withal, an instinct for the jugular and the carotid artery, as unerring as that of any carnivorous animal.

RUFUS CHOATE, referring to John Quincy Adams. 1 Brown, *Works of Choate* 293 (1862).

Attorney and Client

I would rather have clients than be somebody's lawyer.

LOUIS D. BRANDEIS, *Interview*, by Ernest Poole, 71 Amer. Mag. 492 (1911).

To this brave man the Knight repairs
For counsel in his law-affairs,
And found him mounted in his pew,
With books and money plac'd for shew,
Like nest-eggs to make clients lay,
And for his false opinion pay.

SAMUEL BUTLER, *Hudibras*, Pt. III, Canto III, l. 621.

Certain clients come to a lawyer, confide their troubles to him, and then go home light-hearted, feeling that they have rid themselves of all their problems. They go to bed and fall fast asleep like innocent children, in the belief that the lawyer has assumed the professional duty to lie awake and worry on their account. One evening I met a client of mine at the theater. He had been in that day to tell me he was on the brink of bankruptcy. He showed surprise and annoyance at finding me in a place of diversion, and throughout the performance he shot disapproving glances in my direction, as if to let me know that with ruin facing him I should be home bemoaning his fate and that it was, to say the least, indelicate of me to go out seeking entertainment.

PIERO CALAMANDREI, *Eulogy of Judges* 60 (1942) trans. Adams and Phillips.

"I suppose," said Roger quite calmly, "that your idea is that we should invent a good story for you to tell."

"What else is a lawyer for? When truth is good, what need have I of a lawyer? I go to a lawyer when the truth is—how do you say?—inconvenient."

"Well," said Roger, "there may be some countries where lawyers behave like that. And there may be one or two over here who'd do it for you, but not many, and they'd be kicked out pretty quick if they were found out."

"There are not many such?" asked Mr. Glacier.

"Very few," said Roger.

"You have their addresses perhaps?" said Mr. Glacier.

"I have not," said Roger.

HENRY CECIL, *Friends at Court,* ch. 5 (1956).

Who calls a lawyer rogue, may find, too late,
On one of these depends his whole estate.

GEORGE CRABBE, *Tales—The Gentleman Farmer.*

Here . . . Mr. Tulkinghorn has at once his house and office. He keeps no staff; only one middle aged man. . . . who sits in a high Pew in the hall. . . . He wants no clerks. He is a great reservoir of confidences, not to be so tapped. His clients want HIM. He is all in all.

CHARLES DICKENS, *Bleak House,* ch. 10.

If there were no bad people there would be no good lawyers.

CHARLES DICKENS, *Old Curiosity Shop,* ch. 56.

The end and aim of a lawyer is duplex, first, to know, and second to appear to know—the latter brings in clients and the former holds them.

ROGER NORTH, *On the Study of Laws* 28.

Good men have no need of an advocate.

PLUTARCH, *Lives*: *Phocion,* ch. 10.

He who is his own lawyer has a fool for a client.

Proverb.

Ah! Mr. Cleave, don't you mind that adage: it was framed by the lawyers.

LORD LYNDHURST, to a defendant who was arguing his own case. 1 Grant, *Bench and Bar* 151 (1838).

Lawyers' gowns are lined with the willfulness of their clients.

Proverb. HAZLITT, *Proverbs* (1869).

It is not uncommon for the litigant to demand a base and inhuman gratification of his rancor, thinking more of revenge than the defense of his cause. But in this, as in many other things, it is the duty of the advocate to refuse to comply with his client's desires.

QUINTILIAN, *Inst. of Oratory*, bk 12, 9, 10.

Good counsellors lack no clients.

SHAKESPEARE, *Measure for Measure*, I, 2.

Authority

I accede to the authority of that case, although I think it a very strong decision. It does not convince me; it overcomes me.

ALDERSON, B., *Mearing v. Hellings* (1845) 14 M. & W. 711, 712.

The fact is, Lord Coke had no authority for what he states, but I am afraid we should get rid of a good deal of what is considered law in Westminster hall, if what Lord Coke says without authority is not law.

BEST, C.J., *Garland v. Jekyll* (1824) 2 Bing. 273, 296.

The mere repetition of the *cantilena* of lawyers, cannot make it law, unless it can be traced to some competent authority, and if it be irreconcilable to some clear legal principle.

LORD DENMAN, C.J., *O'Connell v. R.* (1844) 11 Cl. & F. 155, 373.

The ABC of the law is generally not questioned before your Lordships, just because it is the ABC.

LORD DUNEDIN, *Johnston v. O'Neill* [1911] A.C. 552, 592.

Decisions of this Court do not have equal intrinsic authority.

FRANKFURTER, J., *Adamson v. California,* 332 U.S. 46, 59 (1947).

The clearer a thing is, the more difficult it is to find any express authority or any dictum exactly to the point.

JAMES, L.J., *Panama & So. Pacific Tel. Co. v. India Rubber, Gutta Percha & Tel. W. Co.* (1875) 10 Ch. App. 515, 526.

There is nothing too absurd but what authority can be found for it.

MANISTY, J., *Henderson v. Preston* (1888) 4 T.L.R. 633.

If no reason had been given, the authority might have had more weight: but, to be sure, the reason is a false one.

LORD MANSFIELD, C.J., *Ingle v. Wordsworth* (1762) 3 Burr. 1284, 1286.

I have arranged all the cases that have been determined in Westminster Hall, in order of time; and when I come to state them, you will be surprised to see they stand so little in the way, as binding authorities against justice, reason, and common sense.

LORD MANSFIELD, C.J., *Pugh v. Duke of Leeds* (1777) 2 Cowp. 714, 718.

In that case the Bench was divided, and the decision was not relished. A decision in an arbitrary question is of great authority; not so when pronounced on wrong principles. The cause was not fully pleaded at first; and some Judges are like the old Bishop, who, having begun to eat the asparagus at the wrong end, did not choose to alter.

LORD PITFOUR, *Sinclair v. Sinclair,* 1768, 1 Hailes Dec. 247, 248.

Great men in judicial places will never want authority.

Proverb. See, COKE, *Second Institute* 553.

The matter is very clearly stated in a work, fortunately not a work of authority, but to which we are all as lawyers indebted, Sir Frederick Pollock's Law of Torts.

LORD WRIGHT, M.R., *Nicholls v. Ely Beet Sugar Factory Ltd.* [1936] Ch. 343, 349. Referring to the English rule that the works of living authors are not considered as authority.

Average

I abhor averages. I like the individual case. A man may have six meals one day and none the next, making an average of three meals per day, but that is not a good way to live.

LOUIS D. BRANDEIS. Fraenkel, *Curse of Bigness, An Interview* 41.

All loss which arises in consequence of extraordinary sacrifices made, or expences incurred, for the preservation of the ship and cargo come within general average, and must be borne proportionably by all who are interested.

LAWRENCE, J., *Birkley v. Presgrave* (1801) 1 East 220, 228.

Banking

If in 1815 the common law halted outside the bankers' door, by 1879 equity had had the courage to lift the latch, walk in and examine the books.

ATKIN, L.J., *Banque Belge Pour l'Etranger v. Hambrouck* [1921] 1 K.B. 321, 335.

That is hardly a practical suggestion. A banker so very careful to avoid risk would soon have no risk to avoid.

LORD MACNAGHTEN, *Bank of England v. Vagliano Brothers* [1891] A.C. 107, 157. One of the judges suggested that bank should not pay until satisfied by inquiry and investigation that all endorsements were genuine.

Bankruptcy

I will be their vassal for life, and dig in the mine of my imagination to find diamonds (or what may sell for such) to make good my engagements, not to enrich myself. And this from no reluctance to allow myself to be called the Insolvent, which I probably am, but because I will not put out of the power of my creditors the resources, mental or literary, which yet remain to me.

SIR WALTER SCOTT, *Journal, January 24, 1826.* At the time bankruptcy was suggested to him and his debts were more than one hundred thousand pounds.

Bench & Bar

It is no grace to a judge first to find that which he might have heard in due time from the bar; or to show quickness of conceit in cutting off evidence or counsel too short; or to prevent information by questions, though pertinent.

BACON, *Essays: Of Judicature.*

It is not, of course, in cases of complication possible for their Lordships to be aware of all the authorities, statutory or otherwise, which may be relevant to the issues which in the particular case require decision. Their Lordships are therefore very much in the hands of counsel, and those who instruct counsel, in these matters, and this House expects, and indeed insists, that authorities which bear one way or the other upon matters under debate shall be brought to the attention of their Lordships by those who are aware of those authorities. This observation is quite irrespective of whether or not the particular authority assists the party which is so aware of it. It is an obligation of confidence between their Lordships and all those who assist in the debates in this House in the capacity of counsel.

BIRKENHEAD, L.C., *Glebe Sugar Refining Co., Ltd. v. Greenock Harbour Trustees,* 1921 S.C. (H.L.) 72, 73.

A suppressed speech may occasion more mental torture than a lost case.

BLECKLEY, J., *Early v. Oliver*, 63 Ga. 11, 18 (1879).

A judge rarely performs his functions adequately unless the case before him is adequately presented.

LOUIS D. BRANDEIS, *Living Law*, 10 Ill. L.R. 461, 470 (1916).

This Court in which we sit is a temple of justice; and the Advocate at the Bar, as well as the Judge upon the Bench, are equally ministers in that temple. The object of all equally should be the attainment of justice.

CRAMPTON, J., *R. v. O'Connell* (1844) 7 Ir. L.R. 261, 312.

I do not like to appear in the character of a drill-sergeant with my cane rapping the knuckles of a private, when I become a colonel from the ranks.

JOHN P. CURRAN, when reproached for too much forbearance on becoming Master of the Rolls. 2 Townsend, *Lives of Twelve Eminent Judges* 261 (1846).

Lord Mansfield treated me, not with contempt indeed, for of that his nature was incapable, but he put me aside with indulgence, as you do a child, when it is lisping its prattle out of season.

THOMAS ERSKINE, referring to his argument in the Dean of St. Asaph libel trial. 1 Townsend, *Lives of Twelve Eminent Judges* 422 (1846).

Shall I ask what a court would be, unaided? The law is made by the Bar, even more than by the Bench.

OLIVER WENDELL HOLMES, *The Law—Speeches* 16 (1913).

The acme of judicial distinction means the ability to look a lawyer straight in the eyes for two hours and not to hear a damned word he says.

JOHN MARSHALL, retort to young lawyer who sought to flatter him by saying that the Chief Justice had reached the "acme of judicial distinction." 4 Beveridge, *Life of Marshall*, ch. 2.

Biography

His Life (Lord Lyndhurst) has been written by Lord Campbell, and fully justified what he himself said when he heard that it was contemplated, that the prospect added another pang to death.

SERJEANT BALLANTINE, *Some Experiences of a Barrister's Life* 145 (1882).

His Life, unlike the Lives of those whose history he has written, has been delivered to posterity by himself, and he escaped the death-pang that others, not without reason, apprehended from his undertaking their biography.

SERJEANT BALLANTINE, *Some Experiences of a Barrister's Life* 185 (1882) referring to Lord Campbell, author of the *Lives of the Chancellors.*

He would not cut off his claws, nor make a tiger a cat, to please anybody.

JAMES BOSWELL. Reply to Hannah More who asked him to mitigate some of Samuel Johnson's asperities in his *Life.* 1 Memoirs H. More 228 (N.Y. 1834).

Mortuary estimates.

FELIX FRANKFURTER, *Mr. Justice Brandeis* 50 (1932). Referring to the inadequacy of biographies of supreme court justices.

Death is now attended with a fresh terror.

SIR CHARLES WETHERELL, referring to the *Lives of the Lord Chancellors,* by Lord Campbell. See, 2 *Life of Lord Campbell,* 219 (1881). (Arbuthnot had called the printer, Curll, "one of the new terrors of death" from his habit of publishing trashy obituaries on the death of any eminent man.)

Blackstone's Commentaries

He it was who first gave to the law the air of a science. He found it a skeleton, and clothed it with life, colour and complexion: he embraced the cold statue, and by his touch it grew into youth, health and beauty.

LORD AVONMORE.

It was not so much his learning that made the book as it was the book that made him learned.

LORD ELLENBOROUGH.

It is a good gentleman's law book, clear but not deep.

HORNE TOOKE.

The prose epic of the common law.

UNKNOWN.

Books

I have not got as much from books as I have from tackling concrete problems. I have generally run up against a problem, have painfully tried to think it out, with a measure of success, and have then read a book and found to my surprise that some other chap was before me.

LOUIS D. BRANDEIS, *Interview*, by Ernest Poole, 71 Amer. Mag. 482 (1911).

It deserves not to be read in schools,
But to be freighted in the Ship of Fools.

COKE, when Sir Francis Bacon presented him with a copy of his *Novum Organum*, on the title page of which appeared the device of a ship sailing through the Pillars of Hercules.

Though backward in accounting, they seemed to be practised in book-keeping.

LORD ELDON, referring to book borrowers, after having lost two volumes of precedents copied by him. 1 Twiss, *Life of Eldon* 98 (1844).

First, there's the Bible,
And then the Koran
Odgers on Libel,
Pope's Essay on Man.

MOSTYN PIGOTT, *The Hundred Best Books*.

He is like a book in breeches.

SYDNEY SMITH. 1 Holland, *Memoir of Smith* 320. (The reference is to Thomas Macaulay).

Books (Law)

Almost any law book that is more than twenty-one years of age, like a single lady who has attained that climacter is said to be too old for much devotion.

HORACE BINNEY, *Leaders of the Old Bar of Philadelphia.*

A masterpiece upon a masterpiece.

Referring to COKE, *on Littleton.*

"I am improving my legal knowledge, Master Copperfield," said Uriah. "I am going through Tidd's Practice. Oh, what a writer Mr. Tidd is, Master Copperfield!"

CHARLES DICKENS, *David Copperfield,* ch. 16.

That underdone-pie-crust-coloured cover, which is technically known as "law-calf".

CHARLES DICKENS, *Pickwick Papers,* ch. 34.

It will some day seem a wonderful thing that men once thought that they could write the history of medieval England without using the Year Books. . . . They come to us from life. Some day they will return to life once more at the touch of some great historian.

FREDERIC WM. MAITLAND, *1 Year Book Series, Selden Society*: *Introduction* XX (1903).

He (Serjeant Maynard) had such a relish of the old year-books, that he carried one in his coach to divert his time in travel and said he chose it before any comedy.

ROGER NORTH, 1 *Life of Lord Keeper Guilford* 27 (1826).

Every Christmas, during all the time of his practice he read Littleton all over. And this he enjoined himself for a task: for that book having gained an authority, as a tract of law, and the foundation of conveyancing, he judged it necessary to be punctually remembered, without giving time the advantage to obliterate, or corrupt any part of it from his just thoughts.

ROGER NORTH, 1 *Life of Lord Keeper Guilford* 104 (1826).

Brain

The brain is like the hand. It grows with using.

LOUIS D. BRANDEIS, in *Filene Cooperative Assn. Echo,* May 1905. See, Mason, *Brandeis, Lawyer and Judge in Modern State* 84 (1933).

Brevity

Praised be he who can state a cause in a clear, simple and succinct manner, and then stop.

BELT, J., *Jungwirth v. Jungwirth,* 115 Ore. 668, 672 (1925).

Nothing conduces to brevity like a caving in of the knees.

OLIVER WENDELL HOLMES. Bowen, *Yankee From Olympus,* ch. 30. Holmes sometimes wrote his opinions standing up.

With as little bewordling and as few reasons as possible.

HUTCHESON, J., *Commissioner Int. Rev. v. McLean,* 127 F.2d 942, 944 (1942).

Bribery

Though the bribe be small, yet the fault is great.

COKE, *Third Institute* 147.

They that buy will sell.

COKE, *Third Institute* 148.

Men are more often bribed by their loyalties and ambitions than by money.

JACKSON, J., *United States v. Wunderlich*, 342 U.S. 98, 103 (1951).

A basket justice, a jill justice, a good forenoon justice.

Proverb. RAY, *Proverbs* (1678).

He that buyeth magistracy will sell justice.

Proverbs. RAY, *Proverbs* (1678).

Burke, Sir Edmund

Oft have we wonder'd that on Irish ground,
No poisonous reptile has e'er been found;
Reveal'd the secret stands of Nature's work—
She saved her venom to produce her Burke.

ROBERT DALLAS, counsel for the defense in the trial of Warren Hastings. Burke was one of the Managers of the impeachment.

Cases

But a more scandalous transaction,
Paltry, vexatious cause of action,
Or a more lame, more flat, more stale,
Dull and unprofitable tale,
I never met in all my reading,
In the whole course of law-proceeding,
Than this same woful trumpt-up story,
My learned brother has just laid before ye.

JOHN ANSTEY, *Pleader's Guide*, bk 2 (1802).

It is a sound precept not to take the law from the rules, but to make the rule from the existing law. For the proof is not to be sought from the words of the rule, as if it were the text of law. The rule, like the magnetic needle points at the law, but does not settle it.

BACON, *De Augmentis Scientiarum*, bk 8, c. 3, Aph. 85.

The hardship of the particular case is no reason for melting down the law. For the sake of fixedness and uniformity, law must be treated as a solid, not as a fluid. It must have, and always retain, a certain degree of hardness, to keep its outlines firm and constant. Water changes shape with every vessel into which it is poured; and a liquid law would vary with the mental conformation of judges, and become a synonym for vagueness and instability.

BLECKLEY, J., *Southern Star Lightning Rod Co. v. Duvall*, 64 Ga. 262, 268 (1879).

Some cases tax the anxious diligence of a court not by their difficulty but their simplicity.

BLECKLEY, C.J., *Wells v. Savannah*, 87 Ga. 397, 398 (1891).

In the ornithology of litigation this case is a tomtit, furnished with a garb of feathers ample enough for a turkey.

BLECKLEY, C.J., *Lukens v. Ford*, 87 Ga. 541, 542 (1891).

I have, of course, as often a bad case as a good one; and what with disagreeable and formidable opponents and imbecile judges, I lead a life worse than a convict in the treadmill.

LORD CAMPBELL, letter to his brother, December 19, 1835. 2 *Life of Lord Campbell* 76 (1881).

I often wished in after-life that all the causes were apple-pie causes.

LORD ELDON. When a senior fellow at University College, two undergraduates complained to him that the cook had sent them an apple-pie that could not be eaten. He ordered the pie to be produced but in the meanwhile other students had consumed it. So Eldon found it impossible to decide "that that was not eatable, which was actually eaten". 1 Twiss, *Life of Lord Eldon* 92 (1844).

Of a nature worthy the judicature of a Roman senate rather than of a single judge.

LORD HARDWICKE, L.C., *Penn v. Lord Baltimore* (1750) 1 Ves. Sr. 444, 446.

Neither law nor equity consists merely of cases and precedents, but of general rules and principles by the reason of which, the several cases coming before the courts of justice are to be governed.

LORD HARDWICKE. L.C., *Gorton v. Hancock* (1744) Harg. Mss. 383, f. 122 (as cited in 2 Yorke, *Life of Lord Hardwicke* 492).

Great cases like hard cases make bad law. For great cases are called great, not by reason of their real importance in shaping the law of the future, but because of some accident of immediate overwhelming interest which appeals to the feelings and distorts the judgment.

HOLMES, J., *Northern Securities Co. v. United States,* 193 U.S. 197, 400 (1904).

General propositions do not decide concrete cases.

HOLMES, J., *Lochner v. New York,* 198 U.S. 45, 76 (1905).

If a man keeps a case six months, it is supposed to be decided on "great consideration". It seems to me that intensity is the only thing. A day's impact is better than a month of dead pull.

OLIVER WENDELL HOLMES, 1 *Holmes-Pollock Letters* 154.

I long have said there is no such thing as a hard case. I am frightened weekly but always when you walk up to the lion and lay hold the hide comes off and the same old donkey of a question of law is underneath.

OLIVER WENDELL HOLMES, 1 *Holmes-Pollock Letters* 156.

Some litigants find that on leaving the Courts
They have found themselves fame in the legal Reports.
For reasons they never will quite understand
They have added a bit to the law of the land.

Their case has decided some interesting law,
Which maybe their barristers never foresaw—
Thus litigant laymen acquire legal fame
Whose lawyers may never accomplish the same.

J.P.C., *Poetic Justice* 4 (1947).

This case reminds me of one in which I likened the Plaintiff's case to a colander, because it was so full of holes.

JESSEL, M.R., *Ex parte Hall* (1882) 19 Ch.D. 580, 584.

Tibullus: How now, Ovid! Law-cases in verse? . . .
Ovid: Troth, if I live, I will new dress the Law
In sprightly Poesy's habiliments.

BEN JONSON, *Poetaster,* I, 3.

The law does not consist in particular cases; but in general principles, which run through the cases, and govern the decision of them.

LORD MANSFIELD, C.J., *Rust v. Cooper* (1777) 2 Cowp. 629, 632.

Hard cases make bad law.

Proverb. 3 LEAN, *Collect.* 479 (1902). Ram, *Legal Judgment* 116 (1871) attributes to Lord Tenterden.

Points more than all the lawyers in Bohemia can learnedly handle.

SHAKESPEARE, *Winter's Tale,* IV, 4.

I am sure none of us [judges] ought to make the parties' case better than the law has made it.

SOMERS, L.K., *The Bankers' Case* (1699) 14 How. St. Tr. 39, 45.

Cases (Popular Names)

Dog and the Potman: Or "Go It, Bob". *Baker v. Snell* [1908] 2 K. B. 352.

SIR FREDERICK POLLOCK'S designation. See, 25 L.Q.R. 317.

Snail in the Bottle. *Donoghue v. Stevenson* [1932] A. C. 562.

SIR FREDERICK POLLOCK'S designation. See, 49 L.Q.R. 22 (1933).

Certainty

If a man will begin with certainties, he shall end in doubts; but if he will be content to begin with doubts, he shall end in certainties.

BACON, *Advancement of Learning*, bk 1.

I was much troubled in spirit, in my first years upon the bench, to find how trackless was the ocean on which I had embarked. I sought for certainty. I was oppressed and disheartened when I found that the quest for it was futile. I was trying to reach land, the solid land of fixed and settled rules, the paradise of a justice that would declare itself by tokens plainer and more commanding than its pale and glimmering reflections in my own vacillating mind and conscience. I found "with the voyagers in Browning's *Paracelsus* that the real heaven was always beyond."

BENJAMIN N. CARDOZO, *Nature of the Judicial Process* 166 (1921).

Law, like other branches of social science, must be satisfied to test the validity of its conclusions by the logic of probabilities rather than the logic of certainty.

BENJAMIN N. CARDOZO, *Growth of the Law* 33 (1924).

Certainty is the mother of quietness and repose, and uncertainty the cause of variance and contentions.

COKE, *First Institute* 212.

I cannot avoid noticing an error into which they fall who complain of the uncertainty of law as though it were a weakness. Rather should it be considered the chiefest of all sanctions . . . Many would dare to do wrong, did they know for certain what would follow.

LORD DARLING, *Scintillae Juris*: *Of Laws*.

It is better the law should be certain, than that every Judge should speculate upon improvements in it.

LORD ELDON, *Sheddon v. Goodrich* (1803) 8 Ves. 481, 497.

Certainty generally is illusion, and repose is not the destiny of man.

OLIVER WENDELL HOLMES, *Path of the Law,* 10 Harv. L.R. 457, 465 (1897).

It would be very hard upon the profession, if the law was so certain, that every body knew it: the misfortune is that it is so uncertain, that its costs much money to know what it is, even in the last resort.

LORD MANSFIELD, C.J., *Jones v. Randall* (1774) 1 Cowp. 37, 40. This was in reply to counsel, Dunning, who in arguing this case stated: "The laws of this country are clear, evident, and certain: all the judges know the laws, and knowing them, administer justice with uprightness and integrity."

Chance

Curious results sometimes happen by chance, but when those results happen so largely along the lines of the purposes of those who have control of the supposed chance, it is not strange that outsiders are apt to feel that purpose, and not chance determined the result.

BREWER, J., *Taylor and Marshall v. Beckham,* 178 U.S. 548, 584 (1900).

Chancery

The Chancery is ordained to supply the law, and not to subvert the law.

BACON, *Speech,* May 7, 1617, on taking his seat in Chancery as Lord Keeper.

Chancery, the Pretorian power for mitigating the rigour of law, in case of extremity, by the conscience of a good man.

BACON, *History of King Henry VII.*

This Court is not a Court of conscience.

BUCKLEY, J., *Re Telescriptor Syndicate Ltd.* [1903] 2Ch. 174, 195.

The raw afternoon is rawest, and the dense fog is densest, and the muddy streets are muddiest, near that leaden-headed old obstruction, appropriate ornament for the threshold of a leaden-headed old corporation: Temple Bar. And hard by Temple Bar, in Lincoln's Inn Hall, at the very heart of the fog, sits the Lord High Chancellor in his High Court of Chancery.

CHARLES DICKENS, *Bleak House,* ch. 1.

The Lord High Chancellor ought to be sitting here—as here he is—with a foggy glory round his head, softly fenced in with crimson cloth and curtains, addressed by a large advocate with great whiskers, a little voice, and an interminable brief, and outwardly directing his contemplation to the lantern in the roof, where he can see nothing but fog. On such an afternoon, some score of members of the High Court of Chancery bar ought to be—as here they are—mistily engaged in one of the ten thousand stages of an endless cause, tripping one another up on slippery precedents, groping kneedeep in technicalities, running their goat-hair and horse-hair warded heads against walls of words, and making a pretence of equity with serious faces, as players might.

CHARLES DICKENS, *Bleak House,* ch. 1.

Your chancery lawyers
Whose subtilty thrives
In spinning out suits
To the length of three lives;
Such suits as the clients
Do wear out in slavery

Whilst pleader makes conscience
A cloak for his knavery.

English Drinking Song (18th Cent.)

Chancery mends no man's bargain, though it sometimes mends his assurance.

LORD FINCH, L.C., *Maynard v. Moseley* (1676) 3 Swanst. 653, 655.

Full oft within the spatious walls
When he had fifty winters o'er him,
My grave Lord Keeper led the Brawls:
The Seal and Maces, danc'd before him.
His bushy beard, and shoe-strings green
His high-crown'd hat and sattin doublet,
Mov'd the stout heart of England's Queen,
Tho' Pope and Spaniard could not trouble it.

THOMAS GRAY, *A Long Story*. Sir Christopher Hatton, Lord Chancellor under Elizabeth was called the "dancing chancellor".

Hell and Chancery are always open.

Proverb. THOMAS FULLER, *Proverbs* (1732).

It is always term time in the court of conscience.

Proverb. THOMAS FULLER, *Proverbs* (1732).

Change

Modification implies growth. It is the life of the law.

BRANDEIS, J., *Washington v. Dawson & Co.*, 264 U.S. 219, 236 (1924).

Law grows, and though the principles of law remain unchanged, yet (and it is one of the advantages of the common law) their application is to be changed with the changing circumstances of the times.

Some persons may call this retrogression, I call it progression of human opinion.

COLERIDGE, C.J., *R. v. Ramsey* (1883) 1 C. & E. 126, 135.

The law is like apparel, which alters with the time. *Le ley est come apparel, que alter ove le temps.*

DODDRIDGE, J., *Jones v. Powell* (1628) Palm. 536, 538.

Lawes were not made for their own sakes, but for the sake of those who were to be guided by them; and though it is true they are and ought to be sacred, yet, if they be or are become unusefull for their end, they must either be amended if it may be, or new lawes be substituted.

SIR MATTHEW HALE, *Considerations Touching the Amendments of Lawes* (In Hargrave, *Law Tracts* 269).

He that thinks a state can be exactly steered by the same lawes in every kind, as it was two or three hundred years since, may as well imagine, that the cloaths that fitted him when he was a child should serve him when he is grown a man. The matter changeth the custom, the contracts the commerce; the dispositions, educations and tempers of men and societies change in a long tract of time; and so must their lawes in some measure be changed, or they will not be usefull for their state and condition. And besides all this, as I before said, time is the wisest thing under heaven.

SIR MATTHEW HALE, *Considerations Touching the Amendment of Lawes* (In Hargrave, *Law Tracts* 269).

I set out on this ground which I suppose to be self-evident, "that the earth belongs in usufruct to the living," that the dead have neither powers nor rights over it. . . . On similar ground it may be proved that no society can make a perpetual constitution, or even a perpetual law. The earth belongs always to the living generation. They may manage it then, and what proceeds from it, as they please, during their usufruct. They are masters too of their own persons, and consequently may govern them as they please. But persons and property make the sum of the objects of government. The constitution and the laws of their predecessors extinguished them, in their natural course, with those whose will gave them being. This could preserve that being till it ceased to be itself, and no longer. Every constitution, then, and every law, naturally expires at the end of nineteen years.

THOMAS JEFFERSON, *Letter to James Madison, September 6, 1789.*

As the usages of society alter, the law must adapt itself to the various situations of mankind.

LORD MANSFIELD, C.J., *Barwell v. Brooks* (1784) 3 Doug. 371, 373.

Charity

Secret charities are often, if not uniformly, a genuine index of the real character of the donor.

BAUGH, J., *Applegate v. McFadin,* 20 S.W.2d 396, 398 (Tex. Ct. Civ. App., 1929).

I readily assume that the motive which leads old women to make bequests to this society is concern for the welfare of the dear dogs. As one who has more than once experienced the grief of losing a beloved spaniel, I can respect and applaud that motive: though I do not think my respect and applause can be expected when it becomes a matter of the dear guinea-pigs and the dear rats. . . . On the reasoning and assumption of Chitty, J., I conceive that a society, whose object was to secure legislation making illegal the manufacture and sale of rat-traps and rat poisons, would have to be held established for charitable purposes; and that the more readily if the tribunal insisted on "standing neutral" on the question whether rats are, or are not, vermin that are a menace to mankind.

MACKINNON, L.J., *Commissioners of Inland Rev. v. National Anti-Vivisection Soc.* [1946] K.B. 185, 211.

Christianity

There is no act which Christianity forbids, that the law will not reach: if it were otherwise, Christianity would not be, as it has always been held to be, part of the law of England.

BEST, C.J., *Bird v. Holbrook* (1828) 4 Bing. 628, 641.

Christianity is part of the law of England.

LORD ELDON, *In Re Bedford Charity* (1819) 2 Swans. 470, 527.

My Lords, with all respect for the great names of the lawyers who have used it, the phrase, "Christianity is part of the law of England" is really not law; it is rhetoric.

LORD SUMNER, *Bowman v. Secular Soc. Ltd.* [1917] A.C. 406, 464.

Church and State

The "establishment of religion" clause of the First Amendment means at least this: Neither a state nor the Federal Government can set up a church. Neither can pass laws which aid one religion, aid all religions, or prefer one religion over another. . . . In the words of Jefferson, the clause against establishment of religion by law was intended to erect "a wall of separation between church and State."

BLACK, J., *Everson v. Board of Education,* 330 U.S. 1, 15 (1947).

The laws of the realm do admit nothing against the law of God.

HOBART, C.J., *Colt and Glover* (1617) Hobart 140, 149.

Believing with you that religion is a matter which lies solely between man and his God, that he owes account to none other for his faith or his worship, that the legislative powers of government reach actions only, and not opinions, I contemplate with sovereign reverence that act of the whole American people which declared that their legislature should "make no law respecting an establishment of religion, or prohibiting the free exercise thereof," thus building a wall of separation between Church and State.

THOMAS JEFFERSON (when President), Reply to Greetings from Committee of the Danbury Baptist Assn. of Connecticut, January 1, 1802.

I cannot think . . . that it was a brilliant day in our legal annals when the affairs of the Free Church of Scotland were brought before the House of Lords, and the dead hand fell with a resounding slap upon the living body.

FREDERIC WM. MAITLAND, *Moral Personality and Legal Personality* in 3 Coll. Papers 319. In the case of *The Free Church of Scotland v. Overtoun* [1904] A.C. 515, involving a church dissolution, the House of Lords refused to sanction the use of funds for purposes other than according to the terms of the trust, although the religious views of a large number of the members had changed. This decision was immediately displaced by legislation — 5 Edw. VII, ch. 12.

Sir Richard Rich (King's Solicitor): Admit there were an act of Parliament that the realme should take me for king, would you not, Mr. More take me for king?

Sir Thomas More: That would I.

Sir Richard Rich: Were there an act of Parliament that all the realme should take me for Pope, would not you then Mr. More, take me for Pope?

Sir Thomas More: Suppose the Parliament would make a law that God should not be God, would you then, Mr. Rich, say that God were not God?

Sir Richard Rich: That I would not since no Parliament may make any such law.

Sir Thomas More: No more could the Parliament make the King the Supreme Head of the Church.

SIR THOMAS MORE. Roper, *Life of More.*

The "wall of separation between church and State" that Mr. Jefferson built at the University which he founded did not exclude religious education from that school. The difference between the generality of his statements on the separation of church and state and the specificity of his conclusions on education are considerable. A rule of law should not be drawn from a figure of speech.

REED, J., *Illinois ex rel McCollum v. Board of Education,* 333 U.S. 203, 247 (1948).

Congress shall make no law respecting an establishment of religion, or prohibiting the free exercise thereof; or abridging the freedom of speech, or of the press; or the right of the people peaceably to assemble, and to petition the government for a redress of grievances.

United States Constitution, First Amendment (1791).

Circumstances

Circumstances alter cases.

THOMAS C. HALIBURTON, *The Old Judge,* ch. 15 (1843).

The character of every act depends upon the circumstances in which it is done.

HOLMES, J., *Schenck v. United States,* 249 U.S. 47, 52 (1919).

The case is altered, quoth Plowden.

This became a proverbial saying when a case broke down on the facts. Sir Edmund Plowden was a devout Catholic. To assist at mass in his day was a crime. Summoned for his attendance but feeling that he had been entrapped he cross examined the celebrant and demanded of him if he would swear that he was a "priest". The answer was "no" and Plowden retorted: "The case is altered, no priest, no mass, no mass, no violation of the law."

See, 1 WOOLRYCH, *Lives of the Serjeants* 117, citing MS. Cooper's *Athenae Cantab.* I, 502.

Citations

Stanton J.: Where have you seen a gentleman vouch on a writ of dower?

Miggeley (Of Counsel): Sir, in Trinity term last, past, and of that I vouch the record.

Stanton J.: If you find it, I will give you my hat. (Jeo vous dorra mon chaperon).

See, Anon. Y.B. 4 Edw. II (Seld. Soc. VI) 168 (1311).

Court: What say you to the cases quoted?

Counsellor Bore'um:

My Lord, these cases I have noted;
Mere *nisi prius* cases, loose,
Loose law, my Lord, quite out of use—
My learned friend is fond of citing
Old cases, which he's seldom right in?
Settling the law as some great men do,
On points reported arguendo.

JOHN ANSTEY, *Pleader's Guide*, bk 2 (1802).

Counsel Randle Jackson: In the book of nature, my Lords, it is written—

Lord Ellenborough: Will you have the goodness to mention the page, Sir, if you please?

LORD CAMPBELL, 3 *Lives of the Chief Justices* 239 (1857).

With such a farrago of authorities, it cannot be but there is much refuse, which ever doth weaken or lessen the weight of the argument.

COKE, 10 Rep.: *Preface.*

Citizens

I should think myself a weak reasoner and a bad citizen, were I not, though a royalist in London, a republican in Paris. I should deem it a fair consequence of my being a royalist in London, that I should become a republican in Paris. Thus doing, I should alike respect the rights and follow the example of my sovereign, who while an Anglican in England, is a Presbyterian in Scotland, and a Lutheran in Hanover.

JEREMY BENTHAM, *Letter to the Minister of the Interior of the French Republic*, 10 Works 282. On August 26, 1792, Bentham was one of a number of foreigners who were honored with the title of Citizen of France, by the National Assembly.

Unless this Court is willing to say that citizenship of the United States means at least this much to the citizen, then our heritage of constitutional privileges and immunities is only a promise to the ear to be broken to the hope, a teasing illusion like a munificent bequest in a pauper's will.

JACKSON, J., *Edwards v. California*, 314 U.S. 160, 186 (1941). California's "anti-okie" law made it a misdemeanor to bring into the state a non-resident indigent person.

Civil Service

Peers shall teem in Christendom,
    And a Duke's exalted station
Be attainable by com
    Petitive examination!

WM. S. GILBERT, *Iolanthe*, Act I.

Clarity

The power of clear statement is the great power at the bar.

DANIEL WEBSTER, *Letter to R.M. Blatchford*, 1849. See Harvey, *Reminiscences of Daniel Webster* 118.

Clerk

An ancient clerk, skilful in precedents, wary in proceeding, and understanding in the business of the court, is an excellent finger of a court; and doth many times point the way to the judge himself.

BACON, *Essays: Of Judicature.*

His clerk, assistant, housekeeper, secretary, confidential plotter, adviser, intriguer, and bill of costs increaser, Miss Brass—a kind of amazon at common law.

CHARLES DICKENS, *Old Curiosity Shop*, ch. 33.

It is the justice's clerk that makes the justice.

Proverb. FULLER, *Proverbs* (1732).

Code

Justinian's Pandects only make precise,
What simply sparkled in men's eyes before,
Twitched in their brow or quivered on their lip,
Waited the speech they called but would not come.

ROBERT BROWNING, *Ring and the Book: Count Guido Franceschini.*

No one ever supposed that a system complete in all its parts, could be struck out at a heat, by the most able lawgiver that ever lived.

GIBSON, J., *Pennock v. Hart*, 8 Serg. & Rawle 369, 378 (Pa. 1822).

The most celebrated system of jurisprudence known to the world begins, as it ends with a Code.

SIR HENRY MAINE, *Ancient Law* 1. Referring to the Twelve Tables and the Code of Justinian.

My true glory is not in having won forty battles; . . . Waterloo will blot out the memory of those victories. . . . But nothing can blot out my Civil Code. That will live forever.

NAPOLEON. 1 De Montholon, *Recits de la Captivite de Napoleon* 401.

My code is lost.

NAPOLEON, when he first heard that a commentary on his code had been published.

I will go down to posterity with the Code in my hand.

NAPOLEON. Butler, *Reminiscences* 43 (Amer. ed. 1824).

Mr. Prin . . . did discourse with me . . . about the laws of England, telling me the many faults in them; and among others, their obscurity through multitude of long statutes, which he is about to abstract out of all of a sort; and as he lives, and Parliaments come, get them put into laws, and the other statutes repealed, and then it will be a short work to know the law, which appears a very noble good thing.

SAMUEL PEPYS, *Diary, April 25, 1666.*

Coke, Sir Edward

The common speech is that fowre Ps have overthrown and put him down, that is, Pride, Prohibitions, Praemunire and Prerogative.

JOHN CHAMBERLAIN, *Letter to Dudley Carleton, November 14, 1616.*

He is held too great an oracle amongst the people, and they may be mislead by anything that carries such an authority as all things do that he either speaks or writes.

CHARLES I. (The King in 1631 ordered that all papers of Coke be seized immediately upon his death.)

The jewel of his mind was put into a fair case, a beautiful body with a comely countenance, a case which he did wipe and keep clean, delighting in good clothes well worn; being wont to say that the outward neatness of our bodies might be a monitor of purity to our souls.

THOMAS FULLER, *Worthies: Norfolk.*

He that should search all glories of the gown,
And steps of all raised servants of the crown,
He could not find than thee, of all that store,
Whom fortune aided less, or virtue more.

BEN JONSON, *Underwoods.*

That wonderful Edward Coke was loose—masterful, masterless man.

FREDERIC WM. MAITLAND, *English Law and the Renaissance.* Rede Lecture (1901).

Commendation (Self)

I thank God for three things: That I never gave my body to physic, my heart to cruelty, nor my hand to corruption; and I commend myself for three things: Obtaining so fair a fortune with my first wife, my successful study of the law, and the independent manner in which I obtained all my public employments, *nec prece, nec pretio,* without either prayers or pence.

COKE. Seward's *Anecdotes* 211.

Commerce

The Court admits that the commerce involved in this case is foreign commerce, but subjects it to the state police power on the ground that it is not very foreign.

JACKSON, J., *Bob-Lo Excursion Co. v. Michigan,* 333 U.S. 28, 44 (1948).

If it is interstate commerce that feels the pinch, it does not matter how local the operation which applies the squeeze.

JACKSON, J., *United States v. Women's Sportswear Assn.*, 336 U.S. 460, 464 (1949).

It describes the commercial intercourse between nations, and parts of nations, in all its branches, and is regulated by prescribing rules for carrying on that intercourse.

MARSHALL, C.J., *Gibbons v. Ogden*, 22 U.S. (9 Wheat.) 1, 189 (1824).

Common Employment

Lord Abinger planted it,[1] Baron Alderson watered it[2] and the Devil gave it increase.

Source unknown. This doctrine was abrogated by statute in 1948, 11 and 12 Geo. 6, c. 41.

Common Law

This unwritten or common law is properly distinguishable into three kinds: 1. General customs; which are the universal rule of the whole kingdom, and form the common law, in its stricter and more usual signification. 2. Particular customs; which for the most part affect only the inhabitants of particular districts. 3. Certain particular laws; which by custom are adopted and used by some particular courts, of pretty general and extensive jurisdiction.

BLACKSTONE, *Commentaries*, bk 1, 67.

In many cases, the common law will control Acts of Parliament, and sometimes adjudge them to be utterly void: for when an Act of Parliament is against common right and reason, or repugnant, or

[1] Priestley v. Fowler (1837) 3 M. & W. 1.
[2] Hutchinson v. The York (1850) 5 Exch. 343.

impossible to be performed, the common law will control it, and adjudge such Act to be void.

COKE, *Bonham's Case,* 8 Rep. 118 (1610).

Any proposition the result of which would be to shew that the Common Law of England is wholly unreasonable and unjust, cannot be part of the Common Law of England.

LORD ESHER, M.R., *Emmens v. Pottle* (1885) 16 Q.B.D. 354, 357.

Its origin . . . is as undiscoverable as the Head of the Nile.

SIR MATTHEW HALE, *History of the Common Law,* ch. 3.

That confusing forest of learned judgments which constitutes the Common Law of England.

A. P. HERBERT, *Uncommon Law*: *Fardell v. Potts.*

The statute is like a tyrant; where he comes he makes all void; but the common law is like a nursing father, makes void only that part where the fault is, and preserves the rest.

CHIEF JUSTICE HOBART. See Twisden, C.J. in the case of *Maleverer v. Redshaw* (1669) 1 Mod. 35.

The common law is not a brooding omnipresence in the sky but the articulate voice of some sovereign or quasi-sovereign that can be identified.

HOLMES, J., *Southern Pacific Co. v. Jensen,* 244 U.S. 205, 222 (1917).

For if there is any virtue in the Common Law whereby she stands for more than intellectual excellence in a special kind of learning, it is that Freedom is her sister, and in the spirit of freedom her greatest work has ever been done. By that spirit our lady has emboldened her servants to speak the truth before kings, to restrain the tyranny of usurping license, and to carry her ideal of equal public justice and ordered right into every quarter of the world.

SIR FREDERICK POLLOCK, *The Genius of the Common Law* 124 (1912).

Mastering the lawless science of our law,
That codeless myriad of precedent,
That wilderness of single instances,
Through which a few, by wit or fortune led,
May beat a pathway out to wealth and fame.

TENNYSON, *Aylmer's Field.*

The common law is nothing else but statutes worn out by time; all our law began by consent of the Legislature, and whether it is now law by usage or writing, it is the same thing.

WILMOT, C.J., *Collins v. Blantern* (1767) 2 Wils. K.B., 341, 348.

Communism

So long as accused persons who are Republicans, Dixiecrats, Socialists, or Democrats must put up with such a jury, it will have to do for Communists.

JACKSON, J., *Dennis v. United States,* 339 U.S. 162, 175 (1950).

The Communist Party is a conspiratorial and revolutionary junta, organized to reach ends and to use methods which are incompatible with our constitutional system.

JACKSON, J., *American Communications Assn. v. Douds,* 339 U.S. 382, 424 (1950).

Your crime is worse than murder. . . . Who knows but that millions more of innocent people may pay the price of your treason. Indeed by your betrayal you undoubtedly altered the course of history to the disadvantage of our country.

KAUFMAN, J., sentencing to death the atom spies, Julius and Ethel Rosenberg, New York Times, April 6, 1951, p. 10.

I should suspect that quite a few members of the Charles' Law Faculty are still what the citizens of Prague call "radishes"—red on the outside and white inside.

JAROSLAV MAYDA, *Lawyers Under Communism,* 39 A.B.A.J. 1071 (1953).

Concurrence

Having listened all day to things which I do not think I ever heard of before, I can safely say I am of the same opinion, and for the same reasons.

BARON BRAMWELL. (When first sitting as Lord Justice on the Chancery side of the Court).

Confessions

I beseech your Lordships, be merciful to a broken reed.

BACON, acknowledging his confession (1621).

I do plainly and ingenuously confess that I am guilty of corruption; and do renounce all defence, and put myself upon the grace and mercy of your Lordships.

BACON, *Confession and Submission to Parliament* (1621).

Congressional Record

The Congressional Record is not the United States Code.

CHARLES P. CURTIS, *A Better Theory of Legal Interpretation,* in *Jurisprudence in Action* 143.

Conservatism

We have a maxim in the House of Commons, and written on the walls of our house, that old ways are the safest and surest ways.

COKE, *Speech, May 8, 1628.*

Conspiracy

Conspiracy, that darling of the modern prosecutor's nursery.

L. HAND, J., *Harrison v. United States,* 7 F.2d 259, 263 (1925).

The Constitution does not make conspiracy a civil right.

JACKSON, J., *Dennis v. United States,* 341 U.S. 494, 572 (1951).

Constitution

The Constitution itself had been extorted from the grinding necessity of a reluctant nation.

JOHN QUINCY ADAMS, *Jubilee Discourse on the Constitution* 55 (1839).

The Constitution, in all its provisions, looks to an indestructible Union, composed of indestructible States.

CHASE, C.J., *Texas v. White,* 74 U.S. (7 Wall.) 700, 725 (1868).

Now the opinion of Cato becomes more certain, that the constitution of the republic is the work of no single time or of no single man. (*Nunc fit illud Catonis certius, nec temporis unius nec hominis esse constitutionem rei publicae; perspicuum est enim, quanta in singulos reges rerum bonarum et utilium fiat accessio.*)

CICERO, *De Re Publica,* II, 21 (37).
McIlwain, *Constitutionalism, Ancient and Modern* (1940) 27 attributes to Cicero the first use of the word "constitution" in its accepted modern sense.

The Constitution of the United States is a law for rulers and people, equally in war and in peace, and covers with the shield of its protection all classes of men, at all times, and under all circumstances.

DAVIS, J., *Ex parte Milligan,* 71 U.S. (4 Wall.) 2, 120 (1866).

The American Constitution is, so far as I can see, the most wonderful work ever struck off at a given time by the brain and purpose of man. It has had a century of trial, under the pressure of exigencies caused by an expansion unexampled in point of rapidity and range; and its exemption from formal change, though not entire, has certainly proved the sagacity of the constructors, and the stubborn strength of the fabric.

W. E. GLADSTONE, *Kin Beyond Sea,* 127 No. Amer. Rev. 185 (1878).

A constitution is not intended to embody a particular economic theory, whether of paternalism and the organic relation of the citizen to the State or of *laissez-faire.* It is made for people of fundamentally differing views.

HOLMES, J., *Lochner v. New York,* 198 U.S. 45, 75 (1905).

We are under a Constitution, but the Constitution is what the judges say it is, and the judiciary is the safeguard of our liberty and of our property under the Constitution.

GOVERNOR CHARLES EVANS HUGHES, *Speech, Elmira Chamber of Commerce, May 3, 1907.*

It is a good canvas, on which some strokes only want retouching.

THOMAS JEFFERSON, *Letter to James Madison, July 31, 1788.*

In questions of power, then, let no more be heard of confidence in man, but bind him down from mischief by the chains of the Constitution.

THOMAS JEFFERSON, *Kentucky Resolutions,* November 1798.

Some men look at constitutions with sanctimonious reverence, and deem them like the ark of the covenant, too sacred to be touched. They ascribe to the men of the preceding age a wisdom more than human, and suppose what they did to be beyond amendment.

THOMAS JEFFERSON, *Letter to Samuel Kercheval, July 12, 1816.*

We must never forget that it is a constitution we are expounding.

MARSHALL, C.J., *McCulloch v. Maryland,* 17 U.S. (4 Wheat.) 316, 407 (1819).

A constitution, intended to endure for ages to come, and consequently, to be adapted to the various crises of human affairs.

MARSHALL, C.J., *McCulloch v. Maryland,* 17 U.S. (4 Wheat.) 316, 415 (1819).

The people made the constitution, and the people can unmake it. It is the creature of their will, and lives only by their will. But this supreme and irresistible power to make or unmake, resides only in the whole body of the people; not in any subdivision of them.

MARSHALL, C.J., *Cohens v. Virginia,* 19 U.S. (6 Wheat.) 264, 389 (1821).

I yield slowly and reluctantly to the conviction that our constitution cannot last. . . . Our opinions are incompatible with a united government even among ourselves. The union has been prolonged thus far by miracles, I fear they cannot continue.

JOHN MARSHALL, *Letter to Joseph Story, September 22, 1832.* 4 Beveridge's *Life of Marshall* 559.

There is a higher law than the Constitution.

WILLIAM H. SEWARD, Speech in Senate, March 11, 1850, *California Union and Freedom,* Congr. Globe, v. 19 App. Pt. 1, 265.

The Constitution of the United States is not a mere lawyers' document: it is a vehicle of life, and its spirit is always the spirit of the age.

WOODROW WILSON, *Constitutional Government in the United States* 69 (1927).

Constitution (Amendments)

Of all these judges, only one, who may respectfully be called an eccentric exception, ever indicated the belief that the Fourteenth Amendment was a shorthand summary of the first eight Amendments theretofore limiting only the Federal Government.

FRANKFURTER, J., *Adamson v. California,* 332 U.S. 46, 62 (1947). Referring to Mr. Justice Harlan.

The Fourteenth Amendment does not enact Mr. Herbert Spencer's Social Statics.

HOLMES, J., *Lochner v. New York,* 198 U.S. 45, 75 (1905).

There is nothing that I more deprecate than the use of the Fourteenth Amendment beyond the absolute compulsion of its words to prevent the making of social experiments that an important part of the community desires, in the insulated chambers afforded by the several States, even though the experiments may seem futile or even noxious to me and to those whose judgment I most respect.

HOLMES, J., *Truax v. Corrigan,* 257 U.S. 312, 344 (1921).

The First Amendment is not confined to safeguarding freedom of speech and freedom of religion against discriminatory attempts to wipe them out. On the contrary, the Constitution, by virtue of the First and the Fourteenth Amendments, has put those freedoms in a preferred position.

STONE, C.J., *Jones v. Opelika,* 316 U.S. 584, 608 (1942).

Constitution (English)

When one scrutinizes the English Constitution, it is like looking at the nests of birds or at the curious and intricate work of beavers and insects; its strange contrivances seem not so much the ordered and foreseen result of human wisdom as a marvellous outcome of instinct, of a singular political sense and apprehension, feeling its sure way for centuries, amid all sorts of obstacles, through and around and over them, with the busy persistence of a tribe of ants.

JAMES BRADLEY THAYER, *Legal Essays* 191 (1908).

Constitutional Law

A great principle of constitutional law is not susceptible of comprehensive statement in an adjective.

CARDOZO, J., *Carter v. Carter Coal Co.,* 298 U.S. 238, 327 (1936).

The petitioner may have a constitutional right to talk politics, but he has no constitutional right to be a policeman.

HOLMES, J., *McAuliffe v. Mayor,* 155 Mass. 216, 220 (1892).

Constitutional law like other mortal contrivances has to take some chances.

HOLMES, J., *Blinn v. Nelson,* 222 U.S. 1, 7 (1911).

Constitutionality

A statute which is ultimately declared unconstitutional is presumed to have been known by all to be a nullity from the time of its enactment, even though the fact of its nullity is not known until declared a long time afterwards by a five to four decision.

CARSWELL, J., *Holland v. Atlantic Stevedoring Co.,* 210 App. Div. (N.Y.) 129, 130 (1924).

The particular phraseology of the constitution of the United States confirms and strengthens the principle, supposed to be essential to all written constitutions, that a law repugnant to the constitution is void; and that courts, as well as other departments, are bound by that instrument.

MARSHALL, C.J., *Marbury v. Madison,* 5 U.S. (1 Cranch) 137, 180 (1803).

Let the end be legitimate, let it be within the scope of the constitution, and all means which are appropriate, which are plainly adapted to that end, which are not prohibited, but consist with the letter and spirit of the constitution, are constitutional.

MARSHALL, C.J., *McCulloch v. Maryland,* 17 U.S. (4 Wheat.) 316, 421 (1819).

Contemporaneous

Great weight has always been attached, and very rightly attached to contemporaneous exposition.

MARSHALL, C.J., *Cohens v. Virginia,* 19 U.S. (6 Wheat.) 264, 418 (1821).

Contempt of Court

Justice is not a cloistered virtue: she must be allowed to suffer the scrutiny and respectful, even though outspoken, comments of ordinary men.

LORD ATKIN, *Ambard v. Atty. Gen. for Trinidad* [1936] A.C. 322, 335.

An ill-disposed person may exhibit contempt of court in divers ways—for example, he may scandalize the court itself, which may be done not merely by the extreme measure of hurling missiles at the presiding judge, or loudly contemning his learning or authority, but by ostentatiously reading a newspaper in his presence, or laughing uproariously at a joke made by someone else. Such contempts, committed as they are *in facie curiae,* are criminal offenses, and may be punished summarily by immediate imprisonment without the right of appeal. It speaks well both for the great good sense of the judges and for the deep-rooted legal instincts of our people that such offences are seldom heard of. It would be impossible nicely to define what measure of freedom of manners should be allowed in a court of justice, which, as we know, is neither a church nor a theatre, but, as a matter of practice, the happy mean between an awe-struck and unmanly silence and free-and-easy conversation is well preserved.

AUGUSTINE BIRRELL, *In the Name of Bodleian: Contempt of Court.*

The object of the discipline enforced by the Court in case of contempt of Court is not to vindicate the dignity of the Court or the person of the Judge, but to prevent undue interference with the administration of justice.

BOWEN, L.J., *Helmore v. Smith* (1887) 35 Ch. D. 449 455.

The law of contempt is not made for the protection of judges who may be sensitive to the winds of public opinion. Judges are supposed to be men of fortitude, able to thrive in a hardy climate.

DOUGLAS, J., *Craig v. Harney,* 331 U.S. 367, 376 (1947).

Judges as persons, or courts as institutions, are entitled to no greater immunity from criticism than other persons or institutions. Just because the holders of judicial office are identified with the interests of justice they may forget their common human frailties and fallibilities. There have sometimes been martinets upon the bench as there have also been pompous wielders of authority who have used the paraphernalia of power in support of what they called their dignity. Therefore judges must be kept mindful of their limitations and of their ultimate public responsibility by a vigorous stream of criticism expressed with candor however blunt.

FRANKFURTER, J., *Bridges v. California,* 314 U.S. 252, 289 (1941).

Contracts

Necessitous men are not, truly speaking, free men, but, to answer a present exigency, will submit to any terms that the crafty may impose upon them.

LORD HENLEY, L.C., *Vernon v. Bethell* (1762) 2 Eden 110, 113.

The movement of the progressive societies has hitherto been a movement from status to contract.

SIR HENRY MAINE, *Ancient Law,* ch. 5.

That which in any contract is left to be implied and need not be expressed is something so obvious that it goes without saying; so that, if, while the parties were making their bargain, an officious bystander were to suggest some express provision for it in their agreement, they would testily suppress him with a common "Oh, of course!"

MACKINNON, L.J., *Shirlaw v. Southern Foundries (1926) Ltd.* [1939] 2 K.B. 206, 227.

If a man will improvidently bind himself up by a voluntary deed, and not reserve a liberty to himself by a power of revocation, this court will not loose the fetters he hath put upon himself, but he must lie down under his own folly.

LORD NOTTINGHAM, L.C., *Villers v. Beaumont* (1682) 1 Vern. 100, 101.

Conveyancing

I, John of Gaunt
Do give and do grant
To Sir John Burgoyne
And the heirs of his loin
Both Sutton and Potton
Till the world goes rotten.

Anon.

The science of conveyancing to sing:
A noble theme which Coke himself supposes
To be at least as old as Lawyer Moses.

S.G.B. GRANT, *The Conveyancer's Guide* (1820).

Copyright and Patent

Half a century writes *Finis* to most authors, while in the case of the few who prove to be for all time, the feeling of mankind would be one of resentment were there now living in Paternoster Row or Madrid or Florence a capitalist who could say, "Hamlet is mine," "Sancho Panza is mine," "The 'Inferno' belongs to me." Who would not feel that this disreputable *bourgeois* was the enemy, not the friend, of the world-wide genius of Shakespeare, of Cervantes, of Dante?

AUGUSTINE BIRRELL, *Law and History of Copyright* 25 (1899). Argument against proposal of perpetual copyright.

The patent system . . . added the fuel of interest to the fire of genius.

ABRAHAM LINCOLN, *Lecture on Discoveries, Inventions and Improvements*, February 11, 1859.

Ideas are free. But while the author confines them to his study, they are like birds in a cage, which none but he can have a right to let fly: for, till he thinks proper to emancipate them, they are under his own dominion.

YATES, J., *Millar v. Taylor* (1769) 4 Burr. 2303, 2378.

Coram Nobis

The wild ass of the law which the courts cannot control.

SIMS, J., *Anderson v. Buchanan,* 292 Ky. 810, 822 (1943).

Corporations

The director is really a watch-dog, and the watch-dog has no right, without the knowledge of his master, to take a sop from a possible wolf.

BOWEN, L.J., *In re North Australian Territory Co.* [1892] 1 Ch. 322, 341.

They cannot commit treason, nor be outlawed, nor excommunicate, for they have no souls.

COKE, *Sutton's Hospital Case* (1612) 10 Rep. 32b.

The law does not permit the stockholders to create a sterilized board of directors.

COLLIN, J., *Manson v. Curtis,* 223 N.Y. 313, 323 (1918).

The corporation is, and must be, the creature of the State. Into its nostrils the State must breathe the breath of a fictitious life for otherwise it would be no animated body but individualistic dust.

FREDERIC WM. MAITLAND, *Introduction,* XXX, to Gierke, *Political Theories of the Middle Ages.*

As touching corporations: that they were invisible, immortall, and that they had no soule, and therefore no subpoena lieth against them, because they have no conscience nor soule; a corporation, is a body aggregate, none can create soules but God; but the King creates them, and therefore they have no soules.

MANWOOD, C.B., *Tipling v. Pexall,* 2 Bulstrode 233.

You never expected justice from a company, did you? They have neither a soul to lose, nor a body to kick.

LORD THURLOW. See, 1 Holland, *Memoir of Sydney Smith* 331.

A corporation cannot blush. It was a body it was true; had certainly a head—a new one every year—an annual acquisition of intelligence in every new lord mayor. Arms he supposed it had, and long ones too, for it could reach at any thing. Legs, of course, when it made such long strides. A throat to swallow the rights of the community, and a stomach to digest them! But whoever yet discovered, in the anatomy of any corporation, either bowels, or a heart?

HOWEL WALSH, in a corporation case tried at the Tralee assizes. Hone, *Table Book* 524 (1837).

Costs

There is one panacea which heals every sore in litigation, and that is costs. I have very seldom, if ever, been unfortunate enough to come across an instance, where a person has made a mistake in his pleadings which has put the other side to such a disadvantage as that it cannot be cured by the application of that healing medicine.

BOWEN, L.J., *Cropper v. Smith* (1884) 26 Ch. D. 700, 711.

Costs as between party and party are given by the law as an indemnity to the person entitled to them: they are not imposed as a punishment on the party who pays them, nor given as a bonus to the party who receives them.

BRAMWELL, B., *Harold v. Smith* (1860) 5 H. & N. 381, 385.

Courage

The heroic hours of life do not announce their presence by drum and trumpet, challenging us to be true to ourselves by appeals to the martial spirit that keeps the blood at heat. Some little, unassuming, unobtrusive choice presents itself before us slyly and craftily, glib and insinuating, in the modest garb of innocence. To yield to its blandishments is so easy. The wrong, it seems, is venial. . . . Then it is that you will be summoned to show the courage of adventurous youth.

BENJAMIN N. CARDOZO, *Law and Literature* 170 (1931).

I thought I heard my little children plucking at my robe and crying out to me—Now, father, is the time to get us bread.

THOMAS ERSKINE, reply when asked how, in his maiden speech at the bar in the Baillie Case, he had the courage to persist in naming Lord Sandwich, the First Lord of the Admiralty, in the face of judicial warning not to do so. See, 6 Campbell, *Lives of the Lord Chancellors*, ch. 177 (1847).

Court Packing

If they want me to preside over a convention, I can do it.

CHIEF JUSTICE CHARLES EVANS HUGHES. Pusey, 2 *Charles Evans Hughes* 753. Roosevelt's court packing bill of 1937 would have given the president the power to appoint a coadjutor judge for every federal judge who had been on the bench for ten years and had not resigned within six years after reaching the age of seventy.

Courts

A swallow had built her nest under the eaves of a Court of Justice. Before her young ones could fly, a serpent, gliding out of his hole ate them all up. When the poor bird returned to her nest and found it empty, she began a pitiable wailing. A neighbor suggested, by way of comfort, that she was not the first bird who had lost her young. "True," she replied, "but it is not only my little ones that I mourn, but that I should have been wronged in that very place where the injured fly for justice."

AESOP, *Fables.*

The place of justice is an hallowed place; and therefore not only the bench but the foot-pace and precincts and purprise thereof, ought to be preserved without scandal and corruption.

BACON, *Essays: Of Judicature.*

It (the court as an institution) is the lengthened shadow of many men.

FIELD, C.J., Observance of the 250th Anniversary of the Supreme Judicial Court, 312 Mass. 746.

Humanity is the second virtue of courts, but undoubtedly the first is justice.

SCOTT, J., *Evans v. Evans* (1790) 1 Hag. Con. 35.

Courts are not the only agency of government that must be assumed to have capacity to govern.

STONE, J., *United States v. Butler*, 297 U.S. 1, 87 (1936).

Crime

When a felon's not engaged in his employment,
Or maturing his felonious little plans,
His capacity for innocent enjoyment
Is just as great as any honest man's.
Our feelings we with difficulty smother
When constabulary duty's to be done.
Ah, take one consideration with another,
A policeman's lot is not a happy one.

WILLIAM S. GILBERT, *Pirates of Penzance*, Act II.

When the enterprising burglar's not a-burgling,
When the cut-throat isn't occupied in crime,
He loves to lie a-basking in the sun.
And listen to the merry village chime.
When the coster's finished jumping on his mother,
He loves to be a-basking in the sun.
Ah, take one consideration with another,
The policeman's lot is not a happy one.

WILLIAM S. GILBERT, *Pirates of Penzance,* Act II.

Criminal Justice

If rogues did but know all the pains that the law has taken for their benefit, honest men would have nothing left they could call their own.

JEREMY BENTHAM, *Rationale of Judicial Evidence,* 6 Works 205.

I oft have heard of Lydford law,
How, in the morn, they hang and draw,
And sit in judgment after.
At first I wonder'd at it much,
But since I find the reason's such,
As it deserves no laughter.

WILLIAM BROWNE. See 6 Chalmers, *British Poets* 335 (1810).

Indeed one would rather that twenty guilty persons should escape the punishment of death, than one innocent person should be executed.

SIR JOHN FORTESCUE, *De Laudibus Legum Angliae,* ch. 27.

My object all sublime
I shall achieve in time—
To let the punishment fit the crime—
The punishment fit the crime.

WILLIAM S. GILBERT, *The Mikado,* Act II.

I think Sir Godfry should decide the suit;
Who sent the thief that stole the cash, away,
And punished him that put it in his way.

POPE, *Imitations of Horace,* II, ii.

First hang and draw,
Then hear the cause by Lidford law.

Proverb. FULLER, *Worthies: Devonshire* (1662).

"You're a young gentleman that doesna approve of Caapital Punishment," said Hermiston. "Weel, I'm an auld man that does."

ROBERT L. STEVENSON, *Weir of Hermiston,* ch. 3.

Cross Examination

You seem to think that the art of cross-examining is to examine crossly.

BARON ALDERSON, to counsel cross-examining with more temper than skill. See, Ballantine, *Some Experiences of a Barrister's Life* 124 (2nd ed. 1882).

Judge: Really, this is a long way from the point.
Serj. Ballantine: If I were to begin any nearer, the witness would discover my object.

BALLANTINE, *Some Experiences of a Barrister's Life* 127 (2nd ed. 1882).

Would you be surprised to hear that—?

LORD BOWEN Phrase used repeatedly by Coleridge when cross-examining the "Claimant" in the famous Tichborne Case. The expression which became a byword is said to have been invented by Bowen who at the time was a junior counsel appearing with Coleridge against the claimant. The intent of the phrasing was to abstain from giving in the form of the question any indication as to whether it would be correctly answered in the affirmative or in the negative. D.N.B., Supp. 1.

More cross-examinations are suicidal than homicidal.

EMORY R. BUCKNER. See, ch. xii in Wellman's *Art of Cross Examination.*

Battledore and shuttlecock's a wery good game, vhen you ain't the shuttlecock and two lawyers the battledores, in vich case it gets too excitin' to be pleasant.

CHARLES DICKENS, *Pickwick Papers*, ch. 20.

If by cross-examination to credit you prove that a man's oath cannot be relied on, and he has sworn he did not go to Rome on May 1, you do not, therefore, prove that he did go to Rome on May 1; there is simply no evidence on the subject.

SCRUTTON, L.J., *Hobbs v. Tinling* [1929] 2 K.B. 1, 21.

Custom

One of the main triangles of the laws of England; those laws being divided into common law, statute law and custom.

COKE, *First Institute* 110b.

No degree of antiquity can give sanction to a usage bad in itself.

YATES and ASTON, J.J., *Leach v. Three of the King's Messengers* (1765) 19 How. St. Tr. 1027.

Damages

Nominal damages are a mere peg on which to hang costs.

MAULE, J., *Beaumont v. Greathead* (1846) 2 C.B. 494, 499.

The very definition of a good award is, that it gives dissatisfaction to both parties.

PLUMER, M.R., *Goodman v. Sayers* (1820) 2 Jac. & W. 249, 259.

Danger

Danger invites rescue.

CARDOZO, J., *Wagner v. International Ry.*, 232 N.Y. 176, 180 (1921).

Death

Old Lord Keeper Sir Nicholas Bacon had his barber rubbing and combing his head. Because it was very hot, the window was open to let in a fresh wind. The Lord Keeper fell asleep, and awaked all distempered and in great sweat. Said he to his barber, Why did you let me sleep? Why, my Lord, saithe he, I durst not wake your Lordship. Why then, saith my Lord, you have killed me with kindness. So removed into his bed chamber and within a few days died.

BACON, *Apothegms,* No. 23.

Stay friend, until I put aside my beard, for that never committed treason.

SIR THOMAS MORE, to executioner, before placing head on block. Roper, *Life of More.*

I pray you, Master Lieutenant, see me safe up; and for my coming down let me shift for myself.

SIR THOMAS MORE, at the steps of the scaffold. Roper, *Life of More.*

Debt

It is the policy of the law that the debtor be just before he be generous.

FINCH, J., *Hearn 45 St. Corp. v. Jano,* 283 N. Y. 139, 142 (1940).

You must know then, once more, that nobody can be arrested in Scotland for debt. . . . As a compulsitor, therefore, of payment—that being a thing to which no debtor is naturally inclined, as I have too much reason to warrant from the experience I have had with my own—we had first the letters of four forms, a sort of gentle invitation, by which our sovereign lord the king, interesting himself, as a monarch should, in the regulation of his subjects' private affairs, at first by mild exhortation, and afterwards by letters of more strict enjoyment and more hard compulsion. . . . You suppose, now, a man's committed to prison, because he cannot pay his debt? Quite otherwise; the truth is, the king is so good as to interfere at the request of the creditor, and to send the debtor his royal command to do him justice within a certain time, fifteen days, or six, as the case may be. Well, the man resists and disobeys—what follows? Why, that he be lawfully and rightfully declared a rebel to our gracious sovereign, whose command he has disobeyed, and that by three blasts of a horn at the market-place of Edinburgh, the metropolis of Scotland. And he is then legally imprisoned, not on account of any civil debt, but because of his ungrateful contempt of the royal mandate.

SIR WALTER SCOTT, *The Antiquary*, ch. 39. This passage may be found cited in the Law Reports. See, *Thom v. Black* (1828) 7 Shaw 159, in which Lord Gillies said, "The law on this subject cannot be better expressed than it is by Monkbarns in a work of fiction, with which we are all well acquainted."

Deceit

The statute enjoins truth; this label exhales deceit.

McREYNOLDS, J., *United States v. Schider*, 246 U.S. 519, 522 (1918).

Deceive not thy physician, confessor, nor lawyer.

Proverb. HERBERT, *Jacula Prudentum* (1651).

Decisions

Decided cases are the anchors of the law, as laws are of the state.

BACON, *De Augmentis Scientiarum*, bk 8, Aph. 73.

If we would guide by the light of reason, we must let our minds be bold.

BRANDEIS, J., *Jay Burns Baking Co., v. Bryan*, 264 U.S. 504, 520 (1924).

To say of a judge that his decisions are fine in the sense that they are exquisite essays, exposing a dazzling erudition, is not to my way of thinking a way to compliment him. Decisions should simply be just, within the limits of human possibility. If we bear in mind the seriousness of the function they are supposed to perform, which is that of bringing peace to men, we cannot evaluate opinions on purely esthetic criteria unless we hold that justice can be reduced to the level of a literary diversion or a schoolboy's theme.

PIERO CALAMANDREI, *Eulogy of Judges* 78 (1942) trans. Adams and Phillips.

Nor should it be forgotten that if style is to be prized above all else in opinions, credit for their excellence should be given to the lawyers, since many of the stylistic gems which adorn the judge's opinions are culled from the lawyer's briefs. But the conscientious judge knows that whereas it may be proper for him to borrow rhetorical ornaments and erudition from the lawyer in order to make his dialectical premises more brilliant, when the time comes to render judgment, he must forget literature and search within himself for the unadorned word of justice which, disdainful of beautiful phrases, is most appropriately expressed in monosyllables.

PIERO CALAMANDREI, *Eulogy of Judges* 79 (1942) trans. Adams and Phillips.

In his written judgments as they appear in the law reports, he betrays an utter disregard of rhythm, and his hereditary love of parenthesis is constantly breaking out.

LORD CAMPBELL, 3 *Lives of the Chief Justices* (1857) 236. Referring to Lord Ellenborough.

Write an opinion, and read it a few years later when it is dissected in the briefs of counsel. You will learn for the first time the limitations of the power of speech, or, if not those of speech in general, at all events your own.

BENJAMIN N. CARDOZO, *Law and Literature* 8 (1931).

The picture cannot be painted if the significant and the insignificant are given equal prominence. One must know how to select. All these generalities are as easy as they are obvious, but, alas! the application is an ordeal to try the souls of men.

BENJAMIN N. CARDOZO, *Law and Literature* 8 (1931).

I seem to discern six types or methods which divide themselves from one another with measurable distinctness. There is the type magisterial or imperative; the type laconic or sententious; the type conversational or homely; the type refined or artificial, smelling of the lamp, verging at times upon preciosity or euphuism; the type demonstrative or persuasive; and finally the type tonsorial or agglutinative, so called from the shears and the pastepot which are its implements and emblem.

BENJAMIN N. CARDOZO, *Law and Literature* 10 (1931).

John Marshall has made his decision now let him enforce it.

ANDREW JACKSON. Attributed to the President following the decision in *Worcester v. Georgia*, 31 U.S. 515 (1832) upholding the rights of the Cherokee Indians to their lands.

An opinion is huddled up in conclave, perhaps by a majority of one, delivered as if unanimous, and with the silent acquiescence of lazy or timid associates, by a crafty chief judge.

THOMAS JEFFERSON, *Letter to Thomas Ritchie, December 25, 1820.*

Judicial decisions are not babies brought by constitutional storks but are born out of the travail of economic circumstance.

MAX LERNER, *Fate of the Supreme Court,* 142 Nation 379 (1936).

A per curiam opinion is one where we agree to pool our weaknesses.

HENRY S. MANLEY, *Nonpareil Among Judges,* 34 Corn. L.Q. 52 (1948) — quoting "a judge of the New York Court of Appeals".

Give your judgment, but give no reasons. As you are a man of integrity, sound sense, and information, it is more than an even chance that your judgments will be right; but, as you are ignorant of the law, it is ten to one that your reasons will be wrong.

LORD MANSFIELD, advice to a new Colonial Judge. See, 27 How. St. Tr. 1060.

Pray let us so resolve cases here that they may stand with the reason of mankind, when they are debated abroad. Shall that be reason here that is not reason in any part of the world besides?

LORD NOTTINGHAM, L.C., *Duke of Norfolk's Case* (1681) 3 Ch. Cas. 14, 33.

The only mode of pronouncing a correct judgment is altogether to abstain from giving any reasons for it. Let the appeal judges find that out for themselves.

CHARLES PHILLIPS, when unanimously reversed. Robinson, *Bench and Bar* 55 (1894).

The idea that the language of a judicial opinion in one case has any peculiar sanctity as applied to another case is quite without foundation. Judicial opinions are written to guide the judge as to the law, not to standardize the language to be used in instructions to the jury.

POUND, C.J., *People v. Rutigliano,* 261 N.Y. 103, 107 (1933).

Defense

The laws of God and man both give the party an opportunity to make his defence, if he has any. I remember to have heard it observed by a very learned man upon such an occasion, that even God himself did not pass sentence upon Adam before he was called upon to make his defence. Adam (says God) where are thou? Hast thou eaten of the tree whereof I commanded thee that thou shouldst not eat? And the same question was put to Eve also.

FORTESCUE ALAND, J., *R. v. Chancellor* (1723) 1 Stra. 557, 567.

No advocate without very good cause shall refuse to act for any person tendering a reasonable fee under pain of deprivation of his office of advocate.

SCOTLAND, Rules of Court, ch. 1, s. 2, 4. (Adopted May 27, 1532).

Defense (Unpopular Cause)

While I live and have my health, I must walk the mountain ranges of my profession, swept by the storms of human hate and passion. Neither self respect nor my love for you will permit me to seek obscurity and consequent shelter of deep valleys and smooth meadows.

MATTHEW HALE CARPENTER, *Letter to his wife.* At the time of the Hayes-Tilden election contest he appeared for Tilden and was much criticized.

I will for ever, at all hazards, assert the dignity, independence, and integrity of the English Bar; without which, impartial justice, the most valuable part of the English Constitution, can have no existence. From the moment that any advocate can be permitted to say, that he will or will not stand between the Crown and the subject arraigned in the court where he daily sits to practise, from that moment the liberties of England are at an end.

THOMAS ERSKINE, arguendo, *Trial of Thomas Paine* (1792) 22 How. St. Tr. 358, 412.

I was twice called to the council of him who was my master, when all the world coveted the honor; and I owe him the same service now, when that duty is thought dangerous by many.

MALESHERBES, *Letter, December 11, 1792 to the National Convention*, requesting permission to defend Louis XVI. Soon after the King's trial Malesherbes was arrested, tried for treason and executed. See, 23 *Nouvelle Biographie Universelle* 28 (1860).

Let such be told, Sir, that these criminals, charged with murder, are not yet legally proved guilty, and therefore, however criminal, are entitled, by the laws of God and man, to all legal counsel and aid; that my duty as a man obligated me to undertake; that my duty as a lawyer strengthened the obligation. . . . This and much more might be told with great truth; and I dare affirm that you and this whole people will one day rejoice that I became an advocate for the aforesaid "criminals" charged with the murder of our fellow citizens.

JOSIAH QUINCY, JR., *Letter, March 26, 1770, to his father,* referring to his defense of the British soldiers involved in the Boston Massacre. In, *Memoir of Josiah Quincy, Jr.* by his son.

In due time, gentlemen of the jury, when I shall have paid the debt of nature, my remains will rest here in your midst with those of my kindred and neighbors. It is very possible they may be unhonored, neglected, spurned! But perhaps years hence, when the passion and excitement which now agitate this community shall have passed away, some wandering stranger, some lone exile, some Indian, some negro, may erect over them an humble stone, and thereon this epitaph: HE WAS FAITHFUL.

WILLIAM H. SEWARD, arguendo, in defense of William Freeman, Auburn, N.Y. 1846. The defendant was deaf and obviously insane but his commission of double murder aroused the community. The defendant had previously been imprisoned and mistreated for a theft which he had not committed.

Definition

It is one of the maxims of the civil law, that definitions are hazardous.

SAMUEL JOHNSON, *Rambler,* May 28, 1751.

Delay

Fresh justice is the sweetest.

BACON, *Speech, May 7, 1617,* on taking his seat as Lord Keeper.

I thought ye had some law affair of your ain to look after; I have ane mysell—a ganging plea that my father left me, and his father afore left to him. It's about our back yard; ye'll maybe hae heard of it in the Parliament House, Hutchinson against MacKitchinson; it's a weel kenn'd plea—it's been four times in afore the fifteen, and deil onything the wisest o' them could make o't, but just to send it out again to the outer-house. O it's a beautiful thing to see how lang and how carefully justice is considered in this country.

WALTER SCOTT, *The Antiquary,* ch. 2.

When More sometime had Chancellor been
No more suits did remain.
The like will never more be seen
Till More be there again.

Saying.

The law's delay.

SHAKESPEARE, *Hamlet,* III, 1.

Democracy

Democracy in any sphere is a serious undertaking. It substitutes self-restraint for external restraint. It is more difficult to maintain than to achieve. It demands continuous sacrifice by the individual and more exigent obedience to the moral law than any other form of government. Success in any democratic undertaking must proceed from the individual. It is possible only where the process of perfecting the individual is pursued. His development is attained mainly in the processes of common living. Hence the industrial struggle is essentially an affair of the Church and its imperative task.

LOUIS D. BRANDEIS, *Letter to Robert W. Bruere,* February 25, 1922. (As quoted by Richberg, 31 Col. L. R. 1099).

Dictum

Obiter dicta, like the proverbial chickens of destiny, come home to roost sooner or later in a very uncomfortable way to the Judges who have uttered them, and are a great source of embarrassment in future cases.

BOWEN, L.J., *Cooke v. New River Co.* (1888) 38 Ch. D. 56, 71.

Dicta are not always ticketed as such, and one does not recognize them always at a glance.

BENJAMIN N. CARDOZO, *Nature of the Judicial Process* 30 (1921).

A case is only an authority for what it actually decides. I entirely deny that it can be quoted for a proposition that may seem to follow logically from it. Such a mode of reasoning assumes that the law is necessarily a logical code, whereas every lawyer must acknowledge that the law is not always logical at all.

LORD HALSBURY, L.C., *Quinn v. Leathem* [1901] A.C. 495, 506.

I recognize, of course, that the rule of stare decisis binds us to follow that court [U.S. Supreme] in respect of things decided by it. I know of no rule of stare "dictis" which binds us to follow it in respect of things merely said by it.

HUTCHESON, J., *Hercules Gasoline Co. v. Comm'r,* 147 F.2d 972, 974 (1945).

An *obiter dictum,* in the language of the law, is a gratuitous opinion, an individual impertinence, which, whether it be wise or foolish, right or wrong, bindeth none—not even the lips that utter it.

The Old Judge. Quoted on title page of Birrell, *Obiter Dicta* (1885).

No "guidance" is more misleading, no "kindly light" is more of a will-o'-the-wisp than an obiter dictum sometimes contrives to be.

LORD SUMNER, *Sorrell v. Smith* [1925] A.C. 700, 743.

An opinion given in Court, if not necessary to the judgment given of record, but that it might have been as well given if no such, or a contrary, opinion had been broached is no judicial opinion, nor more than a gratis dictum.

VAUGHAN, C.J., *Bole v. Horton* (1670) Vaugh. 360, 382.

Diligence

Diligence is always valuable, particularly in defending causes . . . It is the one virtue that contains in itself all the rest. (*Diligentia, inquam, quae cum omnibus in rebus tum in causis defendendis plurimum valet . . . diligentia, qua una virtute omnes virtutes reliquae continentur.*)

CICERO, *De Oratore*, II, 35.

Dining

I approve of the dining system; it puts people in good humor, and makes them agree, when they otherwise might not: a dinner lubricates business.

LORD STOWELL. 2 Townsend, *Lives of Twelve Eminent Judges* 362 (1846).

Discovery

A common law trial is and always should be an adversary proceeding. Discovery was hardly intended to enable a learned profession to perform its functions either without wits or on wits borrowed from the adversary.

JACKSON, J., *Hickman v. Taylor*, 329 U.S. 495, 516 (1947).

Discretion

The discretion of a Judge is the law of tyrants: it is always unknown. It is different in different men. It is casual, and depends upon constitution, temper, passion. In the best it is oftentimes caprice; in the worst it is every vice, folly, and passion, to which human nature is liable.

LORD CAMDEN, C.J., *Hindson v. Kersey* (1765), cited, 8 How. St. Tr. 57 fn.

The exercise of a discretion has been characterized as odious; but where the necessity exists for its exercise, a judge is bound not to shrink from the responsibility devolving on him.

CRAMPTON, J., *Conway v. Queen* (1845) 1 Cox C.C. 210, 217.

Absolute discretion is a ruthless master. It is more destructive of freedom than any of man's other inventions.

DOUGLAS, J., *United States v. Wunderlich,* 342 U.S. 98, 101 (1951).

Sir John Fineux, sometime Chief Justice of the King's Bench, was often heard to say, "Who so taketh from a Justice the order of his discretion, taketh surely from him more than half his Office."

See: CAMDEN, *Remains Concerning Britain*: *Wise Speeches* (1674).

"Discretion" means when it is said that something is to be done within the discretion of the authorities that that something is to be done according to the rules of reason and justice, not according to private opinion; according to law, and not humour. It is to be, not arbitrary, vague, and fanciful, but legal and regular. And it must be exercised within the limit, to which an honest man competent to the discharge of his office ought to confine himself.

LORD HALSBURY, L.C., *Sharp v. Wakefield* [1891] A.C. 173, 179.

The reason, if reason is to be found anywhere, seems to be this—that it requires more discretion to dispose of your own property than to dispose of other people's.

JESSEL, M.R., *Re D'Angibau* (1880) 15 Ch.D. 228, 233. Referring to the fact that although an infant could not dispose of his own property, he could exercise a power.

The writer of this opinion has known a popular judicial officer grow quite angry with a suitor in his court, and threaten him with imprisonment, for no ostensible reason, save the fact, that he wore an overcoat made of wolf skins! Moreover, it cannot safely be denied that mere judicial discretion is sometimes very much interfered with by prejudice, which may be swayed and controlled by the merest trifles—such as the toothache, the rheumatism, the gout, or a fit of indigestion, or even through the very means by which indigestion is frequently sought to be avoided.

PETERS, J., *Ex Parte Chase,* 43 Ala. 303, 310 (1869).

Discrimination

Our constitution is color-blind.

HARLAN, J., *Plessy v. Ferguson,* 163 U.S. 537, 559 (1896).

By the Louisiana statute, the validity of which is here involved, all railway companies (other than street railroad companies) carrying passengers in that State are required to have separate but equal accommodations for white and colored persons.

HARLAN, J., *Plessy v. Ferguson,* 163 U.S. 537, 552 (1896). The Court held that this statute did not violate constitutional provisions. Mr. Justice Harlan alone dissented. In his opinion he turned the words of the statute "equal but separate" into "separate but equal" and it is his terminology that has since prevailed.

Dispute

Coke: Mr. Bacon, if you have any tooth against me, pluck it out, for it will do you more hurt than all the teeth in your head will do you good.

Bacon: Mr. Attorney, I respect you: I fear you not: and the less you speak of your own greatness, the more I will think of it.

Altercation in the Exchequer, 1601 (Bacon, letter to Cecil).

Dissent

Comparatively speaking at least, the dissenter is irresponsible. The spokesman of the court is cautious, timid, fearful of the vivid word, the heightened phrase. He dreams of an unworthy brood of scions, the spawn of careless *dicta,* disowned by the *ratio decidendi,* to which all legitimate offspring must be able to trace their lineage. The result is to cramp and paralyze. One fears to say anything when the peril of misunderstanding puts a warning finger to the lips. Not so, however, the dissenter. He has laid aside the role of the hierophant, which he will be only too glad to resume when the chances of war make him again the spokesman of the majority. For the moment, he is the gladiator making a last stand against the lions.

BENJAMIN N. CARDOZO, *Law and Literature* 34 (1931).

The dissenter speaks to the future, and his voice is pitched to a key that will carry through the years. . . . The prophet and the martyr do not see the hooting throng. Their eyes are fixed on the eternities.

BENJAMIN N. CARDOZO, *Law and Literature* 36 (1931).

The law is not a series of calculating machines where definitions and answers come tumbling out when the right levers are pushed.

WILLIAM O. DOUGLAS, *The Dissent, a Safeguard of Democracy,* 32 J. Am. Jud. Soc. 105 (1948).

In this Court dissents have gradually become majority opinions.

FRANKFURTER, J., *Graves v. N.Y. ex rel O'Keefe,* 306 U.S. 466, 491 (1939).

A dissent in a court of last resort is an appeal to the brooding spirit of the law, to the intelligence of a future day.

CHARLES EVANS HUGHES, *Supreme Court of the United States* 68 (1928).

Some states have inflicted upon their judges the cruel and inhuman punishment of prohibiting dissenting opinions, —a crude and humiliating device of doubtful constitutionality.

HENRY W. TAFT, 4 N.Y.S. Bar Bull. 17 (1932).

The only purpose which an elaborate dissent can accomplish, if any, is to weaken the effect of the opinion of the majority, and thus engender want of confidence in the conclusions of courts of last resort.

WHITE, J., *Pollock v. Farmers' Loan & Trust Co.*, 157 U.S. 429, 608 (1895).

Dissents

I have the misfortune to differ from the Lord Justice Cotton, and I do so with a deep sense of the probability that he is right.

BOWEN, L.J., *In re Haseldine* (1886) 31 Ch. D. 511, 517.

But on mature consideration, all I can say is that I differ on this question from those judges, and I feel bound to say that when I do differ from two such judges, I entertain much more doubt as to the propriety of my decision than of theirs.

BRETT, L.J., *Blake v. Blake* (1882) 7 P.D. 102, 114. (The judges referred to were Sir C. Cresswell and Lord Penzance).

I ran upon a dissenting opinion not long ago, which I have been harboring in secret in the hope of using it hereafter, if provocation shall seem adequate, upon recalcitrant associates. I found it in the reports of the Supreme Court of Ohio. The dissenting judge delivered himself of this restrained comment upon the rule of the majority: "The majority opinion," he said, "to me seems a labored one, its arguments specious and its conclusions faulty." There was not much left of the majority opinion after that.

BENJAMIN N. CARDOZO, *Address,* New York County Lawyers Yearbook 258 (1927).

I know that this, like every other case, will become the parent stock from which a motley progeny will spring. In those after years when this case, elevated to high authority by the cold finality of the printed page is quoted with the customary, "It has been said," perchance another Court will say, "Mayhaps the potter's hand trembled at the wheel." Possibly when that moment comes these words may give that Court a chance to say, "Yea, and a workman standing hard by saw the vase as it cracked."

CLARKSON, J., *Oliver v. Raleigh*, 212 N.C. 465, 471 (1937).

The careful ambiguities and silences of the majority opinion.

FRANKFURTER, J., *Bridges v. California*, 314 U.S. 252, 279 (1941).

Although I think it useless and undesirable, as a rule, to express dissent, I feel bound to do so in this case and to give my reasons for it.

HOLMES, J., *Northern Securities Co. v. United States*, 193 U.S. 197, 400 (1904).

My brothers differ from me in opinion, and they all differ from one another in the reasons of their opinion; but not withstanding their opinion, I think the plaintiff ought to recover.

HOLT, C.J., *Ashby v. White* (1703) 2 Ld. Raym. 938, 950.

I give up. Now I realize fully what Mark Twain meant when he said, "The more you explain it, the more I don't understand it."

JACKSON, J., *Securities Comm. v. Chenery Corp.*, 332 U.S. 194, 214 (1947).

This is the first instance of a final difference of opinion in this Court, since I sat here. Every order, rule, judgment, and opinion, has hitherto been unanimous. That unanimity never could have happened, if we did not among ourselves communicate our sentiments with great freedom; if we did not form our judgments without any prepossession to first thoughts; if we were not always open to conviction, and ready to yield to each other's reasons. We have all equally endeavoured at that unanimity, upon this occasion . . . but, in vain. We continue to differ. And whoever is right, each is bound to abide by and deliver that opinion which he has formed upon the fullest examination.

LORD MANSFIELD, C.J., *Millar v. Taylor* (1769) 4 Burr. 2303, 2395.

I should now, as is my custom, when I have the misfortune to differ from this court, acquiesce silently in its opinion, did I not believe that the judgment of the circuit court of Virginia gave general surprise to the profession, and was generally condemned.

MARSHALL, C.J., *Bank of U.S. v. Dandridge,* 25 U.S. (12 Wheat.) 64, 90 (1827).

At best, the operation of the rule which the Court today enunciates for the first time may be expected to confound confusion in a field already replete with complexities.

VINSON, C.J., *Trupiano v. United States,* 334 U.S. 699, 716 (1948).

It is an old truism that a conclusion is just as sound and no more so than the premises upon which it is based. I make bold to say that there is contained in this language the most beautiful bouquet of Bourbon blunders, expressed and implied, that has ever been handed to the bench and bar of Ohio.

WANAMAKER, J., *City of Cleveland v. Pub. Util. Comm.,* 100 Ohio St. 121, 147 (1919). Referring to associates' opposing opinion.

Distinction

It has been distinguished with more zest than it has been followed.

LORD BIRKENHEAD, L.C., *Portman v. Viscount Portman* [1922] 2 A.C. 473, 488. Referring to an earlier case.

He was in logic a great critic,
Profoundly skill'd in analytic;
He could distinguish, and divide
A hair 'twixt south, and south-west side.

SAMUEL BUTLER, *Hudibras,* Pt. I, Canto I, l. 65.

This distinction appeared to me to be too thin.

LORD ELDON, *Ex parte Kensington* (1813) 2 V.&B. 79, 84.

Distinction without a difference.

HENRY FIELDING, *Tom Jones*, bk 6, ch. 13.

I have known gentlemen to split a hair, and I may have tried to do it myself. But I never before saw any one decimate a hair and count the pieces before the court.

ALEXANDER HAMILTON, referring to his opponent Theophilus Parsons. Parsons, *Memoir of Theophilus Parsons* 160 (1859).

I have heard it suggested that the difference is one of degree. I am the last man in the world to quarrel with a distinction simply because it is one of degree. Most distinctions, in my opinion, are of that sort, and are none the worse for it.

HOLMES, J., *Haddock v. Haddock,* 201 U.S. 562, 631 (1906).

No two cases are exactly alike. A young attorney found two opinions in the New York Reports where the facts seemed identical although the law was in conflict, but an older and more experienced attorney pointed out to him that the names of the parties were different.

CUTHBERT W. POUND, 5 N.Y.S. B. Bull. 267 (1933).

Having referred to a late decision of the King's Bench, which is, in effect, a complete overruling of the case then before the Lords (Richardson v. Campbell, 5 B. and A. 196) I said: "My learned friend will say that the cases are different. And they are different: the Lord Chief Justice, in giving judgment, says so. My Lords, since the short time that I have been in the profession, nothing has excited my admiration so much as the mingled delicacy and astuteness with which the learned Judges of one court avoid overruling the decisions of other courts. (Here Richardson, Parke, and Bailey smiled, and the Chancellor winked.) It would be indecorous in me to insinuate, even if I dared to imagine, what the opinion of the Judges of the King's Bench is; but I beg your Lordships to consider whether the reasoning of Lord Chief Justice Abbott applies to that part of the case in which it differs from the case before the House, or to that in which the cases are the same."

HENRY CRABB ROBINSON, *Diary*, ch. 26, year 1822.

Doe & Roe

John Doe and Richard Roe his crony,
Good men, and true, who never fail
The needy and distress'd to bail,
Direct unseen the dire dispute,
And pledge their names in ev'ry suit.

JOHN ANSTEY, *Pleader's Guide*, bk 1 (1796).

Doubt

The most learned doubteth most.

COKE, *First Institute* 337 b.

I always thought it better to allow myself to doubt before I decided, than to expose myself to the misery after I had decided, of doubting whether I had decided rightly and justly.

LORD ELDON. See, 3 Twiss, *Life of Lord Eldon* 350 (1844).

He delights to balance a straw, to see a feather turn the scale, or make it even again; and divides a scruple to the smallest fraction. He hugs indecision to his breast, and takes home a modest doubt or a nice point to solace himself with it in protracted, luxurious dalliance. Delay seems, in his mind, to be of the very essence of justice.

WILLIAM HAZLITT, *Spirit of the Age* (1825). (re Lord Eldon)

He had such a diffidence of himself, that he did not dare to do right for fear of doing wrong; decrees were always extorted from him; and had he been left alone, he would never have given any suitor his due for fear of giving him what was not so.

HERVEY, 1 *Memoirs of Reign of George II* 286 (1884), referring to Lord Chancellor King.

I may be wrong, and often am, but I never doubt.

SIR GEORGE JESSEL, reply to Attorney General Coleridge when asked if he had any doubts in reference to the Alabama Claims. Jessel admitted that the story was true but added, "Coleridge, with his constitutional inaccuracy has told it wrong. I can never have said 'Often wrong'." See, 219 Blackwood's Mag. 51 (1926).

Mr. Leach
Made a speech,
    Angry, neat but wrong:
Mr. Hart,
On the other part,
    Was heavy, dull, and long:
Mr. Parker
Made the case darker,
    Which was dark enough without:
Mr. Cooke
Cited his book,
And the Chancellor, said—"I doubt."

SIR GEORGE ROSE, when asked by a reporter to take a note of a case for him during his absence. The Chancellor was Lord Eldon. 3 Twiss, *Life of Lord Eldon* 326.

Due Process

That no man of what estate or condition, shall be put out of land or tenement, nor taken nor imprisoned, nor disinherited, nor put to death, without being brought in answer by due process of law.

Statute of Westminster, 28 Edw. III (1354).

Duty

The rule that you are to love your neighbour becomes in law, you must not injure your neighbour; and the lawyer's question, Who is my neighbour? receives a restricted reply. You must take reasonable care to avoid acts or omissions which you can reasonably foresee would be likely to injure your neighbour. Who, then, in law, is my neighbour? The answer seems to be—persons who are so closely and directly affected by my act that I ought reasonably to have them in contemplation as being so affected when I am directing my mind to the acts or omissions which are called in question.

LORD ATKIN, *Donoghue v. Stevenson* [1932] A.C. 562, 580.

Our country has not given us birth, or educated us under her law, as if she expected no succor from us; or that, seeking to administer to our convenience only she might afford a safe retreat for the indulgence of our ease, or a peaceful asylum for our indolence; but that she might hold in pledge the various and most exalted powers of our mind, our genius, and our judgment, for her own benefit and that she might leave for our private use such portion only, as might be spared for that purpose.

CICERO, *De Re Publica,* I, iv.

You see how the vague circumference of the notion of duty shrinks and at the same time grows more precise when we wash it with cynical acid and expel everything except the object of our study, the operations of the law.

OLIVER WENDELL HOLMES, *Path of the Law,* 10 Harv. L.R. 457, 461 (1897).

Earth

So the earth hath He appointed as the suburbs of heaven to be the habitation of man.

COKE, *First Institute* 4a.

The earth hath in law a great extent upwards, not only of water, as hath been said, but of air and all other things even up to heaven; for *cujus est solum ejus est usque ad coelum.*

COKE, *First Institute* 4a.

Education

The system of competitive examinations is a sad necessity. Knowledge is wooed for her dowry, not her diviner charms.

LORD BOWEN, *Lecture on Education.* See, Manson, Builders of Our Law 113 L.T. 356 (1902).

It is idle to pretend that this task is one for which we can find in the Constitution one word to help us as judges to decide where the secular ends and the sectarian begins in education. Nor can we find guidance in any other legal source. It is a matter on which we can find no law but our own prepossessions.

JACKSON, J., *Illinois ex rel McCollum v. Bd. Educ.*, 333 U.S. 203, 237 (1948).

The fundamental theory of liberty upon which all governments in this Union repose excludes any general power of the State to standardize its children by forcing them to accept instruction from public teachers only. The child is not the mere creature of the State.

McREYNOLDS, J., *Pierce v. Society of Sisters*, 268 U.S. 510, 535 (1925).

A whale-ship was my Yale College and my Harvard.

HERMAN MELVILLE, *Moby Dick*, ch.24.

It is, Sir, as I have said, a small college. And yet, there are those who love it.

DANIEL WEBSTER, arguendo in Dartmouth College Case, U.S. Supreme Court, 1818. See R. Choate, *Eulogy on Webster*, for account of trial by Professor Chauncey A. Goodrich.

Education (Legal)

They must pry into the secret recesses of the human heart, and become well acquainted with the whole moral world, that they may discover the abstract reason of all laws: and they must trace the laws of particular states, especially of their own, from the first rough sketches to the more perfect draughts; from the first causes or occasions that produced them, through all the effects, good and bad, that they produced.

LORD BOLINGBROKE, *On the Study and Use of History: Letter 5* (1739).

He was bred to the law, which is, in my opinion, one of the first and noblest of human sciences; a science which does more to quicken and invigorate the understanding, than all the other kinds of learning put together; but it is not apt, except in persons very happily born, to open and liberalize the mind exactly in the same proportion.

BURKE, *Speech on American Taxation,* April 19, 1774.

This study renders men acute, inquisitive, dextrous, prompt in attack, ready in defence, full of resources. In other countries, the people, more simple, and of a less mercurial cast, judge of an ill principle in government only by an actual grievance; here they anticipate the evil, and judge of the pressure of the grievance by the badness of the principle. They augur misgovernment at a distance, and snuff the approach of tyranny in every tainted breeze.

BURKE, *Speech on Conciliation with America,* March 22, 1775.

No man can be a compleat Lawyer by universality of knowledge without experience in particular Cases, nor by bare experience without universality of knowledge; he must be both speculative and active, for the science of the laws, I assure you, must joyn hands with experience.

COKE, *Book of Entries: Preface.*

Six hours to sleep, as many to righteous law;
Four to your prayers, and two to fill your maw;

The rest bestow upon the sacred Muses.
(Sex horas somno, totidem des legibus aequis,
Quatuor orabis, des epulisque duas;
Quod superest ultra sacris largire Camaenis.)

COKE, (translation of ancient verse) *First Institute* 64 b.

Legal studies . . . sharpen, indeed, but like a grinding stone narrow whilst they sharpen.

SAMUEL T. COLERIDGE, *Table Talks: Duties and Needs of an Advocate.*

We lawyers are always curious, always inquisitive, always picking up odds and ends for our patchwork minds, since there is no knowing when and where they may fit into some corner.

CHARLES DICKENS, *Little Dorrit,* bk 2, ch.12.

Live like a hermit and work like a horse.

LORD ELDON, reply to Wilberforce's question as to what advice he would give students who wanted to be young Grants in the law, 3 *Life of Wilberforce* 9, Journal entry, April 17, 1801.

There is nothing does a young lawyer so much good as to be half starved: it has a fine effect.

LORD ELDON, 1 Twiss, *Life of Eldon* 134 (1844).

Pursue the study of the law, rather than the gain of it; pursue the gain of it enough to keep out of the briers, but give your main attention to the study of it. The next is, not to marry early; for an early marriage will obstruct your improvement; and in the next place, it will involve you in expense. Another thing is, not to keep much company, for the application of a man who aims to be a lawyer must be incessant; his attention to his books must be constant, which is inconsistent with keeping much company.

JEREMIAH GRIDLEY, Advice given to John Adams in 1758, 2 *Works of John Adams* 46.

For the rational study of the law the black-letter man may be the man of the present, but the man of the future is the man of statistics and the master of economics.

OLIVER WENDELL HOLMES, *Path of the Law,* 10 Harv. L.R. 457, 469 (1897).

When I began, the law presented itself as a ragbag of details.

OLIVER WENDELL HOLMES, 1 *Continental Legal History Series: Introduction xlvii.*

Other branches of science, and especially history, are necessary to form a lawyer.

THOMAS JEFFERSON, *Letter to John Garland Jefferson, June 11, 1790.*

I do not see why the study of the law is called dry and unpleasant; and I very much suspect that it seems so to those only who would think any study unpleasant which required a great application of the mind and exertion of the memory.

SIR WILLIAM JONES, *Letter June 3, 1771,* to Lord Chief Justice Wilmot.

Seven hours to law, to soothing slumber seven,
Ten to the world allot, and all to Heaven.

SIR WILLIAM JONES. See, 2 Teignmouth, *Life of Jones,* ch. 11 (1804). Compare Coke, supra.

I am only a mast-fed lawyer.

ABRAHAM LINCOLN. See, Hill, *Lincoln, the Lawyer* 198 (1906).

Extemporaneous speaking should be practised and cultivated. It is the lawyer's avenue to the public. . . . And yet there is not a more fatal error to young lawyers than relying too much on speech-making. If anyone upon his rare powers of speaking, shall claim an exemption from the drudgery of the law, his case is a failure in advance.

ABRAHAM LINCOLN, *Notes for a Law Lecture, July 1, 1850.*

Law schools make tough law.

FREDERIC WM. MAITLAND, *English Law and the Renaissance.* Rede Lecture, (1901).

Taught law is tough law.

FREDERIC WM. MAITLAND, *English Law and the Renaissance.* Rede Lecture (1901).

I have heard Serjeant Maynard say the law is *ars bablativa,* meaning that all the learning in the world will not set a man up in bar practice without a faculty of a ready utterance of it.

ROGER NORTH, *On the Study of the Laws* 29.

Sir Henry Finch used to say, study all the morning, and talk all the afternoon.

ROGER NORTH, *On the Study of Laws* 8.

The schoolmaster of the American Bar.

ROSCOE POUND, —appellation bestowed upon. See, *Annual Survey of American Law: Dedication,* 1947.

A lawyer without history or literature is a mechanic, a mere working mason; if he possesses some knowledge of these, he may venture to call himself an architect.

WALTER SCOTT, *Guy Mannering,* ch. 37.

The subject matter of law is somewhat transcendant, and too high for ordinary capacities.

WILLIAM SHEPPARD, *Touchstone: Preface* (1650).

This lawyer's preparatory education is certainly one of the most cold blooded, prejudiced pieces of invention that ever a man was slave to . . . A fellow should do and think of nothing else than LAW.

THACKERAY, *Letter, January 14, 1832* (to his mother).

On the other side of the third landing . . . sits Mr. Paley, who took the highest honors, and who is a fellow of his college, who will sit and read and note cases until two o'clock in the morning; who will rise at seven and be at the pleader's chambers as soon as they are open, where he will work until an hour before dinner-time. . . . He has not been throwing himself away: he has only been bringing a great intellect laboriously down to the comprehension of a mean subject, and in his fierce grasp of that, resolutely excluding from his mind all higher thoughts, all better things, all the wisdom of philosophers and historians, all the thoughts of poets; all wit, fancy, reflection, art, love, truth altogether—so that he may master that enormous legend of the law, which he proposes to gain his livelihood by expounding.

THACKERAY, *Pendennis*, ch. 29.

Emergency

While emergency does not create power, emergency may furnish the occasion for the exercise of power.

HUGHES, C.J., *Home Building & Loan Assn. v. Blaisdell*, 290 U.S. 398, 426 (1934).

Although an emergency may not call into life a power which has never lived, nevertheless emergency may afford a reason for the exertion of a living power already enjoyed.

WHITE, C.J., *Wilson v. New*, 243 U.S. 332, 348 (1917).

Environment

There is a plain old house in the hills of Oneida, overlooking the valley of the Mohawk, where truth and honor dwelt in my youth. When I go back, as I am about to go, to spend my declining years, I mean to go with the feeling that I can say I have not failed to speak and to act in accordance with the lessons that I learned there from the God of my fathers.

ELIHU ROOT, *N. Y. Const. Conv. 1915*, 4 Rev. Rec. 3505.

Epitaphs

He was splendid
In an undefended.

J.P.C., *Epitaph on a Barrister*, 116 Just. P. 640 (1952).

In Memory of Richard, Baron Westbury,
Lord High Chancellor of England.
He was an eminent Christian,
An energetic and successful Statesman,
And a still more eminent and successful Judge.
During his Three Years of Office he abolished
The Time-honoured Institution of the Insolvent Debtors' Court,
The Ancient Mode of Conveying Land and
The Eternity of Punishment.
Towards the End of his Earthly career
In the Judicial Committee of the Privy Council
He dismissed Hell with Costs,
And took away from the orthodox members of
The Church of England
Their best hope of Eternal Damnation.

EDWARD H. PEMBER. Lord Westbury in his judgment in the case of *Bishop of Salisbury v. Williams and Wilson*, said that the charge that Wilson in his *Essay* had departed from the teaching of the Protestant Church as to Eternal Punishment had not been made out.

Equality

Equality may be as much as anything else equality of misery.

RUDOLPH VON JHERING, *Law as a Means to an End*, ch. 8, sec. 11 (5 Mod. Leg. Phil. Ser. 276).

Equal rights to unequal possessions, equal justice to the rich and poor; this is what men come out to fight for and to defend.

SYDNEY SMITH, *Assize Sermon, March 28, 1824, at York.*

Equity

A correction of law where it is defective owing to its universality.

ARISTOTLE, *Ethica Nicomachea,* bk 5, 10.

Equity is that idea of justice, which contravenes the written law.

ARISTOTLE, *Rhetoric,* bk 1, ch. 13.

Equity does not demand that its suitors shall have led blameless lives.

BRANDEIS, J., *Loughran v. Loughran,* 292 U.S. 216, 229 (1934).

Equity does not act for every shadowy or unsubstantial wrong.

CARDOZO, C.J., *Nann v. Raimist,* 255 N.Y. 307, 319 (1931).

Equity fashions a trust with flexible adaptation to the call of the occasion.

CARDOZO, J., *Adams v. Champion,* 294 U.S. 231, 237 (1935).

Equity acts in personam. *(Aequitas agit in personam.)*

COWPER, L.K., *Toller v. Carteret* (1705), 2 Vern. 494, 495.

He who will have equity, or comes hither for equity, must do equity.

COWPER, L.C., *Demandray v. Metcalf* (1715) Prec. Ch. 419, 420.

Upon that occasion Lord Chief Justice De Grey said he never liked Equity so well as when it was like Law. The day before I had heard Lord Mansfield say he never liked Law so well as when it was like Equity.

LORD ELDON, *Lord Dursley v. Fitzhardinge Berkeley* (1801) 6 Ves. 251, 260.

A man must come into a court of equity with clean hands.

EYRE, C.B., *Dering v. Earl of Winchelsea* (1787) 1 Cox Eq. 318, 319.

Equality is equity.

RICHARD FRANCIS, *Maxims of Equity* (1728).

And it was said by Lord Somers, that equity did delight in equality, and that the distribution according to the statute was most agreeable to natural justice.

HOLT, C.J., *Petit v. Smith* (1695) 1 P. Wms. 7, 9.

The rules of Courts of Equity are not, like the rules of the Common Law, supposed to have been established from time immemorial. It is perfectly well known that they have been established from time to time—altered, improved, and refined from time to time. In many cases we know the names of the Chancellors who invented them.

JESSEL, M.R., *Re Hallett* (1879) 13 Ch. D. 696, 710.

To apply one general law to all particular cases, were to make all shoes by one last, or to cut one glove for all hands, which how unfit it would prove, every man can readily perceive.

WILLIAM LAMBARDE, *Archeion* 69 (1635).

Equity had come not to destroy the law, but to fulfil it.

FREDERIC WM. MAITLAND, *Lectures on Equity* 17 (1909). See similar statement by Bacon, under Chancery.

We ought to think of equity as supplementary law, a sort of appendix added on to our code, or a sort of gloss written around our code, an appendix, a gloss, which used to be administered by courts especially designed for that purpose, but which is now administered by the High Court of Justice as part of the code.

FREDERIC WM. MAITLAND, *Lectures on Equity* 18 (1909).

Equity without common law would have been a castle in the air, an impossibility.

FREDERIC WM. MAITLAND, *Lectures on Equity* 18 (1909).

Equity is a right wiseness that considereth all the particular circumstances of the Deed the which also is tempered with the Sweetness of Mercy. And such an Equity must always be observed in every Law of Man, and in every general Rule thereof; And that knew he well that said thus, *Laws covet to be ruled by Equity.*

CHRISTOPHER ST. GERMAN, *Doctor and Student,* Dial. I, c. 16.

Equity is a roguish thing: for law we have a measure, know what to trust to; equity is according to the conscience of him that is chancellor, and as that is larger or narrower, so is equity. 'Tis all one as if they should make the standard for the measure we call a foot, a chancellor's foot; what an uncertain measure would this be? One chancellor has a long foot, another a short foot, a third an indifferent foot: 'tis the same thing in the chancellor's conscience.

JOHN SELDEN, *Table-Talk*: *Equity.*

He who seeks equity must do equity.

JOSEPH STORY, *Equity Jurisprudence,* section 77 (1836). Roscoe Pound credits Story with the particular wording of this maxim.

Error

Some courts live by correcting the errors of others and adhering to their own. On these terms courts of final review hold their existence, or those of them which are strictly and exclusively courts of review, without any original jurisdiction, and with no direct function but to find fault or see that none can be found. With these exalted tribunals, who live only to judge the judges, the rule of *stare decisis* is not only a canon of the public good, but a law of self-preservation. At the peril of their lives they must discover error abroad and be discreetly blind to its commission at home.

BLECKLEY, C.J., *Ellison v. Georgia R.R.*, 87 Ga. 691, 695 (1891).

Error (Ignorance being her inseparable twin) doth in her proceeding so infinitely multiply herself, produceth such monstrous and strange chimaeras, floateth in such and so many uncertainties and sucketh down the poison from the contagious breath of Ignorance, as all such into whom she infuseth any of her poisoned breath, she dangerously infects or intoxicates.

COKE, 5 Rep.: *Preface.*

Eskgroviana

And so, gentlemen, having shown you that the pannell's argument is utterly impossibill, I shall now proceed to show you that it is extremely improbabill.

LORD ESKGROVE. See, Cockburn, *Memorials of His Time* 123 (1856). Although Eskgrove was a judge of ability he was famous for the absurdity of his words and actions.

And not only did you murder him, whereby he was bereav-ed of his life, but you did thrust, or push, or pierce, or project, or propell the lethal weapon through the belly-band of the regimental breeches which were His Majesty's.

ibid. 121. When condemning a tailor to death for murdering a soldier by stabbing.

All this you did; and God preserve us! joost when they were sitten doon to their denner!

ibid. 123. When condemning to death persons who broke into a house and assaulted and robbed the occupants.

Estimate

An estimated value is a precarious measure of justice, compared with the specific thing.

LORD MANSFIELD, C.J., *Fisher v. Prince* (1762) 3 Burr. 1363, 1365.

Ethics (Legal)

Boswell: I asked him whether, as a moralist, he did not think that the practice of the law, in some degree, hurt the nice feeling of honesty.

Johnson: Why no, Sir, if you act properly. You are not to deceive your clients with false representations of your opinion: you are not to tell lies to a judge.

BOSWELL, *Life of Samuel Johnson*: 1768.

Boswell: But what do you think of supporting a cause which you know to be bad?

Johnson: Sir, you do not know it to be good or bad until the Judge determines it. I have said that you are to state facts fairly; so that your thinking, or what you call knowing, a cause to be bad, must be from reasoning, must be from supposing your arguments to be weak and inconclusive. But, Sir, that is not enough. An argument which does not convince yourself, may convince the Judge, to whom you urge it: and if it does convince him, why, then, Sir, you are wrong, and he is right. It is his business to judge; and you are not to be confident in your own opinion that a cause is bad, but to say all you can for your client, and then hear the Judge's opinion.

ibid.

Boswell: But, Sir, does not affecting a warmth when you have no warmth, and appearing to be clearly of one opinion when you are in reality of another opinion, does not such dissimulation impair one's honesty? Is there not some danger that a lawyer may put on the same mask, in common life, in the intercourse with his friends?

Johnson: Why no, Sir. Everybody knows you are paid for affecting warmth for your client; and it is, therefore, properly no dissimulation; the moment you come from the bar you resume your usual behaviour. Sir, a man will no more carry the artifice of the bar into the common intercourse of society, than a man who is paid for tumbling upon his hands will continue to tumble upon his hands when he should walk on his feet.

ibid.

The difference between the true lawyer and those men who consider the law merely a trade is that the latter seek to find ways to permit their clients to violate the moral standards of society without overstepping the letter of the law, while the former look for principles which will persuade their clients to keep within the limits of the spirit of the law in common moral standards.

PIERO CALAMANDREI, *Eulogy of Judges* 62 (1942) trans. Adams and Phillips.

Ethical considerations can no more be excluded from the administration of justice, which is the end and purpose of all civil laws, than one can exclude the vital air from his room and live.

JOHN F. DILLON, *Laws and Jurisprudence of England and America,* Lecture I (1894).

There is a vague popular belief that lawyers are necessarily dishonest. . . . Let no young man choosing the law for a calling for a moment yield to the popular belief—resolve to be honest at all events; and if in your own judgment you cannot be an honest lawyer, resolve to be honest without being a lawyer. Choose some other occupation, rather than one in the choosing of which you do, in advance, consent to be a knave.

ABRAHAM LINCOLN, *Notes for a Law Lecture, July 1, 1850.*

The ultimate justification of the law is to be found, and can only be found, in moral considerations.

LORD MACMILLAN, *Law and Other Things* 41 (1937).

I will join with my adversary in waiving a jury trial wherever and whenever it can possibly be done without the sacrifice of a fundamental right.

I will join with my adversary in supporting a trial justice in fair comment upon the evidence and reasonable direction to a jury on the facts.

I will join with my adversary in fair concession of undisputed facts.

I will not put an adversary to his proof in respect to facts whose existence my client admits.

I will refrain from merely formal or technical objections to the admission of evidence.

I will co-operate with the trial justice and my adversary to secure a speedy, prompt and complete presentation of the facts of the case.

I will neither make nor oppose interlocutory motions unless they are of real and practical importance.

I will take no appeal unless I am satisfied that a substantial error has been committed and that a new trial should reasonably give a different result.

JOSEPH M. PROSKAUER, *Credo* (1928). See, 13 N.Y. Co. Lawyers Assn. Bar Bull. 146 (1956).

An eminent lawyer cannot be a dishonest man. Tell me a man is dishonest, and I will answer he is no lawyer. He cannot be, because he is careless and reckless of justice; the law is not in his heart, is not the standard and rule of his conduct.

DANIEL WEBSTER, *Speech, Charleston, S.C. Bar, May 10, 1847.*

For your duty to particular clients you may consider that some are rich, yet with such there must be no endeavour to lengthen causes, to continue fees. Some are poor, yet their business must not be neglected, if their cause be honest, they are not the worst clients; though they fill not your purses, they will fill the ears of God with prayers for you; and he who is the defender of the poor will repay your charity. Some clients are of mean capacity, you must take the more pains to instruct yourself to understand their business. Some are of quick capacity and confidence, yet you must not trust to their information. Some are peaceable; detain them not, but send them home the sooner. Some are contentious; advise them to reconcilement with their adversary. Amongst your clients and all others endeavour to gain and preserve that estimation and respect which is due to your degree and to a just, honest, and discreet person.

BULSTRODE WHITELOCK, *Memorials of English Affairs* 354. His speech on the call of the sergeants, 1648.

Evidence

Irrelevance can be highly enlightening. The witness who starts with what she had for breakfast and remembers it was Thursday because her husband's sister had come down with the measles when she shouldn't have if she had only gone to the other doctor, the one with glasses—should be a delight to the judge's heart and make the jury feel at home. Behind this leisurely sweep of incident they can follow her as they please, and it will give them at least her barometric pressure at the time when she signed the note at the bank without reading it. After listening to enough of it, any idiot would know that she was an accommodation endorser who had done it to help her husband and had got nothing out of it for herself.

CURTIS BOK, *I Too, Nicodemus* 322 (1946).

It is for ordinary minds, and not for psychoanalysts, that our rules of evidence are framed. They have their source very often in considerations of administrative convenience, of practical expediency, and not in rules of logic.

CARDOZO, J., *Shepard v. United States*, 290 U.S. 96, 104 (1933).

Judges, the case speaks for itself, than which there is no more powerful advocacy. *Res loquitor ipsa, judices, quae semper valet plurimum.*

CICERO, *Pro Milone*, xx.

Oh, Sammy, Sammy, vy worn't there a alleybi.

CHARLES DICKENS, *Pickwick Papers*, ch. 34.

Chops and tomata sauce.

CHARLES DICKENS, *Pickwick Papers*, ch. 34. (From Pickwick's letter to Mrs. Bardell, introduced in evidence in the breach of promise action).

"You must not tell us what the soldier, or any other man, said, Sir," interposed the judge, "it's not evidence."

CHARLES DICKENS, *Pickwick Papers*, ch. 34.

They (rules of evidence) are founded in the charities of religion, in the philosophy of nature, in the truths of history, and in the experience of common life.

THOMAS ERSKINE, arguendo, *Trial of Thomas Hardy* (1794) 24 How. St. Tr. 966.

It is certainly a maxim that all evidence is to be weighed according to the proof which it was in the power of one side to have produced, and in the power of the other to have contradicted.

LORD MANSFIELD, C.J., *Blatch v. Archer* (1774) 1 Cowp. 63, 65.

Human nature constitutes a part of the evidence in every case.

POTTER, J., *Greene v. Harris*, 11 R.I. 5, 17 (1875).

Some circumstantial evidence is very strong, as when you find a trout in the milk.

HENRY D. THOREAU, *Journal, November 11, 1850.*

Fair Trade

To forbid the competition of a cocoanut grove with the American cow.

LETTS, J., *Carolene Products Co. v. Wallace*, 27 F. Supp. 110, 113 (1939). Referring to the purpose of the Filled Milk Act.

Thirsty folk want beer, not explanations.

LORD MACNAGHTEN, *Montgomery v. Thompson* [1891] A.C. 217, 225. Case involved the fraudulent use of the trade name, Stone Ale.

Fair Use

Books are published with an expectation, if not a desire, that they will be criticised in reviews, and if deemed valuable that parts of them will be used as affording illustrations by way of quotation, or the like—and if the quantity taken be neither substantial nor material, if, as it has been expressed by some Judges, a "fair use" only be made of the publication, no wrong is done and no action can be brought.

LORD HATHERLEY, *Chatterton v. Cave* (1878) 3 App. Cas. 483, 492.

Faith

I die the King's servant, but God's first.

SIR THOMAS MORE.

Is not this house as nigh heaven as mine own?

SIR THOMAS MORE, when imprisoned in the Tower of London and his wife urged him to obtain his freedom by yielding to the king. Roper, *Life of More.*

Feeling

Men's feelings are as different as their faces.

BULLER, J., *Good v. Elliott* (1790) 3 T.R. 693, 701.

Fees

As for lawyers' fees, I must leave it to the conscience and merit of the lawyer.

BACON, *Speech, May 7, 1617,* on taking his seat in Chancery as Lord Keeper.

Voila! the non suit of cow beef.

THOMAS ERSKINE, on receiving fee from Admiral Keppel for defending him in court martial proceeding. The charge was pronounced "malicious and ill-founded."

I dislike sending in professional charges to friendly people, but we have a saying here that offices like individuals have to live.

REGINALD L. HINE, *Confessions of an Un-Common Attorney* 26 (1945).

The matter of fees is important, far beyond the mere question of bread and butter involved. Properly attended to, fuller justice is done to both lawyer and client. An exorbitant fee should never be claimed. As a general rule never take your whole fee in advance, nor any more than a small retainer. When fully paid beforehand, you are more than a common mortal if you can feel the same interest in the case, as if something was still in prospect for you, as well as for your client.

ABRAHAM LINCOLN, *Notes for a Law Lecture, July 1, 1850.*

I have just received yours of the 16th, with check on Flagg & Savage for twenty-five dollars. You must think I am a high-priced man. You are too liberal with your money. Fifteen dollars is enough for the job. I send you a receipt for fifteen dollars, and return to you a ten dollar bill.

ABRAHAM LINCOLN, *Letter to George P. Floyd, February 21, 1856.*

The form of their pleading is 1st, the advocates and their clients stand each on either side of the door through the bar, at the bar, and the advocates plead in Scotch before them, and in the then time of their pleading their clients will put a double piece or more, with an ordinary fee with the poorest, and will say to their advocates "thumb it thumb it," and then will the advocates plead accordingly as they feel it weigh.

LOWTHER, *Our Journall into Scotland* (1629) 31. Reprint, 1894.

To lying awake thinking of your case.

Saying. Suggested item on lawyer's bill.

'Tis like the breath of an unfee'd lawyer; you gave me nothing for 't.

SHAKESPEARE, *King Lear*, I, 4.

There was a young lady of Ci'cester,
Who went to consult her solicitor,
When he asked for his fee,
She said "Fiddle-de-dee,
I only looked in as a visitor."

Unknown.

While in bed the sick man's lying,
While in Court your client's cause you're trying,
That's the time to get your fee.
For, when the sick man has recovered,
And the lawsuit's won or smothered,
He will never think of thee.

Unknown. Inscribed on the walls of the University of Bologna, Italy in the Thirteenth Century.

Fiction

Fiction (in law) a wilful falsehood, uttered by a judge, for the purpose of giving to injustice the colour of justice.

JEREMY BENTHAM, *Scotch Reform*, 5 Works 13.

There are many pleasant fictions of the law in constant operation, but there is not one so pleasant or practically humorous as that which supposes every man to be of equal value in its impartial eye, and the benefits of all laws to be equally attainable by all men, without the smallest reference to the furniture of their pockets.

CHARLES DICKENS, *Nicholas Nickleby*, ch. 46.

Any assumption which conceals, or affects to conceal, the fact that a rule of law has undergone alteration its letter remaining unchanged, its operation being modified.

SIR HENRY MAINE, *Ancient Law*, ch. 2.

Fictions of law hold only in respect of the ends and purposes for which they were invented.

LORD MANSFIELD, C.J., *Morris v. Pugh* (1761) 3 Burr. 1241, 1243.

It is the creature of the court, and is moulded to the purposes of justice, according to the view which its inventors have taken of its capacity to effect those purposes.

MARSHALL, Cir. J., *Livingston v. Jefferson*, 15 Fed. Cas. (No. 8411) 660, 663 (1811).

Flag

The flag is but a bit of bunting to one who insists on prose.

HOLMES, C.J. On motion that the court adjourn on February 4, 1901, the one hundredth anniversary of the day John Marshall took his seat as Chief Justice of the United States, 178 Mass. 627.

Flattery

Parliaments, palaces of princes, and pulpits should be free from adulation and flattery.

COKE, *Third Institute* 209.

Fraud

Fraud includes the pretense of knowledge when knowledge there is none.

CARDOZO, C.J., *Ultramares Corp. v. Touche*, 255 N.Y. 170, 179 (1931).

Fraud is infinite in variety; sometimes it is audacious and unblushing; sometimes it pays a sort of homage to virtue, and then it is modest and retiring; it would be honesty itself if it could only afford it.

LORD MACNAGHTEN, *Reddaway v. Banham* [1896] A.C. 199, 221.

Freedom

Many an appeal to freedom is the masquerade of privilege or inequality seeking to intrench itself behind the catchword of a principle.

BENJAMIN N. CARDOZO, *Mr. Justice Holmes,* 44 Harv. L.R. 682, 687 (1931).

Freedom is a thing with which the nature of man has been endowed by God. For this reason if it be taken away from man it strives of its own energy always to return.

SIR JOHN FORTESCUE, *De Laudibus Legum Angliae,* ch. 42.

Freedom of the Press

The liberty of the press is indeed essential to the nature of a free state; but this consists in laying no previous restraints upon publications, and not in freedom from censure for criminal matter when published.

BLACKSTONE, *Commentaries,* bk 4, 151.

To censure the licentiousness, is to maintain the liberty, of the press.

BLACKSTONE, *Commentaries,* bk 4, 153.

The liberty of the press consists in printing without any previous licence, subject to the consequences of law. The licentiousness of the press is Pandora's Box, the source of every evil. Miserable is the condition of individuals, dangerous is the condition of the State, if there is no certain law, or, which is the same thing, no certain administration of law, to protect individuals, or guard the State.

LORD MANSFIELD, C.J., *R. v. Shipley* (1784) 4 Doug. 73, 170.

If it poisons the minds of the people, it likewise administers an antidote. The same waggons, the same flys and stages, that carry down into the county the lies and abuse of faction, carry down also the lies and abuse of the ministry. If any one is bit by the tarantula of opposition, he is cured by the music of the court.

ALEXANDER WEDDERBURN, *Speech, House of Commons, (1770)* 16 Parl. Hist. 1290.

Freedom of Speech

Free speech is not so absolute or irrational a conception as to imply paralysis of the means for effective protection of all the freedoms secured by the Bill of Rights.

FRANKFURTER, J., *Bridges v. California,* 314 U.S. 252, 282 (1941).

The question in every case is whether the words used are used in such circumstances and are of such a nature as to create a clear and present danger that they will bring about the substantive evils that Congress has a right to prevent.

HOLMES, J., *Schenck v. United States,* 249 U.S. 47, 52 (1919).

The most stringent protection of free speech would not protect a man in falsely shouting fire in a theatre and causing a panic.

HOLMES, J., *Schenck v. United States,* 249 U.S. 47, 52 (1919).

Freedom of Thought

It is common knowledge that the thought of man shall not be tried, for the Devil himself knoweth not the thought of man.

BRIAN, J., Y.B. 17 Edw. 4 Pasch., f.2 (1477).

No man . . . shall be examined upon secret thoughts of his heart, or of his secret opinion.

COKE, 12 Rep. 26.

I maintain that opinion is free, and that conduct alone is amenable to the law.

THOMAS ERSKINE, arguendo, *Trial of Thomas Paine* (1792) 22 How. St. Tr. 358, 419.

If there is any principle of the Constitution that more imperatively calls for attachment than any other it is the principle of free thought —not free thought for those who agree with us but freedom for the thought that we hate.

HOLMES, J., *United States v. Schwimmer,* 279 U.S. 644, 654 (1929).

Compulsory unification of opinion achieves only the unanimity of the graveyard.

JACKSON, J., *West Virginia Bd. Educ. v. Barnette,* 319 U.S. 624, 641 (1943).

If there is any fixed star in our constitutional constellation, it is that no official, high or petty, can prescribe what shall be orthodox in politics, nationalism, religion, or other matters of opinion or force citizens to confess by word or act their faith therein.

JACKSON, J., *West Virginia Bd. Educ. v. Barnette,* 319 U.S. 624, 642 (1943).

The danger that citizens will think wrongly is serious, but less dangerous than atrophy from not thinking at all. . . . Thought control is a copyright of totalitarianism, and we have no claim to it. It is not the function of our Government to keep the citizen from falling into error; it is the function of the citizen to keep the Government from falling into error.

JACKSON, J., *American Communications Assn. v. Douds,* 339 U.S. 382, 442 (1950).

If there be any among us who would wish to dissolve this Union or to change its republican form, let them stand undisturbed as monuments of the safety with which error of opinion may be tolerated where reason is left free to combat it.

THOMAS JEFFERSON, *First Inaugural Address, March 4, 1801.*

Human laws reach not thoughts.

Proverb. THOMAS FULLER, *Proverbs* (1732).

Friend

I am on most friendly terms with all the judges, but I suspect that if I should be gathered to Abraham's bosom some of them would think it an advantage to the law, even if they missed a friend.

OLIVER WENDELL HOLMES, (1930), 2 *Holmes-Pollock Letters* 268.

Gain

Every one thirsteth after gain.

COKE, *Third Institute* 196.

Gentleman

As for gentlemen, they be made good cheape in England. For whosoever studieth the lawes of the realme, who studieth in the universities, who professeth liberall sciences, and to be shorte, who can live idly and without manuall labour, and will beare the port, charge, and countenance of a gentleman, he shall be called master, for that is the title which men give to esquires and other gentlemen, and shall be taken for a gentleman.

SIR THOMAS SMITH, *De Republica Anglorum,* bk 1, ch.20 (1583).

Goodwill

We are not here to sell a parcel of boilers and vats, but the potentiality of growing rich beyond the dreams of avarice.

SAMUEL JOHNSON, when asked what he really considered the value of the Thrale Brewery which, as executor, he was trying to sell. Boswell's *Life of Johnson*: 1781.

Government

The prosperity and greatness of empires ever depended, and ever must depend, upon the use their inhabitants do make of their reason in devising wise laws, and the spirit and virtue with which they watch over their just execution: and it is impious to suppose, that men, who have made no provision for their own happiness or security in their attention to their government, are to be saved by the interposition of Heaven in turning the hearts of their tyrants to protect them.

THOMAS ERSKINE, *arguendo, Proceedings against Dean of St. Asaph,* 21 How. St. Tr. 1015 (1783). Argument was in support of the proposition that juries had right to decide on whether or not a publication was libelous.

Men must turn square corners when they deal with the Government.

HOLMES, J., *Rock Island, Ark. & La. R.R. v. United States,* 254 U.S. 141, 143 (1920).

The science of government is the most abstruse of all sciences; if, indeed, that can be called a science, which has but few fixed principles, and practically consists in little more than the exercise of a sound discretion, applied to the exigencies of the state as they arise. It is the science of experiment.

JOHNSON, J., *Anderson v. Dunn,* 19 U.S. (6 Wheat.) 204, 226 (1821).

The idea is Utopian, that government can exist without leaving the exercise of discretion somewhere. Public security against the abuse of such discretion must rest on responsibility, and stated appeals to public approbation.

JOHNSON, J., *Anderson v. Dunn,* 19 U.S. (6 Wheat.) 204, 226 (1821).

No government ought to be so defective in its organization, as not to contain within itself, the means of securing the execution of its own laws against other dangers than those which occur every day.

MARSHALL, C.J., *Cohens v. Virginia,* 19 U.S. (6 Wheat.) 264, 387 (1821).

Government (Laws and Men)

He who bids the law rule may be deemed to bid God and Reason alone rule, but he who bids man rule adds an element of the beast; for desire is a wild beast, and passion perverts the minds of rulers, even when they are the best of men.

ARISTOTLE, *Politics,* III, 16 (trans. Jowett).

A government of laws without men is as visionary as a government of men without laws; the solution will always be a compromise based on experience.

LEARNED HAND, *The Deficiencies of Trials to Reach the Heart of the Matter,* 3 Lectures on Legal Topics, Assn Bar of City of N.Y., 102 (1926).

Headnotes

Possession in Scotland evidence of stealing in England.

Clement's Case (1830) 1 Lewin C.C. 113. A popular version is: Possession of trousers in Scotland-evidence of larceny in England.

The decision depends largely, if not entirely, on facts, which are stated at great length by the court, both in the statement of the case, and in its opinion. These papers are most carefully prepared. While both deal with facts, those facts are stated with clearness, with fullness, with completeness, and with unusual care. They leave nothing untouched. Without treating them with the same fullness, the reporter feels himself unable to prepare a headnote which could convey an adequate and just account of the opinion and decision of the court. Under these circumstances he deems it best not to attempt an impossibility, but to respectfully ask the readers of this headnote to regard the opinion of the court in this case as incorporated into it.

JOHN CHANDLER BANCROFT DAVIS, Headnote to opinion in *Huntting Elevator Co. v. Bosworth,* 179 U.S. 415 (1900).

The reporter does not believe that the opinion in this case was intended to change the settled rule of law, as laid down in the several cases cited, and he has therefore made the head-note conform to those cases, and not to the language of the opinion.

J. W. SHEPERD (reporter), *Drake v. State,* 51 Ala. 30 (1874).

Hindsight

The event is always a great teacher.

BRADLEY, J., *The Nevada,* 106 U.S. 154, 157 (1882).

History

History, in illuminating the past, illuminates the present, and in illuminating the present, illuminates the future.

BENJAMIN N. CARDOZO, *Nature of the Judicial Process* 53 (1921).

The laws of a nation form the most instructive portion of its history.

EDWARD GIBBON, *Decline and Fall of the Roman Empire,* ch. 45.

Historic continuity with the past is not a duty, it is only a necessity.

OLIVER WENDELL HOLMES, *Learning and Science, Speeches* 68 (1913).

A page of history is worth a volume of logic.

HOLMES, J., *N.Y. Trust Co. v. Eisner,* 256 U.S. 345, 349 (1921).

Law in particular becomes then only a rational study, when it is traced historically, from its first rudiments among savages, through successive changes, to its highest improvements in a civilized society.

LORD KAMES, *Historical Law Tracts: Preface.*

Law treated historically becomes an entertaining study; entertaining not only to those whose profession it is, but to every person who hath any thirst for knowledge.

LORD KAMES, *Historical Law Tracts: Preface.*

History involves comparison and the English lawyer who knew nothing and cared nothing for any system but his own hardly came in sight of the idea of legal history.

FREDERIC WM. MAITLAND, *Why the History of English Law Is Not Written,* Inaugural Lecture in Arts School, Cambridge, 1888, in 1 *Coll. Papers* 488.

Such is the unity of all history that any one who endeavours to tell a piece of it must feel that his first sentence tears a seamless web.

FREDERIC WM. MAITLAND, *Prologue to a History of English Law,* 14 L.Q.R. 13 (1898).

To-day we study the day before yesterday, in order that yesterday may not paralyse to-day, and to-day may not paralyse tomorrow.

FREDERIC WM. MAITLAND, *Survey of the Century,* in 3 *Coll. Papers* 439.

Holmes, Oliver Wendell

It has taken a decade to elevate Mr. Justice Holmes from deity to mortality.

WALTON H. HAMILTON, 9 Univ. Chi. L.R. 1 (1941).

I could carve out of a banana, a judge with more backbone than that.

THEODORE ROOSEVELT — attributed to, after Holmes' dissent in *Northern Securities Co. v. United States,* 193 U.S. 197 (1904).

Honesty

He kept his innocency when others let theirs go; . . . which raises his merit to a higher pitch. For to be honest when everybody is honest, when honesty is in fashion and is trump, as I may say, is nothing so meritorious; but to stand alone in the breach—to own honesty when others dare not to do it, cannot be sufficiently applauded, nor sufficiently rewarded.

HOLLIS, M.P., *Speech in behalf of Sir Ranulphe Crew,* 2 pt. 2 Rushworth, *Hist. Coll.* App. 267. (Chief Justice Crew was removed from office for denying the legality of forced loans by Charles I).

Horse Racing

For a generation or more betting at horse races was unlawful. After this prolonged burst of morality the Legislature suddenly discovered the need of "improving the breed of horses" . . . In a backhanded way this legislation restored race track betting by removing the criminal penalties. But let no one suspect that our best citizens repair to Belmont Park and other nearby tracks for the purpose of betting or gambling. Perish the thought, for their minds rest on higher things. Improving the breed of horses is their aim, and their conversation, aside from formal greetings, deals solely with sires and dams, foals and fillies, blood lines, consanguinity and inherited characteristics. These things a judge must believe, even at the risk of being chided as naive, because they are contemporary America.

BONYNGE, J., *Reed v. Littleton,* 159 Misc. (N.Y.) 853, 855 (1936).

The bond . . . was given, not to pay racing debts, but to avoid the consequences of not having paid them.

LORD ROMILLY, M.R., *Bubb v. Yelverton* (1870) L.R. 9 Eq. 471, 474.

House

For a man's house is his castle.

COKE, *Third Institute* 162.

The house of every one is to him as his castle and fortress, as well for his defence against injury and violence, as for his repose.

COKE, *Semayne's Case*, 5 Rep. 91 (b).

Husband and Wife

The common law does not regulate the form of agreements between spouses. Their promises are not sealed with seals and sealing wax. The consideration that really obtains for them is that natural love and affection which counts for so little in these cold Courts.

ATKIN, L. J., *Balfour v. Balfour* [1919] 2 K.B. 571, 579.

The cock swan is an emblem or representation of an affectionate and true husband to his wife above all other fowls; for the cock swan holdeth himself to one female only, and for this cause nature hath conferred on him a gift beyond all others; that is, to die so joyfully, that he sings sweetly when he dies.

COKE, *Case of Swans* (1592) 7 Rep. 17.

While the husband is still declared by statute to be the head of the family, he, like the King of England, is largely a figurehead.

HINES, J., *Curtis v. Ashworth*, 165 Ga. 782, 787 (1928).

When people understand that they must live together, except for a very few reasons known to the law, they learn to soften by mutual accommodation that yoke which they know they cannot shake off; they become good husbands and good wives from the necessity of remaining husbands and wives; for necessity is a powerful master in teaching the duties which it imposes. If it were once understood, that upon mutual disgust married persons might be legally separated, many couples who now pass through the world with mutual comfort, with attention to their common offspring and to the moral order of civil society, might have been at this moment living in a state of mutual unkindness, in a state of estrangement from their common offspring, and in a state of the most licentious and unreserved immorality. In this case, as in many others, the happiness of some individuals must be sacrificed to the greater and more general good.

SCOTT, J., *Evans v. Evans* (1790) 1 Hag. Con. 35, 36.

Idleness

Idleness, the mother of all vice and weakness.

COKE, 10 Rep. *Preface.*

Imitation

Customs and law, in every place
    Like a disease, an heirloom dread,
Still trace their curse from race to race,
    And furtively abroad they spread.
To nonsense, reason's self they turn;
    Beneficence becomes a pest;
Woe unto thee, thou art a grandson born!
    As for the law, born with us, unexpressed
That law, alas, none careth to discern.

GOETHE, *Faust,* I, 4, 449.

I am immensely struck with the blind imitativeness of man when

I see how a doctrine, a discrimination, even a phrase, will run in a year or two over the whole English-speaking world.

OLIVER WENDELL HOLMES, *Law in Science — Science in Law,* 12 Harv. L.R. 443, 455 (1899).

Imprisonment

No restraint be it never so little, but is imprisonment, and foreign employment is a kind of honourable banishment.

COKE, referring to King James' appointment of him to serve on a commission to inquire into conditions in Ireland. See, 11 D.N.B. 237.

Independence

I sat by its cradle, —I followed its hearse.

HENRY GRATTAN, referring to the rise of Irish independence in 1782 and its fall twenty years later. Brougham, *Statesmen of the Time of George III: Grattan.*

Index

A being engaged in looking through an index came to the following entry: "Best (Mr. Justice), his great mind." Turning to the page cited he found the following: "Mr. Justice Best said he had a great mind to commit the man for trial."

Probably apocryphal. Attributed to various authors of law books.

One may recollect generally that certain thoughts or facts are to be found in a certain book; but without a good Index such a recollection may hardly be more available than that of the cabin-boy, who knew where the ship's tea-kettle was, because he saw it fall overboard. In truth, a very large part of every man's reading falls overboard, and unless he has good Indexes he will never find it again.

HORACE BINNEY, *Letter, February 20, 1866 to S. Austin Allibone.*

So essential did I consider an Index to be to every book, that I proposed to bring a Bill into parliament to deprive an author who publishes a book without an Index of the privilege of copyright; and moreover, to subject him, for his offence, to a pecuniary penalty.

LORD CAMPBELL, 3 *Lives of the Chief Justices: Preface.*

Serjeant Waller was called Index; and people went for his opinion, only to bring away a list of quotations to assist other counsel that understood better.

NORTH, 1 *Life of Lord Keeper Guilford* 24 (1826).

Sir Frederick Pollock used to say that a man who would publish a book without an index ought to be banished ten miles beyond Hell where the Devil himself could not go because of the stinging nettles.

ROSCOE POUND, *Book Review,* 60 Yale L.J. 200 (1951).

Indictment

The indictment had never been clearly expressed,
And it seemed that the Snark had begun
And had spoken three hours before anyone guessed
What the pig was supposed to have done.

LEWIS CARROLL, *Hunting of the Snark: The Barrister's Dream.*

The clerk then read the indictment, which was in the usual form. It charged Laura Hawkins, in effect, with the premeditated murder of George Selby, by shooting him with a pistol, with a revolver, shotgun, rifle, repeater, breech-loader, cannon, six-shooter, with a gun, or some other weapon; with killing him with a slung-shot, a bludgeon, carving knife, bowie-knife, pen-knife, rolling-pin, car-hook, dagger, hairpin, with a hammer, with a screwdriver, with a nail, and with all other weapons and utensils whatsoever, at the Southern Hotel and in all other hotels and places wheresoever, on the thirteenth day of March and all others days of the Christian era whensoever.

MARK TWAIN, *The Gilded Age,* v.2, ch. 23.

Inference

Inference is never certainty, but it may be plain enough to justify a finding of fact.

CROUCH, J., *Tortora v. State*, 269 N.Y. 167, 170 (1935).

The law has no mandamus to the logical faculty; it orders nobody to draw inferences.

JAMES BRADLEY THAYER, *Preliminary Treatise on Evidence* 314 (1898).

Injunction

I will grant no injunction merely upon priority of suit; . . . I do not mean to make it a matter of an horse racing or posting who shall be first at Westminster Hall.

BACON, *Speech, May 7, 1617,* on taking his seat in Chancery as Lord Keeper.

I care not who makes th' laws iv a nation iv I can get out an injunction.

FINLEY PETER DUNNE, *Mr. Dooley's Philosophy: Casual Observations.*

Inns of Court

To the noblest Nourceries of Humanity, and Liberty, in the Kingdome: The Innes of Court.

BEN JONSON, *Every Man out of His Humour: Dedication.*

Cheerful Crown-office Row (place of my kindly engendure) . . . a man would give something to have been born in such places.

CHARLES LAMB, *Old Benchers of the Inner Temple.*

Four little winged marble boys used to play their virgin fancies, spouting out ever fresh streams from their innocent-wanton lips, in the square of Lincoln's inn, when I was no bigger than they were figured. They are gone, and the spring closed up. The fashion, they tell me, is gone by, and these things are esteemed childish. Why not then gratify children by letting them stand? Lawyers, I suppose, were children once.

CHARLES LAMB, *Old Benchers of the Inner Temple.*

Gray's Inn for walks,
Lincoln's Inn for a wall,
The Inner Temple for a garden
And the Middle for a hall.

Proverb. FULLER, *Worthies: London* (1662).

The Inner for a Rich Man,
The Middle for a Poor,
Lincoln's for a parchmenter,
And Gray's for the Law.

Anon.

Those bricky towres,
The which on Themmes brode aged backe doe ryde,
Where now the studious lawyers have their bowers,
There whylome wont the Templar Knights to byde,
Till they decayd through pride.

EDMUND SPENSER, *Prothalamion.*

I don't know whether the student of law permits himself the refreshment of enthusiasm, or indulges in poetical reminiscences as he passes by historical chambers, and says, "Yonder Eldon lived—upon this site Coke mused upon Littleton—here Chitty toiled—here Barnwell and Alderson joined in their famous labors—here Byles composed his great work upon bills, and Smith compiled his immortal leading cases . . ." but the man of letters can't but love the place which has been inhabited by so many of his brethren, or peopled by their creations as real to us at this day as the authors whose children they were—and Sir Roger de Coverley walking in the Temple Garden, and discoursing with Mr. Spectator about the beauties in hoops and patches who are sauntering over the grass, is just as lively a figure to me as old Samuel Johnson rolling through the fog with the Scotch gentleman at his heels.

THACKERAY, *Pendennis*, ch. 29.

Insanity

In other cases, reason is not driven from her seat, but distraction sits down upon it along with her, holds her trembling upon it, and frightens her from her propriety.

THOMAS ERSKINE, arguendo, *Trial of James Hatfield* (1800). 4 Erskine's *Speeches* 176. (High, ed.)

Doth not the idiot eat? Doth not the idiot drink? Doth not the idiot know his father and his mother? He does all this because he is a man. Doth he not smile and weep? And think you he smiles and weeps for nothing? He smiles and weeps because he is moved by human joys and sorrows, and exercises his reason, however imperfectly. Hath not the idiot anger, rage, revenge? Take from him his food, and he will stamp his feet and throw his chains in your face. Think you he does this for nothing? He does it all because he is a man, and because, however imperfectly, he exercises his reason.

WILLIAM H. SEWARD, arguendo, in Freeman Case, Auburn, New York, 1846.

To establish a defence on the ground of insanity, it must be clearly proved that, at the time of the committing of the act, the party accused was labouring under such a defect of reason, from disease of the mind, as not to know the nature and quality of the act he was doing; or, if he did know it, that he did not know he was doing what was wrong.

TINDAL, C.J., *M'Naghten's Case* (1843) 10 Cl. & F. 200, 210. The House of Lords had requested the judges to define criminal insanity.

Insurance

The attempted distinction between accidental results and accidental means will plunge this branch of the law into a Serbonian Bog.

CARDOZO, J., *Landress v. Phoenix Ins. Co.,* 291 U.S. 491, 499 (1934). See Milton, *Paradise Lost,* bk 2, l. 592: A gulf profound, as that Serbonian bog Betwixt Damiata and Mount Casius old, Where armies whole have sunk.

Intent

The state of a man's mind is as much a fact as the state of his digestion.

BOWEN, L.J., *Edgington v. Fitzmaurice* (1885) 29 Ch. D. 459, 483.

Detached reflection cannot be demanded in the presence of an uplifted knife.

HOLMES, J., *Brown v. United States,* 256 U.S. 335, 343 (1921).

There is no surer way to find out what parties meant, than to see what they have done.

SWAYNE, J., *Insurance Co. v. Dutcher,* 95 U.S. 269, 273 (1877).

Interest

Interest is a great rascal; but is not an absolute reprobate. Its doom is not perdition at all events. It has a chance of salvation. It is not obliged to commit perjury.

BLECKLEY, J., *Davis v. Central R.R.,* 60 Ga. 329, 333 (1878).

Interpretation

One half of the English language is interpreted by the context.

ALDERSON, B., *Dellevene v. Percer* (1841) 9 Dowl. 244, 245.

I know of only one authority which might justify the suggested method of construction: " 'When I use a word,' Humpty Dumpty said in rather a scornful tone, 'it means just what I choose it to mean, neither more nor less.' 'The question is,' said Alice, 'whether you can make words mean so many different things.' 'The question is,' said Humpty Dumpty, 'which is to be master—that's all' "

LORD ATKIN, *Liversidge v. Anderson* [1942] A.C. 206, 245. Quoting Carroll, *Through the Looking Glass*, ch. 6.

It is never the law itself that is in the wrong; it is always some wicked interpreter of the law that has corrupted and abused it.

JEREMY BENTHAM, *Fragment on Government, Preface,* 1 works 231.

Does not everybody see from hence, that you must first examine the law before you can apply the rule of construction? For the law must not be bent by the construction, but that must be adapted to the spirit and sense of the law.

LORD CAMDEN, C.J., *Entick v. Carrington* (1765) 19 How. St. Tr. 1029, 1060.

"If there's no meaning in it," said the King, "that saves a world of trouble, you know, as we needn't try to find any."

LEWIS CARROLL, *Alice's Adventure in Wonderland,* ch. 12.

The notion that because the words of a statute are plain, its meaning is also plain, is merely pernicious oversimplification.

FRANKFURTER, J., *United States v. Monia,* 317 U.S. 424, 431 (1943).

In law also the emphasis makes the song.

FRANKFURTER, J., *Bethlehem Steel Co. v. N.Y.S. Lab. Rel. Bd.,* 330 U.S. 767, 780 (1947).

Rules of statutory construction are to be resorted to when there is a doubt, ambiguity, or uncertainty, and they are never to be used to create doubt, but only to remove it.

GARDNER, J., *Helvering v. Northwestern Nat. Bank,* 89 F.2d 553, 556 (1937).

The meaning of a sentence may be more than that of the separate words, as a melody is more than the notes, and no degree of particularity can ever obviate recourse to the setting in which all appear, and which all collectively create.

L. HAND, J., *Helvering v. Gregory*, 69 F.2d 809, 810 (1934).

It is one of the surest indexes of a mature and developed jurisprudence not to make a fortress out of the dictionary; but to remember that statutes always have some purpose or object to accomplish whose sympathetic and imaginative discovery is the surest guide to their meaning.

L. HAND, J., *Cabell v. Markham*, 148 F.2d 737, 739 (1945).

Interpretation is the art of proliferating a purpose which is meant to cover many occasions so that it shall be best realized upon the occasion in question.

L. HAND, J., *Brooklyn National Corp. v. Commissioner*, 157 F.2d 450, 451 (1946).

Whoever hath an absolute authority to interpret any written or spoken laws, it is he who is truly the lawgiver to all intents and purposes, and not the person who first wrote or spoke them.

BENJAMIN HOADLY, *Sermon, March 31, 1717.*

We agree to all the generalities about not supplying criminal laws with what they omit, but there is no canon against using common sense in construing laws as saying what they obviously mean.

HOLMES, J., *Roschen v. Ward*, 279 U.S. 337, 339 (1929).

If ever we are justified in reading a statute, not narrowly as through a keyhole, but in the broad light of the evils it aimed at and the good it hoped for, it is here.

JACKSON, J., *United States ex rel Marcus v. Hess*, 317 U.S. 537, 557 (1943).

I should not find any great difficulty in construing Acts of Parliament if I had no opinions to assist me.

SIR GEORGE JESSEL. *Report of Select Committee, 1875: To Improve Manner and Language of Current Legislation, question 1202.*

All laws are promulgated for this end, that every man may know his duty; and, therefore, the plainest and most obvious sense of the words is that which must be put upon them.

SIR THOMAS MORE, *Utopia,* bk 2.

While for the purposes of judicial decision dictionary definitions often are not controlling, they are at least persuasive that meanings which they do not embrace are not common.

STONE, J., *Aschenbrenner v. U.S.F.&G. Co.,* 292 U.S. 80, 85 (1934).

Interpretation (Constitutional)

He protested, he said, against construing this Constitution, as one would a bill of indictment.

Referring to Henry Clay, *Debate on Internal Improvements,* 31 Annals of Congress 1166 (1818).

Th' constitootion iv th' United States is applicable on'y in such cases as it is applied to on account iv its applicability.

FINLEY PETER DUNNE, *Mr. Dooley's Philosophy: President's Message.*

The provisions of the Constitution are not mathematical formulas having their essence in their form; they are organic living institutions transplanted from English soil. Their significance is vital not formal; it is to be gathered not simply by taking the words and a dictionary, but by considering their origin and the line of their growth.

HOLMES, J., *Gompers v. United States,* 233 U.S. 604, 610 (1914).

The interpretation of constitutional principles must not be too literal. We must remember that the machinery of government would not work if it were not allowed a little play in its joints.

HOLMES, J., *Bain Peanut Co. v. Pinson,* 282 U.S. 499, 501 (1931).

If by the statement that what the Constitution meant at the time of its adoption it means to-day, it is intended to say that the great clauses of the Constitution must be confined to the interpretation which the framers, with the conditions and outlook of their time, would have placed upon them, the statement carries its own refutation.

HUGHES, C.J., *Home Bldg. & Loan Assn. v. Blaisdell,* 290 U.S. 398, 442 (1934).

When an act of Congress is appropriately challenged in the courts as not conforming to the constitutional mandate the judicial branch of the Government has only one duty, —to lay the article of the Constitution which is invoked beside the statute which is challenged and to decide whether the latter squares with the former.

ROBERTS, J., *United States v. Butler,* 297 U.S. 1, 62 (1936).

A provision of the Constitution . . . does not mean one thing at one time and an entirely different thing at another time.

SUTHERLAND, J., *Home Bldg. & Loan Assn. v. Blaisdell,* 290 U.S. 398, 448 (1934).

If the provisions of the Constitution be not upheld when they pinch as well as when they comfort, they may as well be abandoned.

SUTHERLAND, J., *Home Bldg. & Loan Assn. v. Blaisdell,* 290 U.S. 398, 483 (1934).

Interpretation (Legislative Intent)

It was by no means uncommon, where the legislature had a particular object in view in making a particular statute, to extend the enactments beyond the immediate and original object, and apply it to other matter suggested by it.

ABBOTT, C.J., *Clarke v. Burdett* (1819) 2 Stark. 504, 505.

The difficulties of so-called interpretation arise when the Legislature has had no meaning at all; when the question which is raised on the statute never occurred to it; when what the judges have to do is, not to determine what the Legislature did mean on a point which was present to its mind, but to guess what it would have intended on a point not present to its mind, if the point had been present.

JOHN CHIPMAN GRAY, *Nature and Sources of the Law: Statutes.* (1921 ed. p. 173).

I have more than once had occasion to say that in construing a statute I believe the worst person to construe it is the person who is responsible for its drafting. He is very much disposed to confuse what he intended to do with the effect of the language which in fact has been employed.

LORD HALSBURY, L.C., *Hilder v. Dexter* [1902] A.C. 474, 477. (Lord Halsbury was himself responsible for drafting the statute).

Do not gloss the Statute; we understand it better than you do, for we made it.

HENGHAM, C.J., Y.B. 33-35 Edw. I (Rolls Ser.) 83 (1305).

The Legislature has the power to decide what the policy of the law shall be, and if it has intimated its will, however indirectly, that will should be recognized and obeyed. The major premise of the conclusion expressed in a statute, the change of policy that induces the enactment, may not be set out in terms, but it is not an adequate discharge of duty for courts to say: We see what you are driving at, but you have not said it, and therefore we shall go on as before.

HOLMES (O.W.), J., *Johnson v. United States,* 163 Fed. 30, 32 (1908).

We do not inquire what the legislature meant; we ask only what the statute means.

OLIVER WENDELL HOLMES, *Theory of Legal Interpretation,* 12 Harv. L.R. 417, 419 (1899).

The sense and meaning of an Act of Parliament must be collected from what it says when passed into a law; and not from the history of changes it underwent in the house where it took its rise. That history is not known to the other house, or to the Sovereign.

WILLES, J., *Millar v. Taylor* (1769) 4. Burr. 2303, 2332.

Intoxication

A drunken man is as much entitled to a safe street, as a sober one, and much more in need of it.

HEYDENFELDT, J., *Robinson v. Pioche,* 5 Cal. 460, 461 (1855).

There is in all men a demand for the superlative, so much so that the poor devil who has no other way of reaching it attains it by getting drunk.

OLIVER WENDELL HOLMES, *Natural Law,* 32 Harv. L.R. 40 (1918).

Investigation

It is the proper duty of a representative body to look diligently into every affair of government and to talk much about what it sees. It is meant to be the eyes and the voice, and to embody the wisdom and will of its constituents. Unless Congress have and use every means of acquainting itself with the acts and the disposition of the administrative agents of the government, the country must be helpless to learn how it is being served; and unless Congress both scrutinize these things and sift them by every form of discussion, the country must remain in embarrassing, crippling ignorance of the very affairs which it is most important that it should understand and direct. The informing function of Congress should be preferred even to its legislative function.

WOODROW WILSON, *Congressional Government* 303 (1885).

Invitee

There is no ground for the argument that the plaintiff was invited upon the tracks. Temptation is not always invitation.

HOLMES, J., *Erie R.R. Co. v. Hilt,* 247 U.S. 97, 101 (1918).

Jest

As for jest, there be certain things which ought to be privileged from it; namely, religion, matters of state, great persons, any man's present business of importance, and any case that deserveth pity.

BACON, *Essays: Of Discourse.*

Jew

He died in a concentration camp of an incurable blood infection—a Jewish grandmother.

JOSEPH GROSS, 11 Shingle 79 (1948).

Judge

Let them be lions, but yet lions under the throne.

BACON, *Essays: Of Judicature.*

The twelve Judges of the realm are as the twelve lions under Salomon's throne: they must be lions, but yet lions under the throne.

BACON, *Speech, 1617.* On the occasion of Justice Hutton being sworn in as judge of the Common Pleas.

They are the depositaries of the laws; the living oracles, who must decide in all cases of doubt, and who are bound by an oath to decide according to the law of the land.

BLACKSTONE, *Commentaries,* bk 1, 69.

Conscious as we are of one another's many imperfections.

LORD BOWEN. (On the opening of the Royal Courts in 1882 the judges were preparing an address to Queen Victoria. It began: "Conscious as we are of our manifold defects." Jessel objected and Bowen suggested the above alternative.)

Laws and customs . . . are often abusively perverted by the foolish and unlearned who ascend the judgment seat before they have learnt the laws.

BRACTON, *De Legibus et Consuetudinibus Angliae,* f. 1 (v. 1, p. 5 Twiss ed. Rolls ser. No. 70).

The great tides and currents which engulf the rest of men, do not turn aside in their course, and pass the judges by.

BENJAMIN N. CARDOZO, *Nature of the Judicial Process* 168 (1921).

It may truly be said that the magistrate is the speaking law, and the law a silent magistrate. (*Vere dici potest, magistratum legem esse loquentem, legem autem mutum magistratum.*)

CICERO, *De Legibus,* III, i.

The law is the rule, but it is mute. The king judgeth by his judges, and they are the speaking law.

COKE, *First Institute* 130. (Generally quoted: The judges are the speaking law.)

Anyone who will may satisfy himself, by taking down a volume of reports, old or new, that any given Judge will run in a particular direction if he fairly can.

LORD DARLING, *Scintillae Juris: Of Judges.*

"If I had me job to pick out," said Mr. Dooley, "I'd be a judge. I've looked over all th' others an that's the on'y wan that suits. I have th' judicyal timperamint. I hate wurruk."

FINLEY PETER DUNNE, *Observations by Mr. Dooley: The Law's Delays.*

I am as sober as a judge.

HENRY FIELDING, *Don Quixote in England,* III, 14.

I would ye should know that the Justices of England sit not in the King's courts above iij houres in a day, that is to say, from viij of the clock in the forenoone til xi, complete. In the afternoones those courts are not holden or kept. But the suters then resort to the perusing of their writings and elsewhere consulting with the Serjeants at law and other their counsaylors. Wherefore the Justices, after they have taken their refection, doe passe and bestow all the residue of the day in the study of the lawes, in reading of holy scripture and using other kind of contemplation at their pleasure. So that their life may seem more contemplative than active. And thus doe they lead a quiet life, discharged of all worldly cares and troubles.

SIR JOHN FORTESCUE, *De Laudibus Legum Angliae,* ch. 51.

And that Nisi Prius nuisance, who just now is rather rife,
The Judicial Humorist—I've got him on the list!
All funny fellows, comic men, and clowns of private life—
They'd none of 'em be missed—they'd none of 'em be missed.

WILLIAM S. GILBERT, *The Mikado,* I.

Judges are apt to be naif, simple-minded men, and they need something of Mephistopheles.

OLIVER WENDELL HOLMES, *Law and the Court,* in *Speeches* 102 (1913).

And there was at that time Deborra, a prophetess, the wife of Lapidoth, who judged the people.

Judges 4:4.

And he (Samuel) went every year about to Bethel, and Galgal, and Masphath, and he judged Israel in the aforesaid places.

1 Kings 7:16.

What a wretched thing a Lord Chief Justice is, always was, and will be!

CHARLES LAMB, *Letter to Bernard Barton, January 23, 1824.* Referring to Leigh Hunt's conviction for libel and his sentencing by Lord Ellenborough. Hunt had written an article reflecting on the Prince Regent whom he called a fat Adonis of fifty.

It is the duty of a Judge to make it disagreeable to counsel to talk nonsense.

LORD CHANCELLOR LYNDHURST, Campbell, *Lives of Lord Chancellors: Lyndhurst, ch. 5.*

The Chief Justice was rich, quiet, and infamous.

THOMAS MACAULAY, *Warren Hastings,* 74 Edinburgh Rev. 105 (1841).

My dear Garrick, a judge on the bench is now and then in your whimsical situation between tragedy and comedy; inclination drawing one way, and a long string of precedents the other.

LORD MANSFIELD, Holliday, *Life of Mansfield* 211 (1797).

The judge should not be young; he should have learned to know evil, not from his own soul, but from late and long observance of the nature of evil in others: knowledge should be his guide, not personal experience.

PLATO, *Republic,* bk 3 (Jowett trans.)

Judges are philologists of the highest order.

POLLOCK, C.B., *Ex parte Davis* (1857) 5 W. R. 522, 523.

We rate the judge who is only a lawyer higher than the judge who is only a philosopher.

CUTHBERT W. POUND, *Address,* Fed. Bar Assn, 1 N.Y.S. Bar Bull. 279, 285 (1929).

A good judge conceives quickly, judges slowly.

Proverb. HERBERT, *Jacula Prudentum* (1651).

Judges are lawyers who knew a governor.

Saying.

Thieves for their robbery have authority
When judges steal themselves.

SHAKESPEARE, *Measure for Measure,* II, 2.

And then the justice,
In fair round belly with good capon lin'd,
With eyes severe and beard of formal cut,
Full of wise saws and modern instances.

SHAKESPEARE, *As You Like It,* II, 7.

Judge Thumb.

The dictum that a husband may beat his wife with a stick no thicker than his thumb was attributed to Sir Francis Buller. The story was generally believed and made the subject of caricature. Foss in his *Biographical Dictionary of the Judges of England* states that searching investigation has produced no substantial evidence that such an opinion was ever rendered by Judge Buller.

Judge (Political Aspiration)

Every judge is politically insolvent.

LOGAN E. BLECKLEY, 49 Alb. L. J. 409 (1894).

I think a judge should extinguish such thoughts when he goes on the Bench.

OLIVER WENDELL HOLMES, 1 *Holmes-Pollock Letters* 192.

A judge has no constituents.

GEORGE SUTHERLAND, 47 Cong. Rec. 2801 (1911). (Said when Senator).

It is dangerous to have a judge who thinks beyond the judicial in his personal ambitions.

MORRISON R. WAITE, *Letter, Nov. 7, 1875,* to his Congressman nephew, J.T. Waite. At the time there was talk of nominating the Chief Justice for the presidency.

Judges (Appraisal)

Let it go. Sit down. Life, liberty, and property are always safe in his hands.

RUFUS CHOATE, to an associate who was rising to contest what he considered an unfair ruling by Chief Justice Lemuel Shaw of Massachusetts. See, 1 Brown, *Works of Choate* 288 (1862).

I regard him as the Indian does his wooden log, curiously carved; I acknowledge he's ugly, but I bow before a superior intelligence.

RUFUS CHOATE, referring to Chief Justice Lemuel Shaw of Massachusetts. See, 1 Brown, *Works of Choate* 289 (1862).

Judge Ashhurst with his lantern jaws,
Throws light upon our English laws.

LORD ERSKINE, attributed to.

Judicial Impartiality

The cold neutrality of an impartial judge.

BURKE, *Preface to Brissot's Address.*

Contrary to the layman's belief, personal friendship between the judge and the lawyer is not an advantage to the client; for a scrupulous judge is so afraid that he will unconsciously favor his friend that in reaction he tends to be unjust to him.

PIERO CALAMANDREI, *Eulogy of Judges* 92 (1942) trans. Adams and Phillips.

He shall know nothing about the parties, everything about the case. He shall do everything for justice; nothing for himself; nothing for his friend; nothing for his patron; nothing for his sovereign. If, on one side, is the executive power, and the legislature and the people, —the sources of his honors, the givers of his daily bread—and on the other an individual nameless and odious, his eye is to see neither, great nor small; attending only to the "trepidations of the balance".

RUFUS CHOATE, *Massachusetts Constitutional Convention, 1853: Debates and Proceedings* 800.

The most satisfactory ideal I have ever been able to form of justice is embodied in the picture of a judge courageous enough "to give the devil his due", whether he be in the right or in the wrong.

JOHN F. DILLION, *Laws and Jurisprudence of England and America* 152 (1894).

There is no guaranty of justice except the personality of the judge.

EUGEN EHRLICH, *Freedom of Decision*, in *Science of Legal Method*, 9 Mod. Leg. Philos. Ser. 65 (1917 trans. by Bruncken).

His private affections are swallowed up in the common cause as rivers lose their names in the ocean.

THOMAS FULLER, *The Holy State*: *The Good Judge* (1642).

A man may judge impartially even in his own cause.

LORD MANSFIELD, C.J., *R. v. Cowle* (1759) 2 Burr. 834, 863.

If the parties will at my hand call for justice, then were it my father stood on the one side, and the devil on the other, his cause being good, the devil should have right.

SIR THOMAS MORE. Roper, *Life of More*.

He whose father is judge goes safe to his trial.

Proverb. THOMAS FULLER, *Proverbs* (1732).

It sometimes happens, also, that he who sits as judge is either our enemy or the friend of our opponent, a circumstance which ought to claim the attention of both sides, but more particularly, perhaps, of that to which the judge seems to incline. For there is sometimes, in unprincipled judges, a foolish propensity to give sentence against their friends, or in favour of parties with whom they are at enmity, and to act unjustly that they may not seem to be unjust.

QUINTILIAN, *Inst. of Oratory,* bk 4, 1, 18 (trans. Watson).

Judicial Independence

There is no human being whose smile or frown; there is no Government, Tory or Liberal, whose favour or disfavour can start the pulse of an English judge upon the Bench, or move by one hair's breath the even equipoise of the scales of justice.

LORD BOWEN, at Mansion House Banquet, May 18, 1887.

That when that case should be, he would do that should be fit for a judge to do.

CHIEF JUSTICE COKE, *Case of the Commendams.* See 1 Coll. Jur. 17. King James directed the judges to stay the action until they should consult with him. The judges refused. They were then asked if they would obey a similar order in the future. Coke refused.

Judges were not to give opinion by fractions, but entirely according to the vote whereupon they should settle upon conference: and that this auricular taking of opinions, single and apart, was new and dangerous.

COKE, *Peacham's Case* (1615) 2 How. St. Tr. 873. (When James I tried to submit a case in advance to the judges.)

Judicial Legislation

The childish fiction employed by our judges, that judiciary or common law is not made by them, but is a miraculous something made by nobody; existing I suppose, from eternity, and merely declared from time to time by the judges.

JOHN AUSTIN, *Jurisprudence: Statute and Judiciary Law* (lect. 37).

Judges ought to remember that their office is *jus dicere,* and not *jus dare;* to interpret law, and not to make law, or give law.

BACON, *Essays: Of Judicature.*

It is the judges . . . that make the common law. Do you know how they make it? Just as a man makes laws for his dog. When your dog does anything you want to break him of, you wait till he does it, and then beat him for it. This is the way you make laws for your dog: and this is the way the judges make law for you and me.

JEREMY BENTHAM, *Truth v. Ashhurst,* 5 Works 235.

[The judge is] not delegated to pronounce a new law, but to maintain and expound the old one.

BLACKSTONE, *Commentaries,* bk 1, 69.

A *casus omissus* does not justify judicial legislation.

BRANDEIS, J., *Ebert v. Poston,* 266 U.S. 548, 554 (1925).

I take judge-made law as one of the existing realities of life.

BENJAMIN N. CARDOZO, *Nature of the Judicial Process* 10 (1921).

He cannot set himself above the law which he has to administer, or make or mould it to suit the exigencies of a particular occasion.

COCKBURN, C.J., *Martin v. Mackonochie* (1878) 3 Q.B.D. 730, 775.

We must not be guilty of taking the law into our own hands, and converting it from what it really is to what we thing it ought to be.

COLERIDGE, C.J., *R. v. Ramsey* (1883) 1 C. & E. 126, 136.

If a statute . . . is apt to reproduce the public opinion not so much of to-day as of yesterday, judge-made law occasionally represents the opinion of the day before yesterday.

ALBERT V. DICEY, *Law and Opinion in England* (lecture xi).

Justices of the Court are not architects of policy. They can nullify the policy of others; they are incapable of fashioning their own solutions for social problems.

FELIX FRANKFURTER, *Mr. Justice Holmes and the Supreme Court* 25 (1938).

The customary law of English-speaking peoples stands, a structure indubitably made by the hands of generations of judges, each professing to be a pupil, yet each in fact a builder who has contributed his few bricks and his little mortar, often indeed under the illusion that he has added nothing. A judge must manage to escape both horns of this dilemma: he must preserve his authority by cloaking himself in the majesty of an overshadowing past; but he must discover some composition with the dominant trends of his time—at all hazards he must maintain that tolerable continuity without which society dissolves, and men must begin again the weary path up from savagery.

LEARNED HAND, *Mr. Justice Cardozo,* 39 Col. L.R. 9 (1939).

I recognize without hesitation that judges do and must legislate, but they can do so only interstitially; they are confined from molar to molecular motions.

HOLMES, J., *Southern Pacific Co. v. Jensen,* 244 U.S. 205, 221 (1917).

The clearest feature of the Court's decision is that it leaves the country under an Act which is not much like any Act passed by Congress.

JACKSON, J., *United States v. Harriss,* 347 U.S. 612, 633 (1954).

Courts are the mere instruments of the law, and can will nothing.

MARSHALL, C.J., *Osborn v. Bank of United States,* 22 U.S. (9 Wheat.) 738, 866 (1824).

Under the common law there is no case unprovided for, —though there be many of which it is extremely difficult, and indeed impossible, to say beforehand what the provision is. For the cases on which no decision has yet been pronounced, as unknown law exists, which must be brought to light whenever the courts are called upon for their decision. For all practical purposes, a law so unknown is the same as a law not in existence. To declare, is substantially to enact it; and the Judges, though called only expounders of law, are in reality legislators.

SIR SAMUEL ROMILLY, *Bentham on Codification*, 29 Edinburgh Rev. 223 (1817).

To vindicate the policy of the law is no necessary part of the office of a judge.

SCOTT, J., *Evans v. Evans* (1790) 1 Hag. Con. 35, 36.

The judicial function is that of interpretation; it does not include the power of amendment under the guise of interpretation.

SUTHERLAND, J., *West Coast Hotel Co. v. Parrish*, 300 U.S. 379, 404 (1937).

Thorpe (Of counsel): I think you will do as others have done in the same case; or else we do not know what the law is.

Hillary, J.: It is the will of the Justices.

Stonore, C.J.: No law is reason.

See, Y.B. 18-19 Edw. III (Rolls Ser.) 78, No. 3 Hil. (1344-45).

However the Court may interpret the provisions of the Constitution, it is still the Constitution which is the law and not the decision of the Court.

CHARLES WARREN, 3 *Supreme Court in U.S. History* 470 (1922).

Judicial Notice

This court knows judicially there is always a chance to lose in any kind of a lawsuit.

CLARKE, J., *Moorman v. Louisville Trust Co.*, 181 Ky. 30, 39 (1918).

The King [Henry IV] demanded of Gascoign, Justice if he saw one in his presence kill J.S, and another that was innocent was indicted for it before him and found guilty of the same death, what he would do in such a case? And he answered, that he would respite judgment, because he knew the party was innocent, and make further relation to his Majesty to grant his pardon; and the King was well pleased that the law was so; but there he could not acquit him, and give judgment of his own private knowledge.

PLOWDEN, 83.

A court must be blind not to see that the so-called tax is imposed to stop the employment of children within the age limits prescribed. Its prohibitory and regulatory effect and purpose are palpable. All others can see and understand this. How can we properly shut our minds to it?

TAFT, C.J., *Child Labor Tax Case,* 259 U.S. 20, 37 (1922).

Judicial Precepts

A popular judge is a deformed thing: and *plaudite's* are fitter for players than magistrates.

BACON, *Speech, Star Chamber, 1617,* to judges before the summer circuit.

That you should:
Draw your learning out of your books, not out of your brain.
Mix well the freedom of your opinion with the reverence of the opinion of your fellows.
Continue the studying of your books, and do not spend time with the old stock.
Fear no man's face, yet turn not stoutness into bravery.
*   *   *
Be a light to jurors to open their eyes, not a guide to lead them by the noses.
Affect not the opinion of pregnancy and expedition by an impatient and catching hearing of the counsellors at the bar.
Let your speech be with gravity, as one of the sages of the law, and not talkative, nor with impertinent flying out to show learning.

* * *

Contain the jurisdiction of your Court within the ancient mere-stones, without removing the mark.

BACON, *Speech 1617,* on the occasion of Justice Hutton being called to be one of the judges of the Common Pleas.

Judges ought to be more learned than witty, more reverend than plausible, and more advised than confident. Above all things, integrity is their portion and proper virtue.

BACON, *Essays: Of Judicature.*

Patience and gravity of hearing is an essential part of justice; and an overspeaking judge is no well-tuned cymbal.

BACON, *Essays: Of Judicature.*

Judges must be chaste as Caesar's wife, neither to be, nor so much as suspected in the least to be unjust.

BACON, *Letter, 1616, to Villiers, Duke of Buckingham* (when he became a Favorite to King James).

The judge is under a duty, within the limits of his power of innovation, to maintain a relation between law and morals, between the precepts of jurisprudence and those of reason and good conscience.

BENJAMIN N. CARDOZO, *Nature of the Judicial Process* 133 (1921).

There are two things against which a judge ought to guard,—precipitancy, and procrastination. Sir Nicholas Bacon was made to say, which I hope never again to hear, that a speedy injustice is as good as justice, which is slow.

CLARKE, M.R., *Atherton v. Worth* (1764) 1 Dick. 375, 377.

There shall be no difference of persons, you shall hear the little as well as the great: neither shall you respect any man's person, because it is the judgment of God. And if any thing seem hard to you, refer it to me, and I will hear it.

Deuteronomy 1:17.

Thou shalt not accept person nor gifts: for gifts blind the eyes of the wise, and change the words of the just.

Deuteronomy 16:19.

Things necessary to be continually had in remembrance:

1. That in the administration of justice I am entrusted for God, the king and country; and therefore,

2. That it be done, first, uprightly; secondly, deliberately, thirdly, resolutely.

3. That I rest not upon my own understanding or strength, but implore and rest upon the direction and strength of God.

4. That in the execution of judgment, I carefully lay aside my own passions and do not give way to them, however provoked.

5. That I be wholly intent upon the business I am about, remitting all other cares and thoughts as unseasonable, and interruptions.

6. That I suffer not myself to be prepossessed with any judgment at all, till the whole business and both parties be heard.

SIR MATTHEW HALE, History of the Common Law xv (4th ed.).

7. That I never engage myself in the beginning of any cause, but reserve myself unprejudiced 'till the whole be heard.

8. That in business capital, though my nature prompt me to pity; yet, to consider that there is also a pity due to the country.

9. That I be not too rigid in matters purely conscientious, where all the harm is diversity of judgment.

10. That I be not biased with compassion to the poor or favour to the rich, in point of justice.

11. That popular or court applause, or distaste, have no influence in any thing I do, in point of distribution of justice.

12. Not to be solicitous what men will say or think, so long as I keep myself exactly according to the rules of justice.

18. To be short, and sparing, at meals, that I may be the better for business.

SIR MATTHEW HALE, ibid.

Credulity is not esteemed a paramount virtue of the judicial mind.

HUSTON, J., *Rankin v. Jauman*, 4 Idaho 394, 401 (1895).

As anger does not become a Judge, so neither doth pity; for one is the mark of a foolish woman, as the other is of a passionate man.

SCROGGS, C.J., *R. v. Johnson* (1678) 2 Show. K.B. 1, 4.

These, then, are those faults which expose a man to the danger of smiting contrary to the law: a Judge must be clear from the spirit of party, independent of all favour, well inclined to the popular institutions of his country; firm in applying the rule, merciful in making the exception; patient, guarded in his speech, gentle and courteous to all. Add his learning, his labour, his experience, his probity, his practised and acute faculties, and this man is the light of the world, who adorns human life and gives security to that life which he adorns.

SYDNEY SMITH, *Assize Sermon, March 28, 1824,* at York.

Judicial Proceedings

It is of great consequence that the public should know what takes place in Court; and the proceedings are under the control of the Judges. The inconvenience therefore arising from the chance of injury to private character is infinitesimally small as compared to the convenience of publicity.

LORD CAMPBELL, C.J., *Davison v. Duncan* (1857) 7 E. & B. 229, 231.

Judicial Process

In cases omitted, the rule of law is to be deduced from similar cases, but with caution and judgment. And here the following rules are to be observed: Let reason be esteemed a fruitful, and custom a barren thing, so as to breed no new cases.

BACON, *Advancement of Learning,* bk 8, Aph. 11.

The narrow compass of human wisdom cannot take in all the cases which time may discover; whence new and omitted cases often present themselves. For these, the remedy or supplement is threefold; namely, by reference to similar cases, by employment of examples which have not yet grown into law, and by juries which decree according to conscience and discretion, whether in the courts of equity or common law.

BACON, *Advancement of Learning,* bk 8, Aph. 10.

What judges do and what they profess to do are not always the same, and the latter is only evidence of the former, —often very misleading evidence.

JETHRO BROWN, *Customary Law in Modern England,* 5 Col. L.R. 561, 567 (1905).

It is when the colors do not match, when the references in the index fail, when there is no decisive precedent, that the serious business of the judge begins.

BENJAMIN N. CARDOZO, *Nature of the Judicial Process* 21 (1921).

No judge writes on a wholly clean slate.

FELIX FRANKFURTER, *The Commerce Clause* 12 (1937).

When the case is difficult or involved, and turns upon a hairsbreadth of law or of fact, that is to say, "when there are many bags on the one side and on the other" and Judge Bridlegoose would have used his "little small dice," I, after canvassing all the available material at my command, and duly cogitating upon it, give my imagination play, and brooding over the cause, wait for the feeling, the hunch—that intuitive flash of understanding which makes the jump-spark connection between question and decision, and at the point where the path is darkest for the judicial feet, sheds its light along the way.

JOSEPH C. HUTCHESON, *Judgment Intuitive,* 14 Corn. L.Q. 274, 278 (1929).

In feeling or "hunching" out his decisions, the judge acts not differently from, but precisely as the lawyers do in working on their cases, with only this exception; that the lawyer, having a predetermined destination in view, —to win his law suit for his client—looks for and regards only those hunches which keep him in the path that he has chosen, while the judge, being merely on his way with a roving commission to find the just solution, will follow his hunch wherever it leads him, and when, following it, he meets the right solution face to face, he can cease his labors.

JOSEPH C. HUTCHESON, *Judgment Intuitive,* 14 Corn. L.Q. 274, 278 (1929).

The problem of judicial interpretation is to hold a just middle way between excess of valour and excess of caution.

SIR FREDERICK POLLOCK, *Judicial Caution and Valour,* 45 L.Q.R. 293, 296 (1929).

For having well and exactly seen, surveyed, overlooked, reviewed, recognized, read, and read over again, turned and tossed over, seriously perused and examined the bills of complaint, accusations, impeachments, indictments, warnings, citations . . . preparatories, productions, evidences, proofs . . . contradictions, supplications, requests, petitions . . . and other such like confects, and spiceries . . . I posit on the end of a table in my closit, all the pokes and bags of the defendant, and then allow unto him the first hazard of the dice. . . . That being done, I thereafter lay down upon the other end of the same table the bags and sachels of the plaintiff. . . . Then do I likeways and semblably throw the dice for him, and forthwith liver him his chance.

RABELAIS, *Gargantua and Pantagruel,* bk 3, ch.39. Trial of Judge Bridlegoose, who decided causes and controversies in law by the chance and fortune of the dice.

But, quoth Trinquamelle, my friend, how come you to know, understand, and resolve, the obscurity of these various and seeming contrary passages, in law, which are laid claim to by the suitors and pleading parties? Even just, quoth Bridlegoose, after the fashion of your other worships: to wit, when there are many bags on the one side, and on the other, I then use my little small dice. . . . I have other large great dice, fair, and goodly ones, which I employ in the fashion that your other worships use to do, when the matter is more plain, clear, and liquid, that is to say, when there are fewer bags. But when you have done all these fine things, quoth Trinquamelle, how do you, my friend, award your decrees, and pronounce judgment? Even as your other worships, answered Bridlegoose; for I give out sentence in his favour unto whom hath befallen the best chance by dice, judiciary, tribunian, pretorial, what comes first. So our laws command.

RABELAIS, *Gargantua and Pantagruel,* bk 3, ch.39.

Judicial Restraint

Nor is it desirable for a lower court to embrace the exhilarating opportunity of anticipating a doctrine which may be in the womb of time, but whose birth is distant.

L. HAND, J., *Spector Motor Service Inc. v. Walsh,* 139 F.2d 809, 823 (1944).

To do so is to allow zeal for our own ideas of what is good in public instruction to induce us to accept the role of a super board of education for every school district in the nation.

JACKSON, J., *Illinois ex rel McCollum v. Bd. of Educ.,* 333 U.S. 203, 237 (1948).

While unconstitutional exercise of power by the executive and legislative branches of the government is subject to judicial restraint, the only check upon our own exercise of power is our own sense of self-restraint.

STONE, J., *United States v. Butler,* 297 U.S. 1, 78 (1936).

Judicial Review

Laws are a dead letter without courts to expound and define their true meaning and operation.

ALEXANDER HAMILTON, *The Federalist,* No. 22.

The interpretation of the laws is the proper and peculiar province of the courts. A constitution is, in fact, and must be regarded by the judges, as a fundamental law. It therefore belongs to them to ascertain its meaning, as well as the meaning of any particular act proceeding from the legislative body.

ALEXANDER HAMILTON, *The Federalist,* No. 78.

I do not think the United States would come to an end if we lost our power to declare an Act of Congress void. I do think the Union would be imperiled if we could not make that declaration as to the laws of the several States.

OLIVER WENDELL HOLMES, *Law and the Court,* in *Speeches* 102 (1913).

We ought to remember the great caution shown by the Constitution in limiting the power of the States, and should be slow to construe the clause in the Fourteenth Amendment as committing to the Court, with no guide but the Court's own discretion, the validity of whatever laws the States may pass.

HOLMES, J., *Baldwin v. Missouri,* 281 U.S. 586, 595 (1930).

It is, emphatically, the province and duty of the judicial department to say what the law is.

MARSHALL, C.J., *Marbury v. Madison,* 5 U.S. (1 Cranch) 137, 177 (1803).

Judicial power is never exercised for the purpose of giving effect to the will of the judge; always for the purpose of giving effect to the will of the legislature; or, in other words, to the will of the law.

MARSHALL, C.J., *Osborn v. Bank of United States,* 22 U.S. (9 Wheat.) 738, 866 (1824).

Judicial Selection

He has made judges dependent on his will alone, for the tenure of their offices, and the amount and payment of their salaries.

Declaration of Independence, ninth specification.

Thou shalt appoint judges and magistrates in all thy gates, which the Lord thy God shall give thee, in all thy tribes: that they may judge the people with just judgment.

Deuteronomy 16:18.

We wish for a Chief Justice who will sustain what has been done in regard to emancipation and the legal tenders. We cannot ask a man what he will do, and if we should, and he should answer us, we should despise him for it. Therefore we must take a man whose opinions are known.

ABRAHAM LINCOLN, at the time of appointing Salmon P. Chase as Chief Justice of the United States. See, 2 Boutwell, *Reminiscences of Sixty Years in Public Affairs* 29 (1902).

I look out for a gentleman, and if he knows a little law so much the better.

LORD CHANCELLOR LYNDHURST. See, Ballantine, *Some Experiences of a Barrister's Life* 148 (2nd ed. 1882).

Fill the seats of justice
With good men, not so absolute in goodness,
As to forget what human frailty is.

SIR THOMAS TALFOURD, *Ion,* V, 3.

Judiciary

The judiciary . . . has no influence over either the sword or the purse; no direction either of the strength or of the wealth of the society; and can take no active resolution whatever. It may truly be said to have neither FORCE nor WILL, but merely judgment. . . . The judiciary is beyond comparison the weakest of the three departments.

ALEXANDER HAMILTON, *The Federalist,* No. 78.

The Judicial Department comes home in its effects to every man's fireside: it passes on his property, his reputation, his life, his all. Is it not, to the last degree important, that he should be rendered perfectly and completely independent, with nothing to influence or controul him but God and his conscience?

JOHN MARSHALL, Virginia Constitutional Convention, 1829-30, *Debates* 616.

I have always thought, from my earliest youth till now, that the greatest scourge an angry Heaven ever inflicted upon an ungrateful and a sinning people, was an ignorant, a corrupt, or a dependent Judiciary.

JOHN MARSHALL, Virginia Constitutional Convention, 1829-30, *Debates* 619.

Jurisdiction

Jurisdiction exists that rights may be maintained. Rights are not maintained that jurisdiction may exist.

CARDOZO, J., *Berkovitz v. Arbib,* 230 N.Y. 261, 274 (1921).

Extraordinary jurisdiction succeeds only by becoming ordinary.

SIR FREDERICK POLLOCK, *The Expansion of the Common Law* 60 (1904).

Jurisprudence

The science of jurisprudence, the pride of the human intellect, which with all its defects, redundancies, and errors, is the collected reason of ages, combining the principles of original justice with the infinite variety of human concerns.

BURKE, *Reflections on the Revolution in France.*

The gladsome light of jurisprudence.

COKE, *First Institute: Epilogue.*

Jurisprudence is a word which stinks in the nostrils of a practising barrister.

ALBERT V. DICEY, 5 Law Mag. and Rev. (4th Ser.) 382 (1880).

There is not, in my opinion, in the whole compass of human affairs, so noble a spectacle as that which is displayed in the progress of jurisprudence; where we may contemplate the cautious and unwearied exertions of a succession of wise men through a long course of ages; withdrawing every case as it arises from the dangerous power of discretion, and subjecting it to inflexible rules; extending the dominion of justice and reason, and gradually contracting, within the narrowest possible limits, the domain of brutal force and of arbitrary will.

SIR JAMES MACKINTOSH, *Discourse on Study of Law of Nature and Nations* 94 (Bost. ed. 1843).

Let us think of jurisprudence for a moment as a science of social engineering, having to do with that part of the whole field which may be achieved by the ordering of human relations through the action of politically organized society.

ROSCOE POUND, *Interpretations of Legal History* 152 (1923).

The knowledge of things human and divine, the science of the just and unjust.

ULPIAN, *Digest,* (Justinian) i, I, 10.

Jurist

A jurist is a person who knows a little about the laws of every country except his own.

LORD BOWEN. Cunningham, *Biographical Sketch* 184.

Jury

That principal criterion of truth in the law of England.

BLACKSTONE, *Commentaries,* bk 3, 348.

In my mind he was guilty of no error, he was chargeable with no exaggeration, he was betrayed by his fancy into no metaphor, who once said that all we see about us, Kings, Lords and Commons, the whole machinery of the State, all the apparatus of the system, and its varied workings, end in simply bringing twelve good men into a box.

HENRY BROUGHAM, *Present State of the Law,* Speech in House of Commons, February 7, 1828.

Then went the jury out, whose names were Mr. Blind-man, Mr. No-good, Mr. Malice, Mr. Love-lust, Mr. Live-loose, Mr. Heady, Mr. High-mind, Mr. Enmity, Mr. Lyar, Mr. Cruelty, Mr. Hate-light, and Mr. Implacable; who every one gave in his private verdict against him among themselves, and afterwards unanimously concluded to bring him in guilty before the Judge.

JOHN BUNYAN, *Pilgrim's Progress,* pt. 1. (15 Harvard Classics 101).

The name of the illustrious Charles Dickens has been called on the jury, but he has not answered. If his great Chancery suit had been still going on, I certainly would have excused him; but, as that is over, he might have done us the honor of attending here, that he might have seen how we went on at common law.

LORD CAMPBELL. See, Heard, *Curiosities of the Law Reporters* 106 (1871).

Our civilisation has decided, and very justly decided, that determining the guilt or innocence of men is a thing too important to be trusted to trained men. It wishes for light upon that awful matter, it asks men who know no more law than I know, but who can feel the things that I felt in the jury box. When it wants a library catalogued, or the solar system discovered, or any trifle of that kind, it uses up its specialists. But when it wishes anything done which is really serious, it collects twelve of the ordinary men standing round. The same thing was done, if I remember right, by the Founder of Christianity.

GILBERT K. CHESTERTON, *Tremendous Trifles: The Twelve Men.*

"I wonder what the foreman of the jury, whoever he'll be, has got for breakfast," said Mr. Snodgrass. . . . "Ah!" said Perker, "I hope he's got a good one." "Why so?" inquired Mr. Pickwick. "Highly important—very important, my dear Sir," replied Perker. "A good, contented, well-breakfasted juryman, is a capital thing to get hold of. Discontented or hungry jurymen, my dear Sir, always find for the plaintiff."

CHARLES DICKENS, *Pickwick Papers,* ch. 34.

If it is possible that such a practice as that which has taken place in the present instance should be allowed to pass without a remedy, trial by jury itself, instead of being a security to persons who are accused, will be a delusion, a mockery, and a snare.

LORD DENMAN, C.J., *O'Connell v. R.* (1884) 11 Cl. & F. 155, 351.

In due time twelve men iv intilligence who have r-read th' pa-apers an' can't remimber what they've r-read, or who can't r-read, or ar-re out iv wurruk, ar-re injooced to sarve, an' th' awful wheels iv justice begins to go round.

FINLEY PETER DUNNE, *Mr. Dooley on Making a Will: On Criminal Trials.*

Whin th' case is all over, the jury'll pitch th' tistimony out iv th' window, an' consider three questions: "Did Lootgert look as though he'd kill his wife? Did his wife look as though she ought to be kilt? Isn't it time we wint to supper?"

FINLEY PETER DUNNE, *Mr. Dooley in Peace and War: On Expert Testimony.*

I have heard an experienced counsellor say that he never feared the effect upon a jury of a lawyer who does not believe in his heart that his client ought to have a verdict. If he does not believe it, his unbelief will appear to the jury, despite all his protestations, and will become their unbelief.

RALPH WALDO EMERSON, *Spiritual Laws.*

A jury too frequently has at least one member more ready to hang the panel than to hang the traitor.

ABRAHAM LINCOLN, *Letter to Erastus Corning,* June 12, 1863.

Gentlemen of the jury, the man stole the boots; consider your verdict.

BARON MARTIN — attributed to — in a larceny case where the facts were beyond dispute. If not literally true it is considered in character.

You are sworn to keep the jury without meat, drink, or fire. Now, water is not fire; water is not meat; and I should certainly hold that water is not drink.

MAULE, J. — attributed to. Before the Juries Act, 1870 (England) the bailiff in charge of the jury was sworn to keep them without meat, drink, or fire until a verdict was reached.

The Jury on the body sat, and gave
their verdict in these terms,
"They found as how that certain slugs
had sent him to the worms."

Old ballad.

The hungry judges soon the sentence sign,
And wretches hang, that jurymen may dine.

POPE, *Rape of the Lock,* III.

A fox should not be of the jury at a goose's trial.

Proverb. FULLER, *Proverbs* (1732).

A London jury; hang half save half.

Proverb. FULLER, *Worthies: London* (1662). Some affirm this of an Essex, others of a Middlesex jury.

The jury, passing on the prisoner's life,
May in the sworn twelve have a thief or two
Guiltier than him they try.

SHAKESPEARE, *Measure for Measure,* II, 1.

They have been grand-jurymen since before Noah was a sailor.

SHAKESPEARE, *Twelfth Night,* III, 2.

Good people, you cannot agree? Go [to John Allen, marshal] and put them in a house until Monday, and let them not eat or drink. On that commandment John put them in a house without [food or drink]. At length on the same day about vesper-time they agreed.

STANTON, J., Anon. Y.B. 4 Edw. II (Seld. Soc. IV) 188 (1310).

The most ingenious and infallible agency for defeating justice that human wisdom could contrive.

MARK TWAIN, *Roughing It,* v. 2, ch. 7 (1872).

The jury system puts a ban upon intelligence and honesty, and a premium upon ignorance, stupidity and perjury.

MARK TWAIN, *Roughing It,* v. 2, ch. 7 (1872).

A man cannot see by another's eye, nor hear by another's ear, no more can a man conclude or infer the thing to be resolved by another's understanding or reasoning.

VAUGHAN, C.J., *Bushell's Case* (1670) Vaugh. 135, 148 (Affirming the right of the jury to find such a verdict as they think right.)

When Scarlett is addressing a jury there are thirteen jurymen.

DUKE OF WELLINGTON. See, Scarlett, *Memoir of Lord Abinger* 193.

Justice

You that turn judgment into wormwood, and forsake justice in the land.

Amos 5:7.

Revenge is a kind of wild justice; which the more man's nature runs to, the more ought law to weed it out.

BACON, *Essays: Of Revenge.*

Justice is not only one of the cardinal virtues, it is the pontifical virtue.

BLECKLEY, C.J., *Lyons v. Planters' Loan & Sav. Bk.,* 86 Ga. 485, 491 (1890).

For justice, tho' she's painted blind,
Is to the weaker side inclin'd.

SAMUEL BUTLER, *Hudibras,* Pt. III, Canto III, l. 709.

Justice, though due to the accused, is due to the accuser also. The concept of fairness must not be strained till it is narrowed to a filament. We are to keep the balance true.

CARDOZO, J., *Snyder v. Massachusetts,* 291 U.S. 97, 122 (1934).

It is the worst oppression, that is done by colour of justice.

COKE, *Second Institute* 48.

Justice is a machine that, when some one has once given it the starting push, rolls on of itself.

JOHN GALSWORTHY, *Justice,* Act II.

If we are to keep our democracy, there must be one commandment: Thou shalt not ration justice.

LEARNED HAND, *Address before the Legal Aid Society of New York, Feb. 16, 1951.* See, 9 *Brief Case,* No. 4, 5.

Equal Justice under Law.
Justice the Guardian of Liberty.

Inscriptions on the United States Supreme Court Building, Washington. Neither is a direct quotation from any identified source. See, 37 A.B.A.J. 788.

Equal and exact justice to all men, of whatever state or persuasion, religious or political.

THOMAS JEFFERSON, *First Inaugural Address, March 4, 1801.*

To no one will we sell, to no one will we refuse or delay right or justice.

Magna Carta, ch. 40 (1215).

Human justice, which sees only the actions, has but one compact with men, namely, that of innocence; divine justice, which sees the thought, has two, that of innocence and repentance.

MONTESQUIEU, *Spirit of the Laws,* bk 26 (trans. Nugent).

Justice is but the interest of the stronger.

PLATO, *Republic, bk 1* (argument of Thrasymachus).

This even-handed justice.

SHAKESPEARE, *Macbeth,* I, 7.

Justice is the constant and perpetual will to allot to every man his due.

ULPIAN, *Digest,* (Justinian) i, I, 10.

Justice, Sir, is the great interest of man on earth. It is the ligament which holds civilized beings and civilized nations together. Wherever her temple stands, and so long as it is duly honored, there is a foundation for social security, general happiness, and the improvement and progress of our race.

DANIEL WEBSTER, *Funeral Oration on Mr. Justice Story, September* 12, 1845.

Justice of the Peace

I'm important in the County,
    I'm a Justice of the Peace,

And I disbelieve Defendants
  When they contradict the P'lice.

J.P.C., *Poetic Justice* 45 (1947).

Long ago lawyers abandoned all hope of describing the duties of a justice in any methodic fashion, and the alphabet has become the one possible connecting thread.

FREDERIC WM. MAITLAND, *Justice and Police* 84 (1885). Provisions re Justices of the Peace were so numerous and various that authors used the alphabetical approach.

Kin

Sir Nicholas Bacon . . . by one of the malefactors mightily importuned for to save his life . . . on account of kindred. "Prithee," said my lord judge, "how came that in?" "Why, if it please you my lord, your name is Bacon, and mine is Hog, and in all ages Hog and Bacon have been so near kindred, that they are not to be separated." "Ay, but" replied Judge Bacon, "you and I cannot be kindred, except you be hanged; for Hog is not bacon until it be well hanged."

BACON, *Apothegms.* (Considered spurious by Spedding).

Knowledge

He who would know anything well, must resolve to be ignorant of many things.

JOHN AUSTIN, *Uses of the Study of Jurisprudence.*

Knowledge is power.

BACON, *Med. Sacrae: de Haeresibus.*

I wax now somewhat ancient; one and thirty years is a great deal of sand in the hour-glass. . . . I have taken all knowledge to be my province.

BACON, *Letter, 1592, to Lord Burghley.*

People must not be wiser than the experience of mankind.

BOWEN, L. J., *Filburn v. People's Palace & Aq. Co.* (1890) 25 Q.B.D. 258, 261.

When a great learned man, who is long in making, dieth, much learning dieth with him.

COKE, *First Institute: Preface.*

For there is no knowledge (seemeth it at the first of never so little moment) but it will stand the diligent observer in stead at one time or other.

COKE, *Fourth Institute: Proeme.*

This morning, Solon, Lycurgus, Demosthenes, Archimedes, Sir Isaac Newton, Lord Chesterfield, and a great many more went away in one post-chaise.

SAMUEL ROGERS, on seeing Brougham depart one day. 1 Greville, *Journal of the Reign of George IV,* Jan. 2, 1828.

What a wonderful versatile mind has Brougham! He knows politics, Greek, history, science; if he only knew a little of law, he would know a little of everything.

Saying. Attributed to various contemporaries of Brougham. Emerson in *Quotation and Originality,* says this scarcasm is from Lord Eldon but you can find the original form of this gibe in Grimm who wrote that Louis XVI after hearing a sermon by the Abbe Maury said, "Si l'Abbe nous avait parle un peu de religion, il nous aurait parle de tout."

Knowledge (Legal)

No attorney is bound to know all the law; God forbid that it should be imagined that an attorney, or a counsel, or even a judge is bound to know all the law.

ABBOTT, C.J., *Montriou v. Jefferys* (1825) 2 C. & P. 113, 116.

Whereby I set the practise of the Law
At as light count as turning of a straw,

For straight I found how John a Stiles did state it,
But I was over stile ere I came at it;
For having thought (so easy was the way)
That one might be a lawyer the first day.

RICHARD BRATHWAITE, *Shepherd's Tales,* E. i (1621).

If again the question were, who is rightly described as learned in the law, I should say it is the man who is an expert in the statutes, and in the customary law observed by individuals as members of the community, and who is qualified to advise, direct the course of a lawsuit, and safeguard a client. (*Sin autem quaereretur, quisnam iurisconsultus vere nominaretur; eum dicerem, qui legum, et consuetudinis eius, qua privati in civitate uterentur, et ad respondendum, et ad agendum, et ad cavendum, peritus esset.*)

CICERO, *De Oratore,* I, 48. (trans. Loeb Classical Lib.)

The knowledge of the law is like a deep well, out of which each man draweth according to the strength of his understanding.

COKE, *First Institute* 71a.

True it was that God hath endowed His Majesty with excellent science, and great endowments of nature; but His Majesty was not learned in the laws of His realm of England, and causes which concern the life, or inheritance, or goods, or fortunes of His subjects, are not to be decided by natural reason but by the artificial reason and judgment of law, which law is an act which requires long study and experience, before that a man can attain to the cognizance of it.

COKE, *Prohibitions del Roy,* 12 Rep. 63, 65. (Reply to James I's argument that since law was founded upon reason he could decide as well as the judges).

If it be common law, I should be ashamed if I could not give you a ready answer; but if it be statute law, I should be equally ashamed if I answered you immediately.

COKE. Woolrych, *Life of Coke* 197.

No man can be a great advocate who is no lawyer.

LORD CHANCELLOR ERSKINE, *Letter, November 13, 1819.* This was in answer to an impertinent person who had made a bet on the number of the Lord Chancellor's decrees which had been reversed and wrote to Erskine for the information. See, 2 Townsend, *Lives of Twelve Eminent Judges* 70 (1846); Campbell, *Lives of the Lord Chancellors: Erskine*, ch. 185 (1847).

But how can you love justice unless you first have sufficient knowledge in the laws, whereby the knowledge of it is won and had, for the philosopher saith, that nothing can be loved except it be known.

SIR JOHN FORTESCUE, *De Laudibus Legum Angliae*, ch. 5.

Lawyers know the law no better than other people; they only know where to find it.

GEORGE III (according to tradition).

Swift was in charge of the departments which handled the estates, corporation matters and appeals. He was an able lawyer. He read all the latest decisions of the courts and most of the current legal periodicals. He knew practically all the law there is. In fact, he knew so much law that whenever some desirable transaction for a client had reached the point of apparent consummation, Swift could think of at least half a dozen confusing legal obstacles which might possibly arise in the future. He could always fill the minds of all concerned with the gravest apprehensions. In short, he knew so much law that he was thoroughly impractical.

FRED L. GROSS, *What is the Verdict?* 8 (1944).

In the year 1598, Sir Edward Coke, then Attorney-General, married the lady Hatton, according to the book of Common Prayer, but without banns or licence; and in a private house. Several great men were then present. . . . They all, by their proctor, submitted to the censure of the Archbishop, who granted them an absolution from the excommunication they had incurred. The act of absolution set forth that it was granted by reason of penitence and the act seemingly to have been done through ignorance of the law.

LORD HARDWICKE, *Middleton v. Croft*, Cunningham's Rep. 61.

If you want to know the law and nothing else, you must look at it as a bad man, who cares only for the material consequences which such knowledge enables him to predict, not as a good one, who finds his reasons for conduct, whether inside the law or outside of it, in the vaguer sanctions of conscience.

OLIVER WENDELL HOLMES, *Path of the Law,* 10 Harv. L.R. 457, 459 (1897).

Alongside of the practitioners to whom the law is a rag-bag from which they pick out the piece and colour that they want, there have been some students who have striven to make their knowledge organic.

OLIVER WENDELL HOLMES, Review of Holdsworth's *History of English Law,* 25 L.Q.R. 412 (1909).

There is no presumption in this country that every person knows the law: it would be contrary to common sense and reason if it were so.

MAULE, J., *Martindale v. Falkner* (1846) 2 C.B. 706, 719.

To say truth, although it is not necessary for counsel to know what the history of a point is, but to know how it now stands resolved, yet it is a wonderful accomplishment, and without it a lawyer cannot be accounted learned in the laws.

ROGER NORTH, *On the Study of the Laws* 40.

The king can make a serjeant, but not a lawyer.

Proverb. THOMAS FULLER, *Proverbs* (1732).

Ignorance of the law excuses no man; not that all men know the law, but because 'tis an excuse every man will plead, and no man can tell how to confute him.

JOHN SELDEN, *Table-Talk: Law.*

No man can be a knowing lawyer in any nation, who hath not well pondered and digested in his mind the common law of the world, from whence the interpretation, extensions and limitations of all statutes and customs must be brought.

LORD STAIR, *Institutions of Law of Scotland* 1 (1681).

Language

I know that, I am talking English, not law.

ARTHUR J. BALFOUR. Retort in the House of Commons to lawyer of the opposition who interrupted to remind him that "trade unions are not corporations". See, Maitland, *Coll. Pap.* 305 citing *The Standard,* April 23, 1904.

I have heard that man speak more poetry than I have ever seen written, though I saw him seldom, and but occasionally.

LORD BYRON, referring to John P. Curran. Moore, *Life of Byron 306* (1860).

"And/or," that befuddling, nameless thing, that Janus-faced verbal monstrosity, neither word nor phrase, the child of a brain of some one too lazy or too dull to express his precise meaning, or too dull to know what he did mean, now commonly used by lawyers in drafting legal documents, through carelessness or ignorance or as a cunning device to conceal rather than express meaning.

FOWLER, J., *Employers Mut. Liability Ins. Co. v. Tollefsen,* 219 Wis. 434 (1935).

The non-lawyer, when annoyed by the way judges sometimes interpret apparently simple statutory language, is the victim of the one-word-one-meaning fallacy, based on the false assumption that each verbal symbol refers to one and only one specific subject. If the non-lawyer would reflect a bit, he would perceive that such an assumption, if employed in the non-legal world, would compel the conclusion that a clothes-horse is an animal of the equine species, and would make it impossible to speak of "drinking a toast".

JEROME FRANK, *Courts on Trial* 299 (1949).

Profanity is vitriol, slang is vinegar, but reporters' English is rancid butter. I don't know that you have the thing to which I refer in England—an intrusion into the language of sentiment, as when they call a house a home.

OLIVER WENDELL HOLMES, 2 *Holmes-Pollock Letters* 131.

Gentlemen, the chimney took fire; it poured out volumes of smoke. Volumes did I say? Whole encyclopedias, gentlemen!

MARRYATT — attributed to; probably apocryphal.

Gobbledygook: Talk or writing which is long, pompous, vague, involved, usually with Latinized words. It is also talk or writing which is merely long, even though the words are fairly simple, with repetition over and over again, all of which could have been said in a few words.

MAURY MAVERICK, *New York Times, May 21, 1944, Mag. p. 11.*

"The last time I was at quarter sessions, the sheriff told us that *dies* —that *dies inceptus*—In short, you don't understand Latin, but it means that a term-day is not begun until it is ended."

"That sounds like nonsense, my dear."

"May be so, my dear: but it may be very good law for all that."

SIR WALTER SCOTT, *Guy Mannering*, ch. 9 (Mr. Bertram to his wife).

Surely, my Lords, this lawyer here hath swallowed
Some 'pothecary's bills, or proclamations.
And now the hard and undigestible words
Come up like stones we use give hawks for physic.
Why, this is Welsh to Latin!

JOHN WEBSTER, *The White Devil*, III, 2 (c. 1608).

Law (Apothegm)

To seek to be wiser than the laws is precisely what good laws forbid.

ARISTOTLE, *Rhetoric*, bk 1, ch. 15.

Moses the lawgiver, and God's first pen.

BACON, *Advancement of Learning,* bk 1.

In this court "the unwritten law" is not worth the paper it isn't written on.

BIDDLE, J., when the theory of the unwritten law was much urged upon the jury in a case in the common pleas of Philadelphia.

Laws, like houses, lean on one another.

BURKE, *Tracts on Popery Laws,* Pt. 1, ch. 3.

Law and arbitrary power are in eternal enmity.

BURKE, *Impeachment of Warren Hastings, February 16, 1788.*

We are in bondage to the law in order that we may be free. (*Legum denique idcirco omnes servi sumus, ut liberi esse possimus.*)

CICERO, *Pro Cluentio* 53.

The laws are silent amidst the clash of arms. (*Silent enim leges inter arma*).

CICERO, *Pro Milone,* iv.

Law is the safest helmet.

SIR EDWARD COKE. (inscription on rings given to friends.)

Now, therefore, O king, confirm the sentence, and sign the decree: that what is decreed by the Medes and Persians may not be altered.

DANIEL 6:8.

Men would be great criminals did they need as many laws as they make.

LORD DARLING, *Meditations in the Tea Room,* XIV.

Every law which the state enacts indicates a fact in human nature.

RALPH WALDO EMERSON, *Essays: History.*

The sparks of all sciences in the world are raked up in the ashes of the law.

SIR HENRY FINCH, *Law, or Discourse,* bk 1, ch. 3.

The Law is the true embodiment
Of everything that's excellent.
It has no kind of fault or flaw,
And I, my Lords, embody the Law.

WILLIAM S. GILBERT, *Iolanthe,* Act I (Lord Chancellor's Song).

The law obliges us to do what is proper, not simply what is just.

GROTIUS, *De Jure Belli ac Pacis,* bk 1, ch. 1 (1625).

Law is a plant that lives long before it throws out bulbs.

OLIVER WENDELL HOLMES, *Introduction: Rational Basis of Legal Institutions* (by various authors).

The life of the law has not been logic: it has been experience.

OLIVER WENDELL HOLMES, *Common Law* 1 (1881).

It cannot be helped, it is as it should be, that the law is behind the times.

OLIVER WENDELL HOLMES, *Law and the Court, Speeches* 101 (1913).

Laws are not made for particular cases, but for men in general.

SAMUEL JOHNSON. Boswell, *Life of Johnson: 1776.*

Now these are the Laws of the Jungle, and many and mighty are they;
But the head and the hoof of the Law and the haunch and the hump
is—Obey!

RUDYARD KIPLING, *The Law of the Jungle.*

Law was the point where life and logic met.

FREDERIC WM. MAITLAND, *Selden Society Year Book Series,* v.1: xxxvii.

Very happily, the more the law is looked into, the more it appears founded in equity, reason and good sense.

LORD MANSFIELD, C.J., *James v. Price* (1773) Lofft 219, 221.

Do not think that I am come to destroy the law or the prophets. I am not come to destroy, but to fulfil.

MATTHEW 5:17.

Law can discover sin, but not remove.

JOHN MILTON, *Paradise Lost,* XII, 1. 290.

Law is neither a trade nor a solemn jugglery, but a science.

SIR FREDERICK POLLOCK, *Contracts* (1885, 2nd Amer. Ed. from 4th Eng.): Dedication to Rt. Hon. Lord Justice Lindley.

Law must be stable and yet it cannot stand still.

ROSCOE POUND, *Interpretations of Legal History* 1 (1923).

In a thousand pounds of law there's not an ounce of love.

Proverb. Ray, *Proverbs* (1678).

Law's like laudanum, it's much more easy to use it as a quack does, than to learn to apply it like a physician.

SIR WALTER SCOTT, *Guy Mannering,* ch. 56.

Old father antic the law.

SHAKESPEARE, *Henry IV,* Pt. I, I, 2.

We must not make a scarecrow of the law,
Setting it up to fear the birds of prey,
And let it keep one shape, till custom make it
Their perch and not their terror.

SHAKESPEARE, *Measure for Measure,* II, 1.

In law, what plea so tainted and corrupt
But, being seasoned with a gracious voice,
Obscures the show of evil?

SHAKESPEARE, *Merchant of Venice,* III, 2.

Still you keep o' the windy side of the law.

SHAKESPEARE, *Twelfth Night,* III, 4.

No laws, however stringent, can make the idle industrious, the thriftless provident, or the drunken sober.

SAMUEL SMILES, *Self-Help,* ch. 1.

We know that the law is good, if a man uses it rightly, knowing that the law is not made for the just, but for the unjust and rebellious.

1 Timothy 1:8.

In crossing France, laws changed as often as one changed horses.

VOLTAIRE, *Dictionnaire Philosophique: Lois.*

The law, —it has honored us, may we honor it.

DANIEL WEBSTER, *Speech, Dinner of Charleston, S.C., Bar, May 10, 1847.*

Law (Definition)

Law is intelligence without passion.

ARISTOTLE, *Politics,* III, 16 (trans. Weldon).

A rule of civil conduct prescribed by the supreme power in a state, commanding what is right and prohibiting what is wrong.

BLACKSTONE, *Commentaries,* bk 1, 44.

For law, remember, is not a dead corpus of blackletter wisdom. It is an elastic tissue which clothes the living body of society.

JOHN BUCHAN, *Homilies and Recreations* 218.

Law is whatever is boldly asserted and plausibly maintained.

AARON BURR. See, 1 Parton, *Life and Times of Aaron Burr* 149 (1889).

Law is the technique of justice.

CELSUS, *Digest,* (Justinian) i, I, 1 (trans. Radin). This inscription will be found on many courthouses.

It is the absolute justice of the State, enlightened by the perfect reason of the State.

RUFUS CHOATE, *Address: Conservative Force of the American Bar, July 3, 1845.*

Law is the highest reason, implanted in nature, which commands what ought to be done and forbids the opposite. (*Lex est ratio summa, insita in natura, quae iubet ea quae facienda sunt, prohibetque contraria.*)

CICERO, *De Legibus,* I, vi.

The design and object of laws is to ascertain what is just, honorable and expedient; and, when that is discovered, it is proclaimed as a general ordinance, equal and impartial to all. This is the origin of law, which, for various reasons, all are under an obligation to obey, but especially because all law is the invention and gift of heaven, the resolution of wise men, the correction of every offence, and the general compact of the state; to live in conformity with which is the duty of every individual in society.

DEMOSTHENES, *Contra Aristogeitan,* I, 16.

The Law of the State or of any organized body of men is composed of the rules which the courts, that is, the judicial organs of that body, lay down for the determination of legal rights and duties.

JOHN CHIPMAN GRAY, *Nature and Sources of the Law,* ch. 4 (2nd ed. 1921, p. 84).

The Law of a great nation means the opinions of half-a-dozen old gentlemen. . . . If those half-a-dozen old gentlemen form the highest tribunal of a country, then no rule or principle which they refuse to follow is Law in that country.

JOHN CHIPMAN GRAY, *Nature and Sources of the Law,* ch. 4 (2nd ed. 1921, p. 84).

The prophecies of what the courts will do in fact, and nothing more pretentious, are what I mean by the law.

OLIVER WENDELL HOLMES, *Path of the Law,* 10 Harv. L. R. 457, 460 (1897).

The law is the last result of human wisdom acting upon human experience for the benefit of the public.

SAMUEL JOHNSON. *Johnsoniana: Piozzi* 58.

It is nothing other than a certain rule of reason for the purpose of the common good, laid down by him who is entrusted with the welfare of the community and promulgated.

ST. THOMAS AQUINAS, *Summa Theologica,* I-II, q. 90, art. 4 (trans Dr. Wu).

Law is common sense as modified by the legislature.

Saying.

Law is law, law is law, and as in such and so forth, and hereby, and aforesaid, provided always, nevertheless, notwithstanding. Law is like a country dance, people are led up and down in it till they are tired. Law is like a book of surgery, there are a great many terrible cases in it. It is also like physic, they that take least of it are best off. Law is like a homely gentlewoman, very well to follow. Law is also like a scolding wife, very bad when it follows us. Law is like a new fashion, people are bewitched to get into it; it is also like bad weather, most people are glad when they get out of it.

GEORGE ALEXANDER STEVENS, *Lecture on Heads* 85 (1799).

Law (A Jealous Mistress)

As the law is a jealous science, and will not have any partnership with the Eastern Muses, I must absolutely renounce their acquaintance for ten or twelve years to come.

SIR WILLIAM JONES, *Letter, October 4, 1774 to Mr. Howard* (after his call to the bar).

As to the profession of the law, I must say of it in general, that it requires the whole man, and must be his north star, by which he is to direct his time, from the beginning of his undertaking it, to the end of his life. It is a business of that nature, that it will not be discontinued, nor scarce endure a cessation; but he that will reap the fruit expected from it, that is, raising of an estate by the strength of that, must pursue the subject without interruption, and he must not only read and talk, but eat, drink, and sleep law.

ROGER NORTH, *On the Study of the Laws* 7.

When I say daily, without intermission or cessation, I do not mean every hour and minute in every day, but only, as the philosophers meant by *nulla dies sine linea,* no day is to pass without somewhat of study or practice of the law, except such as order and necessity will have exempted.

ROGER NORTH, ibid. 8.

I will not say with Lord Hale that "The law will admit of no rival, and nothing to go even with it;" but I will say, that it is a jealous mistress, and requires a long and constant courtship. It is not to be won by trifling favors, but by lavish homage.

JOSEPH STORY, *Miscellaneous Writings* 456 (1835). Speech on his inauguration as Dane Professor of Law, Harvard Univ., August 25, 1829.

The phrase, "The law is a jealous mistress" has been variously attributed but without documentary source. In 1945, after considerable research, M. Eugene Culver (19 Conn. B. J. 90) unearthed this expression of the phrase by Story in 1829. This, however, is not final. See, Roger North, *On the Study of the Laws* (pub. 1824), with Notes by a member of the Inner Temple—Note at p. 55: "Mr. North's observations are correct and sensible; the law is not so jealous a mistress as to exclude every other object from the mind of her devotee, although she will vindicate the first place in his affections."

Law (Letter and Spirit)

Not in the letter but in the spirit; for the letter killeth, but the spirit quickeneth.

2 Corinthians 3:6

If courts of law will adhere to the mere letter of law, the great men who preside in Chancery will ever devise new ways to creep out of the lines of law, and temper with equity.

LORD MANSFIELD, C.J., *Doe d. Perrin v. Blake* (1769) 1 Coll. Jurid. 283, 321.

Wherefore a man ought not to rest upon the letter of an act, nor think that when he has the letter on his side, he has the law on his side in all cases.

PLOWDEN (reporter) *Eyston v. Studd* (1574) 2 Plow. 464.

From this judgment and the cause of it, the reader may observe that it is not the words of the law, but the internal sense of it that makes the law, and our law (like all others) consists of two parts, viz.: of body and soul; the letter of the law is the body of the law, and the sense and reason of the law is the soul of the law, *quia ratio legis est anima legis.* And the law may be likened to a nut which has a shell and within it a kernel; the letter of the law represents the shell and the sense of it the kernel, and as you will be no better for the nut if you make use only of the shell, so you will receive no benefit by the law if you rely only upon the letter, and as the fruit and profit of the nut lies in the kernel and not in the shell, so the fruit and profit of the law consists in the sense more than in the letter.

PLOWDEN (reporter), *Eyston v. Studd* (1574) 2 Plow. 465.

Extreme right wiseness is extreme wrong: as who saith, if thou take all that the words of the law giveth thee, thou shalt sometime do against the law.

CHRISTOPHER ST. GERMAN, *Doctor and Student*, Dial. I, ch. 16.

Law (Publication)

It was not thought fit nor convenient, to publish either those or any of the statutes enacted in those days in the vulgar tongue, lest the unlearned by bare reading without right understanding might suck out errors, and trusting to their conceit, might endamage themselves and some times fall into destruction.

SIR EDWARD COKE, 3 Rep.: *Preface.*

Law (Purpose)

The aim of the law is not to punish sins, but is to prevent certain external results.

HOLMES, J., *Commonwealth v. Kennedy*, 170 Mass. 18, 20 (1897).

The end of the law is peace. The means to that end is war. So long as the law is compelled to hold itself in readiness to resist the attacks of wrong—and this it will be compelled to do until the end of time—it cannot dispense with war. The life of the law is a struggle, —a struggle of nations, of the state power, of classes, of individuals. All the law in the world has been obtained by strife.

RUDOLPH VON JHERING, *The Struggle for Law* (trans. Lalor).

Law (Respect For)

They presume that the law doth speak with all indifferency; that the law hath no side-respect to their persons; that the law is as it were an oracle proceeded from wisdom and understanding.

RICHARD HOOKER, *Laws of Ecclesiastical Polity*, bk 1, ch. 10, 7 (1594).

Let reverence for the laws be breathed by every American mother to the lisping babe that prattles on her lap; let it be taught in schools, seminaries, and in colleges; let it be written in primers, spelling books, and in almanacs; let it be preached from the pulpit, proclaimed in legislative halls, and enforced in courts of justice. And, in short, let it become the political religion of the nation, and let the old and young, the rich and the poor, the grave and the gay of all sexes and tongues and colors and conditions sacrifice unceasingly upon its altars.

ABRAHAM LINCOLN, *Speech, Springfield, Ill., January 27, 1837.*

Let every American, every lover of liberty, every well-wisher to his posterity, swear by the blood of the Revolution never to violate in the least particular the laws of the country, and never to tolerate their violation by others.

ABRAHAM LINCOLN, ibid.

These things my heart prompteth me to teach the Athenians, and to make them understand that lawlessness worketh more harm to the state than any other cause. But a law-abiding spirit createth order and harmony, and at the same time putteth chains upon evil-doers; it maketh rough things smooth, it checketh inordinate desires, it dimmeth the glare of wanton pride and withereth the budding bloom of wild delusion; it maketh crooked judgments straight and softeneth arrogant behavior; it stoppeth acts of sedition and stoppeth the anger of bitter strife. Under the reign of law, sanity and wisdom prevail ever among men.

SOLON, *Fragments* (trans. Linforth).

Law (Symbolic)

Law is the scripture of Justice, the gospel of Right, and Truth is the minister at its altars. Error is a pretender to holy orders, a wolf in sheep's clothing, always striving to usurp the sacred office, or to share in the exercise of its functions.

LOGAN E. BLECKLEY, *Truth at the Bar,* 3 Ga. Bar Rep. 106 (1886).

Our Lady of the Common Law—I say it with the humility that is due from an old and faithful servant—our Lady in these days is no longer an easy one to please. She has become insatiate in her demands. Not law alone, but almost every branch of human knowledge, has been brought within her ken, and so within the range of sacrifice exacted of her votaries. Those who would earn her best rewards must make their knowledge as deep as the science and as broad and universal as the culture of their day. She will not be satisfied with less.

BENJAMIN N. CARDOZO, *Commencement Address to First Graduating Class, 1928*, 13 St. John's L.R. 231, 232 (1939).

The Law was the golden met-wand, and measure to try the causes of the subjects; and which protected his Majesty in safety and peace.

COKE, *Prohibitions del Roy*, 12 Rep. 65.

The law, wherein, as in a magic mirror, we see reflected, not only our own lives, but the lives of all men that have been! When I think on this majestic theme, my eyes dazzle.

OLIVER WENDELL HOLMES, *The Law. Speeches* 17 (1913).

When I think thus of the law, I see a princess mightier than she who once wrought at Bayeux, eternally weaving into her web dim figures of the ever-lengthening past—figures too dim to be noticed by the idle, too symbolic to be interpreted except by her pupils, but to the discerning eye disclosing every painful step and every world-shaking contest by which mankind has worked and fought its way from savage isolation to organic social life.

OLIVER WENDELL HOLMES, *The Law. Speeches* 17 (1913).

When I think of the Law as we know her in the courthouse and the market, she seems to me a woman sitting by the wayside, beneath whose overshadowing hood every man shall see the countenance of his deserts or needs. The timid and overborne gain heart from her protecting smile. Fair combatants, manfully standing to their rights, see her keeping the lists with the stern and discriminating eye of even justice. The wretch who has defied her most sacred commands, and has thought to creep through ways where she was not, finds that his path ends with her, and beholds beneath her hood the inexorable face of death.

OLIVER WENDELL HOLMES, *The Law. Speeches* 18 (1913).

Of Law there can be no less acknowledged, than that her seat is the bosom of God, her voice the harmony of the world. All things in heaven and earth do her homage, the very least as feeling her care, and the greatest as not exempted from her power: both Angels and Men and creatures of what condition soever, though each in different sort and manner, yet all with uniform consent, admiring her as the mother of their peace and joy.

RICHARD HOOKER, *Laws of Ecclesiastical Polity,* bk 1, 16 (1594).

Law Enforcement

Judges must beware of hard constructions and strained inferences; for there is no worse torture than the torture of laws.

BACON, *Essays: Of Judicature.*

Let penal laws, if they have been sleepers of long, or if they be grown unfit for the present time, be by wise judges confined in the execution.

BACON, *Essays: Of Judicature.*

After an existence of nearly twenty years of almost innocuous desuetude these laws are brought forth.

PRESIDENT CLEVELAND, *Message, March 1, 1886 to the Senate.*

The laws sometimes sleep, never die.

COKE, *Second Institute* 161.

The bite of law is in its enforcement.

FRANKFURTER, J., *Fisher v. United States,* 328 U.S. 463, 484 (1946).

It is a public scandal when the law is forced to uphold a dishonest act.

LORD MACNAGHTEN, *Nordenfelt v. Maxim Nordenfelt Guns* [1894] A.C. 535, 573.

Enormous offences call for a greater axe.

SIR FREDERICK POLLOCK, *The Expansion of the Common Law* 82 (1904).

The law hath not been dead, though it hath slept.

SHAKESPEARE, *Measure for Measure,* II, 2.

Law of the Land

This Constitution, and the Laws of the United States which shall be made in Pursuance thereof; and all Treaties made, or which shall be made under the Authority of the United States, shall be the supreme Law of the Land.

Constitution of the United States, Art. VI, cl.2.

No freeman shall be taken or imprisoned or disseised, or outlawed, or exiled, or in any ways destroyed; nor shall we go upon him, nor will we send upon him, but by the lawful judgment of his peers or by the law of the land.

Magna Carta, ch. 39 (1215).

Law Review

Judges have at last awakened, or at all events a number of them not wholly negligible, to the treasures buried in the law reviews.

BENJAMIN N. CARDOZO, *Growth of the Law* 14 (1924).

I have thought in certain moods that there is only one test of merit for a decision, and that is whether it was in favor of the critic or against him. In the old fable of the Greeks, Midas, King of

Phrygia was chosen to decide between Pan and Apollo when they engaged in a musical contest on the flute and lyre. Midas gave his vote to Pan, whereupon Apollo turned his ears into those of an ass. There are times in reading the comments in the law reviews when I wonder whether Phoebus Apollo is at his elfish tricks again.

BENJAMIN N. CARDOZO, Address, December 17, 1931, 1932 N.Y. County Lawyers Yearbook 369, 371.

Lawyer

It is as impossible for a lawyer to wish men out of litigation, as for a physician to wish them in health.

JEREMY BENTHAM, *Commonplace Book,* 10 Works 74.

Advisers of particular men, in particular difficulties, for particular fees.

AUGUSTINE BIRRELL, *Introductory Lecture on Law of Fraud,* University College, December, 1896. See, 13 L.Q.R. 264.

But once a lawyer always a lawyer. Though it is fifteen years since I ceased to practise I find that I still read the law reports first in the morning paper, and that fragments of legal jargon still tend to adorn my dubious literary style.

JOHN BUCHAN, *Homilies and Recreations* 209.

We may justly tax our wrangling lawyers, they do grow old in lawsuits, are so litigious and busy here on earth, that I think they will plead their clients' causes hereafter, some of them in hell.

ROBERT BURTON, *Anatomy of Melancholy: Democritus to the Reader* (1621).

A sergeant of the lawe, war and wys,
That often hadde been at the parvys,
Ther was also, ful riche of excellence.
Discreet he was, and of greet reverence:
He semed swich, his wordes weren so wyse.

Justyce he was ful often in assyse,
By patente, and by pleyn commissioun;
For his science, and for his heigh renoun
Of fees and robes hadde he many oon.
So greet a purchasour was no-wher noon.
Al was fee simple to him in effect,
His purchasing mighte nat been infect,
No-wher so bisy a man as he ther nas,
And yet he semed bisier than he was.
In termes hadde he caas and domes alle,
That from the tyme of king William were falle.
Therto he coude endyte, and make a thing,
Ther coude no wight pinche at his wryting;
And every statut coude he pleyn by rote.

CHAUCER, *Canterbury Tales: Prologue.*

The lawyer's vacation is the space between the question put to a witness and his answer.

RUFUS CHOATE. See, 1 Brown, *Works of Choate* 137 (1862).

The greatest orator among the lawyers, the greatest lawyer among the orators. (*Iuris peritorum eloquentissimus, eloquentium iuris peritissimus.*)

CICERO, *De Oratore,* I, 39 (Referring to Quintus Scaevola).

For the house of a great lawyer is assuredly the oracular seat of the whole community. (*Est enim sine dubio domus iurisconsulti, totius oraculum civitatis.*)

CICERO, *De Oratore,* I, 45.

[Gaius Aquilius] so just and virtuous a man that he seems to be a lawyer by nature rather than training. (*Qui ita iustus est et bonus vir, ut natura, non disciplina consultus esse videatur.*)

CICERO, *Pro Caecina,* xxvii.

A most learned species of profoundly ignorant men. (*Doctissimum genus indoctissimorum hominum.*)

ERASMUS, referring to English lawyers and his impression that they knew little outside their profession. 1 North, *Life of Lord Keeper Guilford* 200 (1826).

One that will not plead that cause wherein his tongue must be confuted by his conscience.

THOMAS FULLER, *The Holy State: The Good Advocate* (1642).

I know you lawyers can, with ease,
Twist words and meaning as you please;
That language, by your skill made pliant,
Will bend to favor every client;
That 'tis the fee directs the sense,
To make out either side's pretense,
When you peruse the clearest case,
You see it with a double face,
For scepticism is your profession;
You hold there's doubt in all expression.

JOHN GAY. *Fables: Dog and the Fox.*

All thieves who could my fees afford
Relied on my orations,
And many a burglar I've restored
To his friends and his relations.

WILLIAM S. GILBERT, *Trial by Jury.*

To protect his clients from being persuaded by persons whom they do not know to enter into contracts which they do not understand to purchase goods which they do not want with money which they have not got.

LORD GREENE. Lord Evershed, *Practical and Academic Characteristics of English Law* 40 (1956) says Lord Greene was fond of quoting this old definition of a lawyer's function.

Come, you of the law, who can talk if you please,
Till the man in the moon will allow it's a cheese.

O. W. HOLMES, Sr., *Lines Recited at Berkshire Jubilee.*

You know my division of able lawyers into kitchen knives, razors, and stings.

OLIVER WENDELL HOLMES, 1 *Holmes-Laski Letters* 692.

In a peaceful Cambridge college,
    Far remote from active law,
I dissect the Courts' decisions—
    I of course detect the flaw:
I correct their learned Lordships,
    (Though I do it from afar);
Though I'm good at academics,
    I'd be useless at the Bar.

J.P.C., *Poetic Justice* 15 (1947).

He did not care to speak ill of any man behind his back, but he believed the gentleman was an attorney.

SAMUEL JOHNSON. Boswell, *Life of Johnson*: *1770.*

Lawyers know life practically. A bookish man should always have them to converse with, they have what he wants.

SAMUEL JOHNSON. Boswell, *Life of Johnson*: 1778.

Woe to you lawyers also! because you load men with oppressive burdens and you yourselves with one of your fingers do not touch the burdens.

Luke 11:46.

Woe to you lawyers! for you have taken away the key of knowledge; you yourselves have not entered in, and those that were entering in you have hindered.

Luke 11:52.

A cock-brained solicitor, a law puddler, a mere and arrant pettifogger, a pork who never read any philosophy, an unbuttoned fellow, a boar in a vineyard, a snout in pickle . . . the shame of all honest attorneys, an unswilled hogshead, a tradesman of the law, whose best ware is only gibberish, a serving man and solicitor compounded into one mongrel—an apostate scarecrow, a vagabond and ignoramous, a beetle, a daw, a horsefly, a nuisance and brazen ass.

JOHN MILTON, *Colasterion,* (A composite of the epithets which Milton applied to an opponent who disagreed with him on the subject of divorce.)

Some allured to the trade of law, grounding their purposes not on the prudent and heavenly contemplation of justice and equity, which was never taught them, but on the promising and pleasing thoughts of litigious terms, fat contentions, and flowing fees.

JOHN MILTON, *Of Education.*

Sometimes a man who deserves to be looked down upon because he is a fool is despised only because he is a lawyer.

MONTESQUIEU, *Persian Letters,* XLIV.

They have no lawyers among them, for they consider them as a sort of people whose profession it is to disguise matters.

SIR THOMAS MORE, *Utopia,* bk 2.

The lawyer is always in a hurry.

PLATO: *Theaetetus.*

Your lawyer in practice spends a considerable part of his life in doing distasteful things for disagreeable people who must be satisfied, against an impossible time limit and with hourly interruptions, from other disagreeable people who want to derail the train; and for his blood, sweat, and tears he receives in the end a few unkind words to the effect that it might have been done better, and a protest at the size of the fee.

WILLIAM L. PROSSER, 1 Jl. Leg. Educ. 260.

St. Ives was a Breton,
Lawyer and not a robber,
A thing that made the people wonder.

Proverb.

A barrister of extended practise, if he has any talents at all, is the best companion in the world.

SIR WALTER SCOTT, *Journal, April 30, 1828.*

Why might not that be the skull of a lawyer? Where be his quiddities now, his quillets, his cases, his tenures, and his tricks?

SHAKESPEARE, *Hamlet,* V, 1.

Dick (the Butcher): The first thing we do, let's kill all the lawyers.

Jack Cade: Nay, that I mean to do.

SHAKESPEARE, *Henry the Sixth,* Pt. 2, IV, 2. (Read in its full context these words show that Shakespeare knew that you cannot set up a totalitarian form of government unless you first get rid of all the lawyers. Edwin M. Otterbourg, 39 A.B.A.J. 424.)

And do as adversaries do in law,
Strive mightily, but eat and drink as friends.

SHAKESPEARE, *Taming of the Shrew,* I, 2.

He piqued himself on understanding the practice of the courts, and in private company he took pleasure in laying down the law.

SMOLLETT, *Sir Launcelot Greaves,* ch. 1 (referring to Tom Clarke, a young lawyer).

There are three sorts of lawyers—able, unable, lamentable.

ROBERT SMITH SURTEES, *Plain or Ringlets,* ch. 40.

There was a society of men among us, bred up from their youth in the art of proving, by words multiplied for the purpose, that white is black and black is white, according as they are paid.

JONATHAN SWIFT, *Gulliver's Travels: Houyhnhnms,* ch. 5.

He is never in the company of a lawyer but he fancies himself in a witness-box.

WARD, *Illustrations of Human Life.* Quoted in 1 Grant, *Bench and Bar* 157 (1841).

I can give it as the condensed history of most, if not all good lawyers, that they lived well and died poor.

DANIEL WEBSTER, *Speech, Charleston, S.C. Bar, May 10, 1847.*

I have given my life to law and politics. Law is uncertain and politics are utterly vain.

DANIEL WEBSTER, to Professor Silliman, May 1852. Lodge, *Life of Webster* 346.

He is the very miracle of a lawyer,
One that persuades men to peace, and compounds quarrels
Among his neighbours, without going to law.

JOHN WEBSTER, *Devil's Law Case,* II, 1 (1619).

[Lawyers] have been known to wrest from reluctant juries triumphant verdicts of acquittal for their clients, even when those clients, as often happens, were clearly and unmistakably innocent.

OSCAR WILDE, *The Decay of Lying.*

A modest lawyer! a silent woman! a paradox in nature.

JOHN WILSON, *The Cheats,* I, 4 (1664).

O lady, lady, all interruption and no sense between us, as if we were lawyers at the bar; but I had forgot Apollo and Littleton never lodge in a head together.

WILLIAM WYCHERLEY, *The Plain Dealer,* IV, 1.

Lawyer (Fledgling)

Young men who feel drawn to the legal profession may rest assured that they will find in it an opportunity for usefulness which is probably unequalled elsewhere.

LOUIS D. BRANDEIS, Interview by Ernest Poole, 71 Amer. Mag. 493 (1911).

"Phunky, Phunky," said the Serjeant; "I never heard the name before. He must be a very young man."

"Yes, he is a very young man," replied the attorney. "He was only called the other day. Let me see—oh, he hasn't been at the Bar eight years yet."

CHARLES DICKENS, *Pickwick Papers*, ch. 31.

Mr. Bellby, the junior—not as junior as he might have been, for Soames only employed barristers of established reputation; it was, indeed, something of a mystery to him how barristers ever managed to establish that which made him employ them.

JOHN GALSWORTHY, *In Chancery*, Pt. 2, ch. 4.

When I went to the Bar as a very young man,
(Said I to myself—said I,)
I'll work on a new and original plan,
(Said I to myself—said I,)
I'll never assume that a rogue or a thief
Is a gentleman worthy implicit belief,
Because his attorney has sent me a brief,
(Said I to myself—said I!)

WILLIAM S. GILBERT, *Iolanthe*, Act. I.

I'll never throw dust in a juryman's eyes,
(Said I to myself—said I,)
Or hoodwink a judge who is not over-wise,
(Said I to myself—said I,)
Or assume that the witnesses summoned in force

In Exchequer, Queen's Bench, Common Pleas, or Divorce,
Have perjured themselves as a matter of course,
(Said I to myself—Said I!)

WILLIAM S. GILBERT, *Iolanthe,* Act I.

Ere I go into court I will read my brief through,
(Said I to myself—said I,)
And I'll never take work I'm unable to do,
(Said I to myself—said I.)
My learned profession I'll never disgrace
By taking a fee with a grin on my face,
When I haven't been there to attend to the case,
(Said I to myself—said I!)

WILLIAM S. GILBERT, *Iolanthe,* Act I.

When I, good friends, was called to the bar,
I'd an appetite fresh and hearty,
But I was, as many young barristers are,
An impecunious party:
I'd a swallow-tail coat of beautiful blue—
A brief which I bought of a booby—
A couple of shirts and a collar or two,
And a ring that looked like a ruby!

WILLIAM S. GILBERT, *Trial By Jury.*

I was speaking of my first brief, when he asked, "Did you not exclaim, —'Thou great first cause, least understood'?"

CRABB ROBINSON, *Diary, November 14, 1815.* Referring to conversation with Charles Lamb, who quoted from Pope's, *Universal Prayer.*

O, how can a modest young man
E'er hope for the smallest progression,—
The profession's already so full
Of lawyers so full of profession!

JOHN GODFREY SAXE, *The Briefless Barrister.*

Lawyer (Philadelphia)

It would (to use a Yankee phrase) puzzle a dozen Philadelphia lawyers.

The Balance, Nov. 15, 1803.

Proverb. There would seem to be little doubt but that the origin of this expression grew out of the Zenger trial. Zenger's New York lawyers were disbarred by the court. Andrew Hamilton (then eighty years of age) came from Philadelphia to defend him and succeeded in obtaining an acquittal. The expression is used both in praise and in opprobrium. Hamilton was given the Freedom of the Corporation by the Mayor of New York. See *Zenger Trial* (1735) 17 How St. Tr. 723. Remarks on the trial by two lawyers, defending the arguments of the Crown repeatedly use the expression in a disparaging manner. See, ibid. 740, 754, 763.

Many historians credit him (Andrew Hamilton) with being the one who, through his successful defense of John Peter Zenger, not only established in the New World the freedom of the press, but also created the appellation you here have enjoyed of being "Philadelphia lawyers".

LOYD WRIGHT, 41 A.B.A.J. 797 (1955).

Legal Aid

For the sake of God, I will help you. (*Pro Deo te adjuvabo.*)

ST. IVES (his maxim).

Legislation

As in other sciences, so in politics, it is impossible that all things should be precisely set down in writing; for enactments must be universal, but actions are concerned with particulars.

ARISTOTLE, *Politics,* bk 2, 8.

It is better that all things be regulated by law, than left to be decided by judges.

ARISTOTLE, *Rhetoric,* bk 1, 1.

It is far easier to conceive justly what would be useful law, than so to construct that same law that it may accomplish the design of the lawgiver.

JOHN AUSTIN, *Jurisprudence: Codification* (Lect. 39 pt. 2).

That law may be set down as good which is certain in meaning, just in precept, convenient in execution, agreeable to the form of government, and productive of virtue in those that live under it.

BACON, *Advancement of Learning,* bk 8, Aph. 7.

The laws of the most kingdoms and states have been like buildings of many pieces, and patched up from time to time according to occasions, without frame or model.

BACON, *An Offer to the King of a Digest to be Made of the Laws of England.*

Legislatures are not grammar schools; and, in this country at least, it is hardly reasonable to expect legislative acts to be drawn with strict grammatical or logical accuracy.

CHRISTIANCY, C.J., *Whipple v. Judge of Saginaw Circuit,* 26 Mich. 342, 344 (1873).

Law has always been unintelligible, and I might say that perhaps it ought to be. And I will tell you why, because I don't want to deal in paradoxes. It ought to be unintelligible because it ought to be in words—and words are utterly inadequate to deal with the fantastically multiform occasions which come up in human life.

LEARNED HAND, *Speech at Seventy-Fifth Anniversary Dinner, Legal Aid Society of N.Y., Feb. 16, 1951, 9 Brief Case,* No. 4, 4.

It might be possible, but I doubt if it would be easy, to compress in the same number of lines more fertile opportunities for doubt and error.

LORD HEWART, C.J., *London County Council v. Lees* [1939] 1 All E. R. 191, 194. Referring to the Sunday Trading Restrictions Act, 1936.

The Constitution does not make it a condition of preventive legislation that it should work a perfect cure. It is enough if the questioned act has a manifest tendency to cure or at least to make the evil less.

HOLMES, J., *Liggett Co. v. Baldridge*, 278 U.S. 105, 115 (1928).

An Act of Parliament can do no wrong, though it may do several things that look pretty odd.

HOLT, C.J., *City of London v. Wood* (1701) 12 Mod. 669, 687.

Algebraic formulae are not lightly to be imputed to legislators.

HOUGH, J., *Edwards v. Slocum*, 287 Fed. 651, 654 (1923).

I'm the Parliamentary Draftsman,
    I compose the country's laws,
And of half the litigation
    I'm undoubtedly the cause.
I employ a kind of English
    Which is hard to understand:
Though the purists do not like it,
    All the lawyers think it's grand.

J.P.C., *Poetic Justice* 31 (1947).

I'm the Parliamentary Draftsman,
    And they tell me it's a fact
That I often make a muddle
    Of a simple little Act.
I'm a target for the critics,
    And they take me in their stride—
Oh, how nice to be a critic
    Of a job you've never tried!

J.P.C., *Poetic Justice* 32 (1947).

Laws are formed by the manners and exigencies of particular times, and it is but accidental that they last longer than their causes.

SAMUEL JOHNSON. Boswell, *Life of Johnson: 1776.*

Three corrective words turn whole legal libraries into waste paper.

JULIUS VON KIRCHMANN, — attributed to (1847).

It was incongruous and impossible of operation; and its absurdities were so great that the framers themselves had no very distinct notion of its meaning.

MAULE, J., *Stratton v. Pettit* (1855) 16 C.B. 420, 432.

The laws should be adapted in such a manner to the people for whom they are framed that it should be a great chance if those of one nation suit another. . . . They should be in relation to the climate of each country, to the quality of its soil, to its situation and extent, to the principal occupation of the natives.

MONTESQUIEU, *Spirit of the Laws,* bk 1.

I first thought it would be possible to reduce laws to simple geometrical demonstrations, so that whoever could read and tie two ideas together would be capable of pronouncing on them; but I almost immediately convinced myself that this was an absurd idea.

NAPOLEON.

The law does not perfectly comprehend what is noblest and most just for all and therefore cannot enforce what is best. The differences of men and actions, and the endless irregular movements of human things, do not admit of any universal and simple rule. And no art whatsoever can lay down a rule which will last for all time.

PLATO, *Statesman* (Jowett trans.)

I will drive a coach and six through the Act of Settlement.

STEPHEN RICE. Macaulay, *History of England,* ch. 12.

It is not enough to attain to a degree of precision which a person reading in good faith can understand; but it is necessary to attain if possible to a degree of precision which a person reading in bad faith cannot misunderstand.

STEPHEN, J., *In re Castioni* [1891] 1 Q.B. 149, 167.

No law of that country must exceed in words the number of letters in their alphabet, which consists only of two and twenty. But, indeed few of them extend even to that length. They are expressed in the most plain and simple terms, wherein those people are not mercurial enough to discover above one interpretation; and to write a comment upon any law is a capital crime. As to the decision of civil causes, or proceedings against criminals, their precedents are so few, that they have little reason to boast of any extraordinary skill in either.

JONATHAN SWIFT, *Gulliver's Travels: Brobdingnag*, ch. 7.

Do you want good laws? Burn those which you have at present, and make fresh ones.

VOLTAIRE, *Dictionnaire Philosophique: Lois.*

Legislature

It is a fundamental principle with the English lawyers that Parliament can do everything, except making a woman a man or a man a woman.

DE LOLME, *Constitution of England*, bk 1, ch. x (1775). Although De Lolme is invariably given as the source of this saying, it appears earlier in a satirical pamphlet pub. in 1648. See, *News from Pembroke and Montgomery* in *The Harleian Miscellany*. The words are there put into the mouth of Philip Herbert, 4th Earl of Pembroke.

I think a Court of Law is bound to proceed upon the assumption that the legislature is an ideal person that does not make mistakes.

LORD HALSBURY, L.C., *Comm'rs. for Special Purpose of Income Tax v. Pemsel* [1891] A.C. 531, 549.

It must be remembered that legislatures are ultimate guardians of the liberties and welfare of the people in quite as great a degree as the courts.

HOLMES, J., *Missouri, Kansas & Texas Ry. v. May*, 194 U.S. 267, 270 (1904).

If the present Congress errs in too much talking, how can it be otherwise, in a body to which the people send one hundred and fifty lawyers, whose trade it is to question everything, yield nothing, and talk by the hour? That one hundred and fifty lawyers should do business together, ought not to be expected.

THOMAS JEFFERSON, *Autobiography.*

No man's life, liberty, or property are safe while the Legislature is in session.

Saying. See, 1 Tucker (N.Y. Surr.) 249 (1866).

The most high and absolute power of the realme of Englande, consisteth in the Parliament. . . . That which is done by this consent is called firme, stable and sanctum, and is taken for lawe. The Parliament abrogateth olde lawes, maketh newe, giveth orders for things past, and for thinges hereafter to be followed, changeth rightes, and possessions of private men, legittimateth bastards, establisheth formes of religion, altereth weightes and measures, giveth formes of succession to the crowne, defineth of doubtfull rightes, whereof is no lawe alreadie made, appointeth subsidies, tailes, taxes, and impositions, giveth most free pardons and absolutions, restoreth in bloud and name as the highest court, condemneth or absolveth them whom the Prince will put to that triall: And to be short, all that ever the people of Rome might do either in Centuriatis comitiis or tributis, the same may be doone by the parliament of Englande, which representeth and hath the power of the whole realme both the head and the bodie. For everie Englishman is entended to bee there present, either in person or by procuration and attornies, of what preheminence, state dignitie, or qualitie soever he bee, from the Prince (be he King or Queene) to the lowest person of Englande. And the consent of the Parliament is taken to be everie mans consent.

SIR THOMAS SMITH, *De Republica Anglorum,* bk 2, ch. 1.

For protection against abuses by legislatures the people must resort to the polls, not to the courts.

WAITE, C.J., *Munn v. Illinois,* 94 U.S. 113, 134 (1876).

Liability

Wherever one of two innocent persons must suffer by the acts of a third, he who has enabled such third person to occasion the loss must sustain it.

ASHHURST, J., *Lickbarrow v. Mason* (1787) 2 T.R. 63, 70.

Legal obligations that exist but cannot be enforced are ghosts that are seen in the law but that are elusive to the grasp.

HOLMES, J., *The Western Maid,* 257 U.S. 419, 433 (1922).

Libel and Slander

It had been adjudged, that where one says of a Lawyer, That he had as much Law as a Monkey, that the words were not actionable; because he hath as much Law, and more also. But if he had said, That he hath no more Law than a Monkey, those words were actionable.

BARCKLEY (BERKELEY) J., *Dickes v. Fenne* (1639) March N.R. 60.

For supposing they were true, the law says they are not the less libellous for that; nay indeed the law says, their being true is an aggravation of the crime.

RICHARD BRADLEY (Atty. Gen. for King, Province of N.Y.) arguendo, *Trial of Peter Zenger* (1735) 17 How. St. Tr. 694.

Dost not know that old Mansfield who writes like the Bible
Says the more 'tis a truth, sir, the more 'tis a libel.

ROBERT BURNS, *Lines written at Stirling.*

Many things that are defamatory may be said with impunity through the medium of speech. Not so, however, when speech is caught upon the wing and transmuted into print. What gives the sting to the writing is its permanence of form. The spoken word dissolves, but the written one abides and "perpetuates the scandal".

CARDOZO, C.J., *Ostrowe v. Lee,* 256 N.Y. 36, 39 (1931).

It hath ever been agreed, that it is not the matter but the manner which is punishable; for libelling against a common strumpet is as great an offense as against an honest woman, and perhaps more dangerous to the breach of the peace; for as the woman said she would never grieve to have been told of her red nose if she had not one indeed, neither is it a ground to examine the truth or falsehood of a libel, because it is *sub judice* whether it be a libel or not.

HUDSON, *Star Chamber* (2 Coll. Jurid., 102).

I adopt, in this case, as perfectly correct, the comprehensive and accurate definition of one of the counsel at the bar, (Gen. Hamilton) that the liberty of the press consists in the right to publish with impunity, truth, with good motives, and for justifiable ends, whether it respects government, magistracy or individuals.

KENT, J., *People v. Croswell,* 3 John. Cas. (N.Y.) 337, 393 (1804). This definition by Alexander Hamilton antedated by almost forty years Lord Campbell's Act of 1843 and is the basis of modern criminal libel statutes.

Whenever a man publishes he publishes at his peril.

LORD MANSFIELD, C.J., *R. v. Woodfall* (1774) Lofft, 776, 781.

The greater the truth the greater the libel.

Maxim. This maxim was applicable to the criminal law of defamation prior to the passage of Lord Campbell's Libel Act of 1845, which permitted the truth to be given in evidence on the subject of malice. The maxim has been attributed to both Lord Mansfield and Lord Ellenborough but the particular wording has not been found in the reports.

And oh, 'twas nuts to the Father of Lies,
(As this wily fiend is named in the Bible)
To find it settled by laws so wise,
That the greater the truth, the worse the libel.

THOMAS MOORE, *A Case of Libel. Odes on Cash, Corn, etc.*

For Sir Philip well knows,
That his innuendos
Will serve him no longer
In verse or in prose;
For twelve honest men have decided the cause,
Who are judges of fact, though not judges of law.

SIR WILLIAM PULTENEY, *Ballad*, published on the occasion of an acquittal of *The Craftsman*, for libel. This version of the ballad Lord Mansfield quoted from memory in the Trial of the Dean of St. Asaph, 21 How. St. Tr. 1037. Ridgeway, ed. of *Speeches of Lord Erskine* (see, 17 How. St. Tr. 672) and Lord Campbell (see, *Lives of Chancellors*: *Erskine*, ch. 178) assert that the last two lines read: For twelve honest men have determined the cause, Who are judges alike of the facts and the laws.

"You are too easily surprised," said Mr. Towkington. "Many words have no legal meaning. Others have a legal meaning very unlike their ordinary meaning. For example, the word 'daffy-down-dilly.' It is a criminal libel to call a lawyer a daffy-down dilly. Ha! Yes, I advise you never to do such a thing. No, I certainly advise you *never* to do it."

DOROTHY SAYERS, *Unnatural Death*, ch. 14. (In Peares' Case (1634) 1 Roll. Abr. 55, it was held actionable to call a lawyer a "daffa-down-dilly".)

A strange wild jurisdiction; where the jurors are judges both of law and of fact, and ignorant country fellows are to determine the nicest points of law.

WILMOT, J., *Doe v. Roe* (1760) 2 Burr. 1046, 1047.

Liberty

Experience should teach us to be most on our guard to protect liberty when the Government's purposes are beneficent. Men born to freedom are naturally alert to repel invasion of their liberty by evil-minded rulers. The greatest dangers to liberty lurk in insidious encroachment by men of zeal, well-meaning but without understanding.

BRANDEIS, J., *Olmstead v. United States,* 277 U.S. 438, 479 (1928).

The liberty of a man's person is more precious to him than all the rest that follow.

COKE, *Second Institute* 46.

It is the common fate of the indolent to see their rights become prey to the active. The condition upon which God hath given liberty to man is eternal vigilance.

JOHN P. CURRAN, *Speech on the Right of Election, July 10, 1790.*

A country preserved at the sacrifice of all the cardinal principles of liberty, is not worth the cost of preservation.

DAVIS, J., *Ex parte Milligan,* 71 U.S. (4 Wall.) 2, 126 (1866).

I often wonder whether we do not rest our hopes too much upon constitutions, upon laws and upon courts. These are false hopes; believe me, these are false hopes. Liberty lies in the hearts of men and women; when it dies there, no constitution, no law, no court can save it; no constitution, no law, no court can even do much to help it. While it lies there it needs no constitution, no law, no court to save it.

LEARNED HAND, *Spirit of Liberty* 189. Speech to newly naturalized citizens, May 21, 1944.

What then is the spirit of liberty? I cannot define it; I can only tell you my own faith. The spirit of liberty is the spirit which is not too sure that it is right; the spirit of liberty is the spirit which seeks to understand the minds of other men and women; the spirit of liberty is the spirit which weighs their interests alongside its own without bias; the spirit of liberty remembers that not even a sparrow falls to earth unheeded; the spirit of liberty is the spirit of Him who, near two thousand years ago, taught mankind that lesson it has never learned, but has never quite forgotten; that there may be a kingdom where the least shall be heard and considered side by side with the greatest.

LEARNED HAND, ibid. 190.

There is no such thing as an achieved liberty; like electricity, there can be no substantial storage and it must be generated as it is enjoyed, or the lights go out.

ROBERT H. JACKSON, *Task of Maintaining Our Liberties*, 39 A.B.A.J. 962 (1953).

Not every defeat of authority is a gain for individual freedom, nor every judicial rescue of a convict a victory for liberty.

ROBERT H. JACKSON, ibid. 964.

But he who has looked carefully into the perfect law of liberty and has remained in it, not becoming a forgetful hearer but a doer of the work, shall be blessed in his deed.

James 1:25.

Civil liberty consists, not in a right to every man to do just what he pleases, but it consists in an equal right to all the citizens to have, enjoy, and do, in peace, security, and without molestation, whatever the equal and constitutional laws of the country admit to be consistent with the public good.

JAY, C.J., *First Charge to Grand Jury as a Federal Judge*, 1st Cir., N.Y., 1790.

To be free is to live under a government by law.

LORD MANSFIELD, C.J., *R. v. Shipley* (1784) 4 Doug. 73, 170.

Freedom is not a mere intellectual abstraction; and it is not merely a word to adorn an oration upon occasions of patriotic rejoicing.

SUTHERLAND, J., *Associated Press v. N.L.R.B.*, 301 U.S. 103, 137 (1937).

For the saddest epitaph which can be carved in memory of a vanished liberty is that it was lost because its possessors failed to stretch forth a saving hand while yet there was time.

SUTHERLAND, J., *Associated Press v. N.L.R.B.*, 301 U.S. 103, 141 (1937).

Life

Life has relations not capable always of division into inflexible compartments. The moulds expand and shrink.

CARDOZO, J., *Glanzer v. Shepard*, 233 N.Y. 236, 241 (1922).

The life of a man is much favoured in law, but the life of the law itself which protects all in peace and safety ought to be more favoured.

COKE, 9 Rep. 68.

A man's life, like a piece of tapestry, is made up of many strands which interwoven make a pattern; to separate a single one and look at it alone, not only destroys the whole, but gives the strand itself a false value.

JUDGE LEARNED HAND, *Proceedings in Memory of Mr. Justice Brandeis*, 317 U.S. xi (1942).

The riders in a race do not stop short when they reach the goal. There is a little finishing canter before coming to a standstill. There is time to hear the kind voice of friends and to say to one's self: "The work is done." But just as one says that, the answer comes: "The race is over, but the work never is done while the power to work remains." The canter that brings you to a standstill need not be only coming to rest. It cannot be while you still live. For to live is to function. That is all there is in living. And so I end with a line from a Latin poet who uttered the message more than fifteen hundred years ago. "Death plucks my ears and says, Live—I am coming."

OLIVER WENDELL HOLMES, Radio Address, Mar. 8, 1931, on his 90th birthday.

I was on the point of asking you for the original of the quotation with which you wind up your speech of thanks (not the least of your minor works and I hope not the last), when I found in Miss Waddell's reprint that *Mors aurem vellens, Vivite, ait, venio,* is the end line of the pseudo-Virgilian *Copa.* The author understood life in a pretty different fashion from yours, but all is fair in quotation and especially of tags. Your approximate dating leaves room for conjecture to place that curious poem anywhere in the whole range of ancient Latin verse. To my mind the rather affected use of out of the way words can hardly be earlier than the silver age, and some of the lines are too good to be much later.

SIR FREDERICK POLLOCK, 2 *Holmes-Pollock Letters* 285.

Literature

I am in one of my moods of wholesale impatience with all fiction and all verging on it, reading instead, with rapture, *Fountainhall's Decisions.* . . . Fountainhall is prime, two big folio volumes, and all dreary and all true, and all terse as an obituary; and about one interesting fact on an average in twenty pages, and ten of them unintelligible for technicalities. There's literature, if you like.

ROBERT L. STEVENSON, *Letter to Henry James, July, 1893.*

The style . . . of the legal decisions of the Supreme Court of the United States . . . in purity, in elegance, and in technical precision, is equaled only by that of the best British authors, and surpassed by that of no English compositions of a similar kind.

NOAH WEBSTER, *Dictionary: Preface* (1828 ed.).

Litigation

To him that goes to law, nine things are requisite: A good deal of money, a good deal of patience, a good cause, a good attorney, good counsel, good evidence, a good jury, a good judge—and lastly, good luck.

Anon. *Hone, Every-day Book, under February 14.*

While lawyers have more sober sense,
Than t' argue at their own expense,
But make their best advantages
Of others' quarrels, like the Swiss.

SAMUEL BUTLER, *Hudibras*, Pt. III, Canto III, l. 455.

The litigious spirit is more often found with ignorance than with knowledge of law. (*Potius ignoratio iuris litigiosa est quam scientia.*)

CICERO, *De Legibus*, I, vi.

Sainthood is not a prerequisite to entering the portals of the courts; and if it were few litigants (and perhaps no lawyers) would enter therein, and the judges could go fishing as often as they heard the call of the waters. Nor will it be amiss to say (as probably will be said) that if such test should be applied to the bench, many judges including this writer) would be "recalled"; for it is here and now frankly conceded that the adoption of such a test would create more vacancies than the bar could furnish saints to fill.

KEY, J., *Heidenheimer v. Beer*, 155 S.W. 352, 356 (Tex. Civ. App., 1913).

Discourage litigation. Persuade your neighbors to compromise whenever you can. Point out to them how the nominal winner is often a real loser—in fees, expenses and waste of time. As a peacemaker the lawyer has a superior opportunity of being a good man.

ABRAHAM LINCOLN, *Notes for a Law Lecture, July 1, 1850.*

And if anyone would go to law with thee and take thy tunic, let him take thy cloak as well.

Matthew 5:40.

Lawsuits are an absolute leprosy, a social cancer. My code has singularly diminished lawsuits, by placing numerous causes within the decision of every individual. But there still remained much for the legislator to accomplish. Not that he could hope to prevent men from quarrelling: that they have done in all ages; but he might have prevented a third party in society, from living upon the quarrels of the two others, and even stirring up disputes, to promote their own interest. It was therefore my intention to establish the rule that lawyers should never receive fees, except when they gain causes.

NAPOLEON. See, Parkes, *History of Court of Chancery* 457* (1828).

You little know what a ticklish thing it is to go to law.

PLAUTUS, *Mostellaria*, V., 1.

The parties before the court are wholly answerable for the conduct of their own cases. Litigation is a game in which the court is umpire. The rules are in the knowledge of the court and will be declared and applied by it as required. It is for the parties to learn the rules and play the game correctly at their peril. The court will not tell the plaintiff what step he ought to take next, neither will it tell the defendant whether the plaintiff has made a slip of which he can take advantage. The umpire will speak when his judgment is demanded; it is not his business if the players throw away chances.

SIR FREDERICK POLLOCK, *The Expansion of the Common Law* 32 (1904).

Once, says an author, where I need not say,
Two travellers found an oyster on their way.
Both fierce, both hungry, the dispute grew strong,
When scale in hand, Dame Justice passed along.
Before her each with clamor pleads the laws,
Explains the matter, and would win the cause.
Dame Justice, weighing long the doubtful right,
Takes, opens, swallows it before their sight.
The cause of strife removed so rarely well,
"There, take," says Justice, "take you each a shell,
We thrive in courthouses on fools like you.
'Twas a fat oyster; live in peace—adieu."

POPE, *Miscellanies*, (trans. from Boileau).

He'll go to law for the wagging of a straw.

Proverb. RAY, *Proverbs* (1678).

Law-suits consume time, and money, and rest, and friends.

Proverb. HERBERT, *Jacula Prudentum* (1651).

Sue a beggar and catch a louse.

Proverb. RAY, *Proverbs* (1678).

It is not the saints of the world who chiefly give employment to our profession.

RYAN, C.J., *Motion to admit Miss Lavinia Goodell to the Bar*, 39 Wis. 232, 245 (1875).

When fools fall out, for ev'ry flaw,
They run horn mad to go to law,
A hedge awry, a wrong plac'd gate,
Will serve to spend a whole estate,
Your case the lawyer says is good,
And justice cannot be withstood;
By tedious process from above
From office they to office move;
Thro' pleas, demurrers, the dev'l and all,
At length they bring it to the hall;
The dreadful hall by Rufus rais'd,
For lofty Gothick arches prais'd.

Unknown. Inscription on an engraving of Westminster Hall by C. Mosley. See: Hone, *Everyday Book* under Jan. 23.

Loss

When baggage is lost, it is not simple privation; it is bereavement.

BLECKLEY, J., *Western R.R. v. Thornton*, 60 Ga. 300, 302 (1878).

Magna Charta

Magna Charta is such a fellow that he will have no sovereign.

COKE, *Speech in the House of Commons, May 17, 1628*, 2 Parl. Hist. 357.

Man

A man's happiness depends upon the state of his digestion, and not the station he fills.

LORD ABINGER. 1 Hardcastle, ed., *Life of Lord Campbell*, ch. 13 (Amer. ed. 1881, p. 394).

The best men are but men, and are sometimes transported with passion.

SIR ROBERT ATKYNS, *Enquiry into the Power of Dispensing with Penal Statutes* (1686). See, *Trial of Sir Edward Hales*, 11 How. St. Tr. 1206.

A great man represents a great ganglion in the nerves of society, or, to vary the figure, a strategic point in the campaign of history, and part of his greatness consists in his being *there.*

HOLMES, C.J. On motion that the court adjourn on February 4, 1901, the one hundredth anniversary of the day John Marshall took his seat as Chief Justice of the United States, 178 Mass. 625.

I only mean that when one thinks coldly I see no reason for attributing to man a significance different in kind from that which belongs to a baboon or to a grain of sand.

OLIVER WENDELL HOLMES, 2 *Holmes-Pollock Letters* 252.

Man with all his wisdom, *toils for heirs he knows not who.*

KIRKPATRICK, C.J., *Nevison v. Taylor,* 8 N.J.L. 43, 46 (1824).

If parts allure thee, think how Bacon shin'd,
The wisest, brightest, meanest of mankind.

POPE, *Essay on Man*, iv, 281. Referring to Sir Francis Bacon.

Mansfield, Lord

Mansfield was not a mere lawyer. When he came to town he "drank champagne with the wits"; he was the friend of Pope.

SAMUEL JOHNSON (indirect quote). Boswell, *Life of Johnson*: *1772*. The expression "drank champagne with the wits" is from Prior's Chameleon.

Much may be made of a Scotchman, if he be caught young.

SAMUEL JOHNSON. Boswell, *Life of Johnson: 1772.*

Graced as thou art, with all the power of words,
So known, so honoured, at the House of Lords.

POPE, *Imitations of Horace,* I, vi.

Marriage

In me heart I think if people marry it ought to be f'r life. Th' laws ar-re altogether too lenient with thim.

FINLEY PETER DUNNE, *Dissertations by Mr. Dooley: Short Marriage Contracts.*

I believe marriages would in general be as happy, and often more so if they were all made by the Lord Chancellor, upon a due consideration of characters and circumstances, without the parties having any choice in the matter.

SAMUEL JOHNSON. Boswell, *Life of Johnson: 1776.*

What was once a holy estate enduring for the joint lives of the spouses, is steadily assuming the characteristics of a contract for a tenancy at will.

LORD RUSSELL of Killowen, *Fender v. St. John-Mildmay* [1938] A.C. 1, 34.

Quoth Dick to Tom,—This Act appears
Absurd, as I'm alive;
To take the Crown at eighteen years,
The Wife at twenty-five.
The myst'ry how shall we explain?
For sure, as Dowdeswell said,
Thus early if they're fit to *reign*
They must be fit to *wed.*
Quoth Tom to Dick, —Thou art a fool,
And little know'st of life;

Alas! 'tis easier far to rule
A kingdom than a wife.

Saying, 1772 in England at the time of the passage of the Royal Marriage Act. The law placed restraints on the freedom of marriage in the case of the Heir-Apparent and other members of the Royal Family. 17 Parl. Hist., 401.

Of all actions of a man's life, his marriage does least concern other people, yet of all actions of our life 'tis most meddled with by other people.

JOHN SELDEN, *Table-Talk*: *Marriage.*

Martyr

One . . . does not prove by his martyrdom that he has kept within the law.

CARDOZO, J., *Hamilton v. Regents,* 293 U.S. 245, 268 (1934).

Maxim

If this is a maxim, is it any the worse? What are maxims but the expression of that which good sense has made a rule.

LORD BRAMWELL, J., *Smith v. Charles Baker & Sons* [1891] A.C. 325, 344.

I detest the attempt to fetter the law by maxims. They are almost invariably misleading: they are for the most part so large and general in their language that they always include something which really is not intended to be included in them.

LORD ESHER, M.R., *Yarmouth v. France* (1887) 19 Q.B.D. 647, 653.

It certainly is very hard upon a Judge, if a rule which he generally lays down, is to be taken up and carried to its full extent. This is sometimes done by counsel, who have nothing else to rely on; but great caution ought to be used by the Court in extending such maxims to cases which the Judge who uttered them never had in contemplation.

LORD MANSFIELD, C.J., *Brisbane v. Dacres* (1813) 5 Taunt., 143, 162.

Memory

For my name and memory, I leave it to men's charitable speeches, and to foreign nations, and the next ages.

BACON, *From His Will.*

Verses at the first were invented for the helpe of memorie and it standeth well with gravitie of our lawyer to cite them.

COKE, *First Institute* 237.

I would sooner trust the smallest slip of paper for truth, than the strongest and most retentive memory, ever bestowed on mortal man.

LUMPKIN, J., *Miller v. Cotton,* 5 Ga. 341, 349 (1848).

I do not remember. (*Non mi ricordo*).

MAJORCHI, an Italian witness, testifying against Queen Caroline (1820) when cross-examined by Lord Brougham, made this statement nine out of ten times. It became a catchword.

Metaphor

Metaphors in law are to be narrowly watched, for starting as devices to liberate thought, they end often by enslaving it.

CARDOZO, J., *Berkey v. Third Ave. Ry. Co.,* 244 N.Y. 84, 94 (1926).

When I can't talk sense, I talk metaphor.

JOHN P. CURRAN. 2 Thomas Moore, *Memoirs* 170 (1853).

Nothing in law is so apt to mislead as a metaphor.

LORD MANSFIELD. Attributed to him by Lord Westbury in *Knox v. Gye* (1872) 42 L.J. Ch. 234, 239.

Meum and Tuum

These two great pronouns, *meum* and *tuum.*

COKE, *Third Institute: Proeme.*

Monster

Thou are a monster; thou hast an English face, but a Spanish heart.

COKE, *Trial of Sir Walter Raleigh* (1603) 2 How. St. Tr. 1, 7.

Morality

Our system of morality is a body of imperfect social generalizations expressed in terms of emotion.

OLIVER WENDELL HOLMES, *Ideals and Doubts*, 10 Ill. L.R. 1, 3 (1915).

Men who are knaves by retail are extremely honest in the gross; they love morality.

MONTESQUIEU, *Spirit of the Laws,* bk 25.

Motive

The illustrious Lucius Cassius, whom the Roman people considered the wisest and most conscientious of judges, was in the habit of asking repeatedly in trials, "who had profited by it?" (*L. Cassius ille quem populus Romanus verissimum et sapientissimum iudicem putabat, indentidem in causis quaerere solebat, "cui bono" fuisset.*)

CICERO, *Pro Roscio Amerino,* xxx, 84.

Murder

Gentlemen of the jury, the charge against the prisoner is murder, and the punishment of murder is death; and that simple statement is sufficient to suggest to us the awful solemnity of the occasion which brings you and me face to face.

JOHN INGLIS, *Address to the Jury, July 8, 1857,* Trial of Madeleine Smith before the High Court of Justiciary, Edinburgh. (Regarded in England as the finest opening by the counsel for the defense in a murder case ever known.)

I have just heard of your deep affliction, and the arrest of your son for murder. I can hardly believe he can be capable of the crime alleged against him. It does not seem possible. I am anxious that he should be given a fair trial at any rate; and gratitude for your long continued kindness to me in adverse circumstances prompts me to offer my humble services gratuitously in his behalf. It will afford me an opportunity to requite, in a small degree, the favors I received at your hand, and that of your lamented husband, when your roof afforded me a grateful shelter, without money and without price.

ABRAHAM LINCOLN, *Letter to Mrs. Hannah Armstrong,* September, 1857.

Mrs. Manning insisted on being hanged in black satin, and ruined the trade in that material in consequence for several years for ladies dresses.

SERJEANT ROBINSON. See, Manson, *Builders of Our Law* 119 (2nd. ed. 1904).

Natural Law

This law of nature, being coeval with mankind, and dictated by God himself, is of course superior in obligation to any other. It is binding over all the globe, in all countries, and at all times: no human laws are of any validity, if contrary to this; and such of them as are valid derive all their force, and all their authority, mediately or immediately, from this original.

BLACKSTONE, *Commentaries*, bk 1, 41.

There is but one law for all, namely that law which governs all law, the law of our Creator, the law of humanity, justice, equity, —the Law of Nature and of Nations.

BURKE, *Impeachment of Warren Hastings*, May 28, 1794.

There is in fact a true law—namely, right reason—which is in accordance with nature, applies to all men, and is unchangeable and eternal. By its commands this law summons men to the performance of their duties; by its prohibitions it restrains them from doing wrong. Its commands and prohibitions always influence good men, but are without effect on the bad. To invalidate this law by human legislation is never morally right, nor is it permissible ever to restrict its operation, and to annul it wholly is impossible. Neither the senate nor the people can absolve us from our obligation to obey this law, and it requires no Sextus Aelius to expound and interpret it. It will not lay down one rule at Rome and another at Athens, nor will it be one rule today and another tomorrow. But there will be one law, eternal and unchangeable, binding at all times upon all peoples; and there will be, as it were, one common master and ruler of men, namely God, who is the author of this law, its interpreter, and its sponsor. The man who will not obey it will abandon his better self, and in denying the true nature of a man, will thereby suffer the severest of penalties, though he has escaped all the other consequences which men call punishment.

CICERO, *De Re Publica*, III, xxii (trans. by Sabine and Smith).

The law of nature is that which God at the time of creation of the nature of man infused into his heart, for his preservation and direction; and this is *lex aeterna,* the moral law, called also the law of nature. And by this law, written with the finger of God in the heart of man, were the people of God a long time governed, before the law was written by Moses, who was the first reporter or writer of law in the world.

COKE, *Calvin's Case* (1608) 7 Rep. 12 b.

Natural law is the dictate of right reason, showing the moral turpitude, or moral necessity of any act from its agreement or disagreement with a rational nature, and consequently that such an act is either forbidden or commanded by God, the author of nature.

GROTIUS, *De Jure Belli ac Pacis* (1625) bk 1, ch. 1.

When the first principles of civil society are violated, and the rights of a whole people are invaded, the common forms of municipal law are not to be regarded. Men may then betake themselves to the law of nature; and if they but conform their actions to that standard, all cavils against them betray either ignorance or dishonesty. There are some events in society to which human laws can not extend; but when applied to them lose all their force and efficacy. In short, when human laws contradict or discountenance the means which are necessary to preserve the essential rights of any society, they defeat the proper end of all laws, and so become null and void.

ALEXANDER HAMILTON, *The Farmer Refuted* (1775).

The natural law always buries its undertakers.

HEINRICH ROMMEN, *Natural Law* (1947) 267 (paraphrasing an expression of Etienne Gilson, French philosopher).

We must say that the natural law, as to first common principles, is the same for all, both as to rectitude and as to knowledge. But as to certain matters of detail, which are conclusions, as it were of those common principles, it is the same for all in the majority of cases, both as to rectitude and as to knowledge; and yet in some few cases it may fail, both as to rectitude, by reason of certain obstacles (just as natures subject to generation and corruption fail in some few cases on account of some obstacle), and as to knowledge, since in some the reason is perverted by passion, or evil habit, or an evil disposition of nature.

ST. THOMAS AQUINAS, *Summa Theologica,* I-II, q.94, art. 4 (trans. English Dominican Fathers).

Every human law has just so much of the character of law as it is derived from the law of nature. But if in any point it differs from the law of nature, it is no longer a law but a corruption of law.

ST. THOMAS AQUINAS, *Summa Theologica,* I-II, q.95, art. 2.

I cannot fancy to myself what the law of nature means, but the law of God. How should I know I ought not to steal, I ought not to commit adultery, unless some body had told me so? Surely 'tis because I have been told so? 'Tis not because I think I ought not to do them, nor because you think I ought not; if so, our minds might change, whence then comes the restraint? From a higher Power, nothing else can bind.

JOHN SELDEN, *Table-Talk*: *Law of Nature.*

Neck Verse

Have mercy on me, O God, according to thy great mercy. And according to the multitude of thy tender mercies blot out my iniquity.

Psalms 50. This psalm was called the "neck verse" since it was the one invariably chosen by persons claiming benefit of clergy to prove that they were able to read.

Negligence

Negligence is the omission to do something which a reasonable man . . . would do, or doing something which a prudent and reasonable man would not do.

ALDERSON, B., *Blyth v. Birmingham Waterworks Co.* (1856) 11 Exch. 781, 784.

Whenever one person is by circumstances placed in such a position with regard to another that every one of ordinary sense who did think would at once recognize that if he did not use ordinary care and skill in his own conduct with regard to those circumstances he would cause danger of injury to the person or property of the other, a duty arises to use ordinary care and skill to avoid such danger.

BRETT, M.R., *Heaven v. Pender* (1883) 11 Q.B.D. 503, 509.

Standards of prudent conduct are declared at times by courts, but they are taken over from the facts of life.

CARDOZO, J., *Pokora v. Wabash Ry. Co.*, 292 U.S. 98, 104 (1934).

I said I could see no difference between negligence and gross negligence—that it was the same thing, with the addition of a vituperative epithet.

ROLFE, B., *Wilson v. Brett* (1843) 11 M. & W. 113, 115.

Negotiable Instrument

It is a key which in the hands of a rightful owner is intended to unlock the door of the warehouse, floating or fixed, in which the goods may chance to be.

BOWEN, L.J., *Sanders Bros. v. MacLean & Co.* (1883) 11 Q.B.D. 327, 341 (referring to a bill of lading).

Nonsuit

A nonsuit . . . is but like blowing out of a candle, which a man at his own pleasure lights again.

JOHN MARCH, *Slander and Arbitrements* 215 (1648).

Nuisance

One ought not to have so delicate a nose, that he cannot bear the smell of hogs.

COKE, 9 Rep. 58.

It would have been wrong, as it seems to me, for this Court in the reign of Henry VI to have interfered with the further use of sea coal in London, because it had been ascertained to their satisfaction, or predicted to their satisfaction, that by the reign of Queen Victoria both white and red roses would have ceased to bloom in the Temple Gardens. If some picturesque haven opens its arms to invite the commerce of the world, it is not for this Court to forbid the embrace, although the fruit of it should be the sights, and sounds, and smells of a common seaport and ship-building town, which would drive the Dryads and their masters from their ancient solitudes.

JAMES, L.J., *Salvin v. North Brancepeth Coal Co.* (1874) 9 Ch. 705, 709.

A nuisance may be merely a right thing in the wrong place, —like a pig in the parlor instead of the barnyard.

SUTHERLAND, J., *Euclid v. Ambler Realty Co.*, 272 U.S. 365, 388 (1926).

Numbers

And it seemeth to me, that the law in this case delighteth herselfe in the number of twelve; for there must not onely be twelve jurors for the tryall of matters of fact but twelve judges of ancient time for tryall of matters of law in the Exchequer Chamber. Also for matters of state there were in ancient time twelve counsellors of state. He that wageth his law must have eleven others with him, which thinke he says true. And that number of twelve is much respected in holy writ, as twelve apostles, twelve stones, twelve tribes etc.

COKE, *First Institute* 155.

Oath

I will not counsel or maintain any suit or proceeding which shall appear to me to be unjust, nor any defense except such as I believe to be honestly debatable under the law of the land.

American Bar Association, model oath for candidates for admission to the bar, 33 A.B.A. Rep. 585 (1908).

Every pleader is bound by oath that he will not knowingly maintain or defend wrong or falsehood, but will abandon his client immediately that he perceives his wrongdoing. That he will never have recourse to false delays or false witnesses, and never allege, proffer, or consent to any corruption, deceit, lie, or falsified law, but loyally will maintain the right of his client, so that he may not faii through his folly, or negligence, nor by default of him, nor by default of any argument that he could urge; and that he will not by blow, contumely, brawl, threat, noise, or villain conduct disturb any judge, party, serjeant, or other in court, nor impede the hearing or the course of justice.

ANDREW HORN, *Mirror of Justice* (c. 1307), 7 Seld. Soc. Pub. 48.

Office

Officialdom, however it displays itself, is the husk and that what is precious is the man within.

BENJAMIN N. CARDOZO, *Law and Literature* 189 (1931).

The officers of our government, from the highest to the lowest, are equally subjected to legal restraint.

JOHNSON, J., *Gilchrist v. Collector of Charleston,* 10 Fed. Cas. 355, 356 (1808).

The only road to the highest stations in this country is that of the law.

SIR WILLIAM JONES, *Letter March 17, 1771, to C. Reviczki.*

No man in this country is so high that he is above the law. No officer of the law may set that law at defiance with impunity. All the officers of the government, from the highest to the lowest, are creatures of the law, and are bound to obey it.

MILLER, J., *United States v. Lee,* 106 U.S. 196, 220 (1882).

In our country, the highest man is not above the people; the humblest is not below the people.

JOSEPH STORY, Speech, Massachusetts Constitutional Convention, 1820. 1 Story, *Life of Joseph Story* 392.

Opinion

Opinion has a significance proportioned to the sources that sustain it.

CARDOZO, C.J., *Petrogradsky M.K. Bank v. National City Bank,* 253 N.Y. 23, 35 (1930).

Order

I should like to stipulate for some kind of order. . . . There is the chronological, the botanical, the metaphysical, the geographical—even the alphabetical order would be better than no order at all.

MAULE, J. See, Robinson, *Bench and Bar* 109 (1894).

Paradox

In the Blue Grass region,
A "Paradox" was born,
The corn was full of kernels
And the "colonels" full of corn.

JOHN MARSHALL. 4 Beveridge, *Life of Marshall,* ch. 2. At a social gathering a game was being played which required each one present to make a rhyme upon a word suddenly given. This doggerel was Marshall's contribution.

Parchment

There is no magic in parchment or in wax.

ASHHURST, J., *Master v. Miller* (1791) 4 T.R. 320, 331.

Is not this a lamentable thing, that of the skin of an innocent lamb should be made parchment? that parchment, being scribbled o'er, should undo a man?

SHAKESPEARE, *Henry VI, pt. II, IV, 2.*

Past

The past cannot be recalled by the most absolute power.

MARSHALL, C.J., *Fletcher v. Peck,* 10 U.S. (6 Cranch) 87, 135 (1810).

Though the Court may order an election *nunc pro tunc* it is beyond the power of the Courts, or of an Act of Parliament to recall a day that has passed, or make a thing which has happened not have happened.

MAULE, J., *Berwick (Mayor of) v. Osward* (1854) 3 El. & Bl. 653, 670.

Perjury

Once forsworn, and ever forlorn.

COKE, *Second Institute* 238.

Perpetuities

Perpetuities were born under some unfortunate constellation.

COKE, 10 Rep. 42 b.

Persecution

Persecution is a very easy form of virtue.

COLERIDGE, C.J., *R. v. Ramsey* (1883) 1 C. & E. 126, 145.

Pleading

Whoe'er has drawn a special plea,
Has heard of old Tom Tewkesbury,
Deaf as a post, and thick as mustard,
He aim'd at wit, and bawl'd and bluster'd,
And died a *nisi prius* leader—
That genius was my special pleader.

JOHN ANSTEY, *Pleader's Guide,* bk 1 (1796).

Good pleading—the heart-string of the common law.

COKE, *First Institute*: *Preface.*

The wisdom of Solomon, accentuated by the legal lore of Coke and Mansfield, could not devise a judgment which this complaint would support.

HUSTON, J., *Wilson v. Thompson,* 4 Idaho 678, 680 (1896).

In law it is good policy to never plead what you need not, lest you oblige yourself to prove what you can not.

ABRAHAM LINCOLN, *Letter to Usher F. Linder, Feb. 20, 1848.*

And know ye this, my son, that this is one of the most honorable, laudable and profitable things in our law; to have the science of well pleading in actions real and personal; and therefore I counsel thee especially to set all thy courage and care to learn this.

LITTLETON, *Tenures,* bk 3, ch. 9, sec. 534 (1481).

The prayer for general relief—that India-rubber prayer.

LUMPKIN, J., *Rutherford v. Jones,* 14 Ga. 521, 525 (1854).

So great is the ascendency of the Law of Actions in the infancy of Courts of Justice, that substantive law has at first the look of being gradually secreted in the interstices of procedure.

SIR HENRY MAINE, *Early Law and Custom* 389 (1907).

Procedure . . . is the prime bread-and-butter subject of the practitioner.

ARTHUR T. VANDERBILT, *Cases and Materials on Modern Procedure* 4 (1952).

Police Power

All rights tend to declare themselves absolute to their logical extreme. Yet all in fact are limited by the neighborhood of principles of policy which are other than those on which the particular right is founded, and which become strong enough to hold their own when a certain point is reached. The limits set to property by other public interests present themselves as a branch of what is called the police power of the State.

HOLMES, J., *Hudson Water Co. v. McCarter,* 209 U.S. 349, 355 (1908).

The power to direct the removal of gunpowder is a branch of the police power, which unquestionably remains, and ought to remain, with the states.

MARSHALL, C.J., *Brown v. Maryland,* 25 U.S. (12 Wheat.) 419, 443 (1827).

Politics

The constitution does not allow reasons of State to influence our judgment: God forbid it should! We must not regard political consequences, how formidable soever they might be: if rebellion was the certain consequence, we are bound to say, "*Fiat justitia ruat coelum.*"

LORD MANSFIELD, C.J., *R. v. Wilkes* (1770) 4 Burr. 2527, 2561. The maxim: "Let justice be done though the heavens fall" became widely popular after its use by Lord Mansfield.

Some odd old Whig
Who never changed his principle, or wig.

POPE, *Imitations of Horace, Epilogue to Satires*, I (Referring to Sir Joseph Jekyl, Master of the Rolls).

Scarcely any political question arises in the United States which is not resolved sooner or later into a judicial question.

ALEXIS DE TOCQUEVILLE, *Democracy in America*, Pt. 1, ch. 16.

Popularity

Experience might inform them that many who have been saluted with the huzzas of a crowd one day, have received their execrations the next; and many who by the popularity of their times have been held up as spotless patriots, have, nevertheless, appeared upon the historian's page, when truth has triumphed over delusion, the assassins of liberty. Why then, can the noble lord think I am ambitious of present popularity, that echo of folly and shadow of renown.

LORD MANSFIELD, reply to Chatham in House of Lords, May 9, 1770, 16 Parl. Hist. 977.

I wish popularity: but, it is that popularity which follows; not that which is run after. It is that popularity which, sooner or later, never fails to do justice to the pursuit of noble ends, by noble means. I will not do that which my conscience tells me is wrong upon this occasion; to gain the huzzas of thousands, or the daily praise of all the papers which come from the press: I will not avoid doing what I think is right; though it should draw on me the whole artillery of libels; all that falsehood and malice can invent, or the credulity of a deluded populace can swallow.

LORD MANSFIELD, C.J., *R. v. Wilkes* (1770) 4 Burr. 2527, 2562.

Possession

Possession is eleven points of the law and they say there are but twelve.

Proverb. RAY, *Proverbs* (1678).

Poverty

Poverty and immorality are not synonymous.

BYRNES, J., *Edwards v. California,* 314 U.S. 160, 177 (1941).

Power

Arbitrary power has seldom or never been introduced into any country at once. It must be introduced by slow degrees, and as it were step by step lest the people should see its approach. The barriers and fences of the people's liberty must be plucked up one by one, and some plausible pretences must be found for removing or hoodwinking, one after another, those sentries who are posted by the constitution of a free country, for warning the people of their danger.

THOMAS ERSKINE, arguendo, *Trial of Thomas Paine* (1792) 22 How. St. Tr. 443.

The prize of the general is not a bigger tent, but command.

OLIVER WENDELL HOLMES, *Law and the Court, Speeches* 100 (1913).

Evil men are rarely given power; they take it over from better men to whom it had been entrusted.

Justices ROBERTS, FRANKFURTER, and JACKSON, dissenting in *Screws v. United States,* 325 U.S. 91, 160 (1945).

Arbitrary power and the rule of the Constitution cannot both exist. They are antagonistic and incompatible forces; and one or the other must of necessity perish whenever they are brought into conflict.

SUTHERLAND, J., *Jones v. Securities and Exchange Comm.,* 298 U.S. 1, 24 (1936).

Prayers

Almighty God, the giver of wisdom, without whose help resolutions are vain, without whose blessing study is ineffectual, enable me, if it be Thy will, to attain such knowledge as may qualify me to direct the doubtful, and instruct the ignorant, to prevent wrongs and terminate contentions; and grant that I may use that knowledge which I shall attain, to Thy glory and my own salvation, for Jesus Christ's sake, Amen.

SAMUEL JOHNSON, *Prayer Before the Study of Law.* Boswell, *Life of Johnson: 1765.*

St. Thomas More, be our advocate and counsel before the Divine tribunal that alone is without error.

Bespeak for us the wisdom to apply the precepts of God's eternal law to the problems of our daily practice.

Intercede for us that we may emulate the sense of humor which made your heart echo with the mirth of heaven.

Pray that we may spurn false oaths and live as you did, faithful to our trust as members of the Bar, even though by doing so we may be called upon to sacrifice our lives as you sacrificed yours.

These things seek for us through the merits of Jesus Christ, Our Lord. Amen.

MILES F. McDONALD, *Prayer for Lawyers.*

O God of all truth, knowledge and judgment, without whom nothing is true or wise, or just, look down with mercy upon Thy servants whom Thou sufferest to sit in earthly seats of judgment, to administer Thy justice to Thy people. Enlighten their ignorance and inspire them with Thy judgments. Grant them grace, truly and impartially to administer Thy justice and to maintain Thy truth in the glory of Thy name. And of Thy infinite mercy so direct and dispose of my heart that I may this day fulfill all my duty in Thy fear, and fall into no error of judgment. Give me grace to hear patiently, to consider diligently, to understand rightly, and to decide justly. Grant me due sense of humility, that I be not mislead by my wilfulness, vanity or egotism. Of myself I humbly acknowledge my own unfitness and unworthiness in Thy sight, and without Thy gracious guidance I can do nothing right. Have mercy upon me, a poor, weak, frail sinner, groping in the dark; and give me grace so to judge others now, that I may not myself be judged when Thou comest to judge the world with Thy truth. Grant my prayer, I beseech Thee, for the love of Thy son, our Saviour, Jesus Christ. Amen.

EDWARD G. RYAN, Chief Justice of Wisconsin Supreme Court. Prayer was found among his papers after his death.

Give therefore to thy servant an understanding heart, to judge thy people, and discern between good and evil. For who shall be able to judge this people, thy people which is so numerous?

3 Kings 3:9 (Solomon's prayer for wisdom).

Preamble

Of all instruments of longwindedness, the most unmerciful is that which is called a Preamble. It is a sort of excrescence growing out of the head of a section.

JEREMY BENTHAM, *Nomography*, ch. 5, in 3 *Works* 249 n.

A key to open the minds of the makers of the Act and the mischiefs which they intended to redress.

DYER, C.J., See, 1 Plowd. 369.

Precedent

Shall not we give judgment because it is not adjudged in the books before? We will give judgment according to reason; and if there be no reason in the books I will not regard them.

ANDERSON, C.J., *Case of the Resceit*, Gouldes. 96. (c. 1600).

Consequence does not draw consequence, but the extension should stop within the next cases; otherwise there will be a gradual lapse into dissimilar cases, and sharpness of wit will have greater power than authority of law.

BACON, *De Augmentis Scientiarum*, bk 8, ch. 3, aph. 16.

Precedents and rules must be followed, unless flatly absurd or unjust.

BLACKSTONE, *Commentaries*, bk 1, 70.

It is of dangerous consequence for judges, in their judgments, to rely too much on precedents, that perhaps went forth through the necessity of the present times.

BRAMSTON, L.C.J., *Hampden's Case* (1637) 3 How. St. Tr. 1245.

Precedents drawn from the days of travel by stage coach do not fit the conditions of travel to-day. The principle that the danger must be imminent does not change, but the things subject to the principle do change. They are whatever the needs of life in a developing civilization require them to be.

CARDOZO, J., *MacPherson v. Buick Motor Co.*, 217 N.Y. 382, 391 (1916).

Precedents will be misleading if separated from the statutes they interpret. Opinions get their color and significance from the subject of the controversy.

CARDOZO, J., *Cott v. Erie R.R. Co.*, 231 N.Y. 67, 73 (1921).

I will look, your Honor, and endeavor to find a precedent, if you require it; though it would seem to be a pity that the Court should lose the honor of being the first to establish so just a rule.

RUFUS CHOATE. See, 1 Brown, *Works of Choate* 292 (1862).

The slaves of custom and established mode,
With packhorse constancy we keep the road,
Crooked or straight, through quags and thorny dells,

True to the jingling of our leader's bells.
To follow foolish precedents, and wink
With both our eyes, is easier than to think.

WILLIAM COWPER, *Tirocinium, "A Review of Schools"*, 1. 251.

To make precedents the fount and origin of the law is to compel their study; to compel their study is to put a premium upon the knowledge so acquired; and to put a premium upon this knowledge is to encourage its overexhibition by the overzealous. We should think of the case lawyer at least with the charity due to one who has been led into temptation.

JOHN W. DAVIS, *The Case for the Case Lawyer*, 3 Mass. L.Q. 102 (1917).

Every precedent had first a commencement.

ELLESMERE, L.C., *Case of Proclamations* (1611) 2 How. St. Tr. 723, 725.

I should be sorry that any opinion of mine should shake the authority of an established precedent; since it is better for the subject that even faulty precedents should not be shaken than that the law should be uncertain.

GROSE, J., *King v. Thompson* (1787) 2 T.R. 18, 24.

All the sentences of precedent judges that have ever been, cannot altogether make a law contrary to natural equity.

THOMAS HOBBES, *Leviathan*, Pt. 2, ch. 26.

It is revolting to have no better reason for a rule of law than that so it was laid down in the time of Henry IV. It is still more revolting if the grounds upon which it was laid down have vanished long since, and the rule simply persists from blind imitation of the past.

OLIVER WENDELL HOLMES, *Path of the Law*, 10 Harv. L.R. 457, 469 (1897).

Constitutional precedents are accepted only at their current valuation and have a mortality rate almost as high as their authors.

ROBERT H. JACKSON, *Task of Maintaining Our Liberties*, 39 A.B.A.J. 962 (1953).

The reason and spirit of cases make law; not the letter of particular precedents.

LORD MANSFIELD, C.J., *Fisher v. Prince* (1762) 3 Burr. 1363, 1364.

The law of England would be a strange science indeed if it were decided upon precedents only. Precedents serve to illustrate principles, and to give them a fixed certainty. But the law of England, which is exclusive of positive law, enacted by statute, depends upon principles; and these principles run through all the cases according as the particular circumstances of each have been found to fall within the one or other of them.

LORD MANSFIELD, C.J., *Jones v. Randall* (1774) Cowp. 37, 39.

Precedent, though it be evidence of law, is not law in itself.

LORD MANSFIELD, C.J., *Jones v. Randall* (1774) Lofft 383, 385.

Our common-law system consists in the applying to new combinations of circumstances those rules of law which we derive from legal principles and judicial precedents; and for the sake of attaining uniformity, consistency and certainty, we must apply those rules, where they are not plainly unreasonable and inconvenient, to all cases which arise; and we are not at liberty to reject them, and to abandon all analogy to them, in those to which they have not yet been judicially applied, because we think that the rules are not as convenient and reasonable as we ourselves could have devised.

PARKE, J., *Mirehouse v. Rennell* (1833) 1 Cl. & F. 527, 546.

It must not be; there is no power in Venice
Can alter a decree established.
'Twill be recorded for a precedent,
And many an error by the same example
Will rush into the state.

SHAKESPEARE, *Merchant of Venice*, IV., 1.

Instead of controlling precedents, forsooth some are found to be only inns for the night, good enough for the time and purpose, but the law, like the traveler, was up and moving on the morrow.

STACY, C.J., *Styers v. Forsyth County,* 212 N.C. 558, 563 (1937).

It is a maxim among these lawyers, that whatever has been done before may legally be done again; and therefore they take especial care to record all the decisions formerly made against common justice and the general reason of mankind. These, under the name of precedents, they produce as authorities to justify the most iniquitous opinions; and the judges never fail of directing accordingly.

JONATHAN SWIFT, *Gulliver's Travels: Houyhnhnms,* ch. 5.

Justice, moral fitness and public convenience . . . when applied to a new subject, make common law without a precedent.

WILLES, J., *Millar v. Taylor* (1769) 4 Burr. 2303, 2312.

Prefaces

Beseeching you that where you shall finde any faultes, which either by my insufficiency, the intricatenes of the worke, or the Printer's recklesnes, are committed, either friendly to pardon, or by some means to admonish me thereof.

RICHARD BELLEW (E), *Cases, Temp. Rich. II: Preface* (1585).

Wherefore accept in good part the Author's pains, and bestowe your own in the perusal of them, before you proceed to censure, and then no doubt you will find very good advantage thereby.

WILLIAM BENDLOES, *Reports: Preface* (1661).

This seems a very little book to introduce to so large a continent. No such enterprise would ever have suggested itself to the home-keeping mind of the Author, who, none the less, when this edition was proposed to him by Messrs. Scribner on terms honorable to them and grateful to him, found the notion of being read in America most fragrant and delightful.

AUGUSTINE BIRRELL, *Obiter Dicta*: *Preface* to American Edition.

I . . . have, for the instruction, at least of the younger generation, undertaken the task of diligently examining the ancient judgments of righteous men, not without much loss of sleep and labour, and by reducing their acts, counsels, and answers, and whatever thereof I have found noteworthy, into one summary, I have brought it into order under titles and paragraphs (without prejudice against any better system), to be commended to perpetual memory by the aid of writing; requesting the reader, if he should find anything superfluous or erroneously stated in this work, to correct and amend it, or to pass it over with eyes half closed, since to retain everything in memory, and to make no mistakes, is an attribute of God rather than of man.

BRACTON, *De Legibus et Consuetudinibus Angliae,* f.1 (v.l, p. 5 Twiss ed. Rolls ser. No. 70).

I found myself reduced to the necessity of either destroying or publishing these papers; (which were originally intended for my own private use, and not for public inspection). For as it was become generally known "that I had taken some account (good or bad) of all the cases which had occured in the Court of King's Bench for upwards of forty years", I was subject to continual interruption and even persecution, by incessant applications for searches into my notes; for transcripts of them; sometimes for the note-books themselves (not always returned without trouble and solicitation), not to mention frequent conversations upon very dry and unentertaining subjects, which my consulters were paid for considering, but I had no sort of concern in. This inconvenience grew from bad to worse, till it became quite insupportable; and from thence arised the present publication.

SIR JAMES BURROW, 1 *Reports*: *Preface* (1765).

I anticipate slippered readers rather than academicians.

GEORGE W. DALZELL, *Benefit of Clergy: Preface* (1955).

The function of the preface is to ingratiate the author with the reader in a naive effort to forestall criticism by a show of modesty.

GEORGE W. DALZELL, *Benefit of Clergy: Preface* (1955).

I still consider the fundamental idea of the work so undoubtedly true and irrefutable that I look upon every word said in opposition to it as lost.

RUDOLPH VON JHERING, *Struggle for Law*, xlvi (Amer. ed. 1915). Preface from the 5th German edition in which Jhering stated that he was making no change in the subject matter.

It is anticipated that in such a work as the present embracing periods of history by no means satisfactorily explored, numerous omissions and errors may be pointed out by those who make it more their business to detect them than to appreciate the contribution to the common stock of knowledge. He will no further notice or answer any disingenuous criticism than by perfecting and extending a future edition of his work.

JOSEPH PARKES, *History of the Court of Chancery: Preface* (1828).

Prescription

Prescription and custom are brothers and ought to have the same age, and reason ought to be the father and congruence the mother, and use the nurse, and time out of memory to fortify them both.

COKE, C.J., *Rowles v. Mason* (1612) 2 Brownl. & Golds. 192, 198.

For whereas prescription and antiquity of time fortifies all other titles, and supposeth the beginning that law can give them: in this case it works clean contrary.

HOBART, C.J., *Slade v. Drake* (1617) Hobart 295, 297.

Presumptions

The presumption does not consecrate as truth the extravagantly improbable.

CARDOZO, C.J., *Matter of Findlay,* 253 N.Y. 1, 8 (1930).

There are breaths of human nature at which presumptions shrink and wither.

CARDOZO, C.J., *Matter of Findlay,* 253 N.Y. 1, 11 (1930).

Experience is not sufficiently uniform to raise a presumption that one who has the means of paying a debt will actually pay it.

CHAPMAN, C.J., *Atwood v. Scott,* 99 Mass. 177, 178 (1868).

If a man stay away from his wife for seven years, the law presumes the separation to have killed him; yet, according to our daily experience, it might well prolong his life.

LORD DARLING, *Scintillae Juris: Of Evidence.*

"That is no excuse," replied Mr. Brownlow. "You were present on the occasion of the destruction of these trinkets, and, indeed, are the more guilty of the two, in the eye of the law; for the law supposes that your wife acts under your direction."

"If the law supposes that," said Mr. Bumble, . . . "the law is a ass—a idiot. If that's the eye of the law, the law's a bachelor; and the worst I wish the law is, that his eye may be opened by experience—by experience."

CHARLES DICKENS, *Oliver Twist,* ch. 51.

In England a man is presoomed to be innocent till he's proved guilty an' they take it f'r granted he's guilty. In this counthry a man is presoomed to be guilty ontil he's proved guilty an' afther that he's presoomed to be innocent.

FINLEY PETER DUNNE, *Mr. Dooley on Making a Will: On Criminal Trials.*

"Presumptions", as happily stated by a scholarly counselor, ore tenus, in another case, "may be looked on as the bats of the law, flitting in the twilight but disappearing in the sunshine of actual facts."

LAMM, J., *Mockowik v. Kansas City, St. J. & C.B. R.R.*, 196 Mo. 550, 571 (1906).

Privilege

The moment confidence ceases, privilege ceases.

LORD ELDON, L.C., *Parkhurst v. Lowten* (1819) 2 Swanst. 194, 216.

Probability

It is always probable that something improbable will happen.

BLECKLEY, J., *Warren v. Purtell*, 63 Ga. 428, 430 (1879).

Profession

I hold every man a debtor to his profession; from the which as men of course do seek to receive countenance and profit, so ought they of duty to endeavour themselves by way of amends, to be a help and ornament thereunto.

BACON, *Maxims of the Law: Preface.*

He did not like his children to come and see him act, and was always regretting—heaven help him! —that he wasn't a barrister-at-law. Look upon this picture and on that. Here we have Macbeth, that mighty thane; Hamlet, the intellectual symbol of the whole world of modern thought; Strafford, in Robert Browning's fine play; splendid dresses, crowded theatres, beautiful women, royal audiences; and on the other side, a rusty gown, a musty wig, a fusty court, a deaf judge, an indifferent jury, a dispute about a bill of lading, and ten guineas on your brief—which you have not been paid, and which you can't recover—why, " 'tis Hyperion to a satyr!"

AUGUSTINE BIRRELL, *Obiter Dicta* (First Ser.): *Actors.* Referring to the noted actor William Charles Macready.

There are abuses incident to every branch of industry, to every profession. It would not be thought very just or wise to arraign the honorable professions of law and physic, because the one produces the pettifogger, and the other the quack.

HENRY CLAY, *Debate on Revision of the Tariff,* 36 Annals of Cong. 2037 (1820).

Commonly, physicians, like beer, are best when they are old; and lawyers, like bread, when they are young and new.

THOMAS FULLER, *The Holy State: The Good Advocate* (1642).

Every calling is great when greatly pursued.

OLIVER WENDELL HOLMES, *The Law. Speeches* 17 (1913).

The lawyers are the cleverest men, the ministers are the most learned, and the doctors are the most sensible.

O. W. HOLMES, Sr., *Poet at the Breakfast Table,* ch. 5.

Historically, there are three ideas involved in a profession, organization, learning, and a spirit of public service. These are essential. The remaining idea, that of gaining a livelihood, is incidental.

ROSCOE POUND, *What is a Profession?* 19 Notre Dame Law. 203, 204 (1944).

An old physician and a young lawyer.

Proverb. HERBERT, *Jacula Prudentum* (1651).

Profession (Legal)

It [the Bar] is an order as ancient as the magistracy, as noble as virtue, as necessary as justice; it is distinguished by a character which is peculiar to itself, and it alone always maintains the happy and peaceful possession of independence.

HENRI D'AGUESSEAU, Speech on opening of French Parliament, 1693. See, Young, *French Bar* (1869) 61.

We must never forget that the profession of law exists in order that the administration of justice shall be carried on.

SIR NORMAN BIRKETT, informal remarks at dinner by New Jersey Bar to American Bar Association officers. See, 32 A.B.A.J. 861 (1946).

Then welcome business, welcome strife,
Welcome the cares and thorns of life,
The visage wan, the pore-blind sight,
The toil by day, the lamp by night,
The tedious forms, the solemn prate,
The pert dispute, the dull debate,
The drowsy bench, the babbling hall,
For thee fair justice, welcome all.

BLACKSTONE, *Farewell to His Muse.*

Law, —in its nature the noblest and most beneficial to mankind, in its abuse and debasement the most sordid and most pernicious.

LORD BOLINGBROKE, *On the Study and Use of History: Letter 5* (1739).

There have been lawyers that were orators, philosophers, historians; there have been Bacons and Clarendons, my lord. There will be none such any more, till, in some better age true ambition, or the love of fame, prevails over avarice; and till men find leisure and encouragement to prepare themselves for the exercise of this profession, by climbing up to the "vantage ground" (so my Lord Bacon calls it) of science, instead of grovelling all their lives below, in a mean but gainful application of all the little arts of chicane. Till this happens, the profession of the law will scarce deserve to be ranked among the learned professions. And whenever it happens, one of the vantage grounds to which men must climb, is metaphysical, and the other, historical knowledge.

LORD BOLINGBROKE. ibid.

Instead of holding a position of independence, between the wealthy and the people, prepared to curb the excesses of either, able lawyers have, to a large extent, allowed themselves to become adjuncts of great corporations and have neglected their obligation to use their powers for the protection of the people. We hear much of the "corporation lawyer", and far too little of the "people's lawyer". The great opportunity of the American bar is and will be to stand again as it did in the past, ready to protect also the interests of the people.

LOUIS D. BRANDEIS, *The Opportunity in the Law,* 39 Am. L. Rev. 559.

Membership in the bar is a privilege burdened with conditions.

CARDOZO, J., *Matter of Rouss,* 221 N.Y. 81, 84 (1917).

The quest is greater than what is sought, the effort finer than the prize, or, rather, that the effort *is* the prize—the victory cheap and hollow were it not for the rigor of the game.

BENJAMIN N. CARDOZO, *Law and Literature* 164 (1931).

Though holding larger trusts than all other vocations combined, and without security, the record of the profession in its fiduciary relations is of unexampled purity.

CHAUNCEY M. DEPEW, *Speech to Graduates of Columbia Law School,* May 17, 1882.

"How do you like the law, Mr. Micawber?" "My dear Copperfield," he replied, "to a man possessed of the higher imaginative powers the objection to legal studies is the amount of detail they involve. Even in our professional correspondence," said Mr. Micawber, glancing at some letters he was writing, "the mind is not at liberty to soar to any exalted form of expression. Still, it is a great pursuit, a great pursuit."

CHARLES DICKENS, *David Copperfield,* ch. 39.

To be a great lawyer, I must give up my chance of being a great man.

BENJAMIN DISRAELI, *Vivian Grey,* bk 1, ch. 9 (1826).

And then there is the blessed assurance that, as a lawyer, his "works do follow him", not into the grave, but into the workaday lives of his clients. Long after he is dead and gone, men and women will be acting upon his advice, will be carrying out his directions, will be ordering their affairs in strict observance of his written word. Estates will go on devolving under the settlements he drew. Husbands, wives, children will go on being protected by the trusts he created. Beneficiaries will rise up and bless him for the wills he made. Year after year, tenants will occupy or trade or farm, relying on the agreements and the leases he approved.

REGINALD L. HINE, *Confessions of an Un-Common Attorney* 112.

Law is the business to which my life is devoted, and I should show less than devotion if I did not do what in me lies to improve it, and, when I perceive what seems to me the ideal of its future, if I hesitated to point it out and to press toward it with all my heart.

OLIVER WENDELL HOLMES, *Path of the Law,* 10 Harv. L.R. 457, 473 (1897).

The law is the calling of thinkers.

OLIVER WENDELL HOLMES, *Profession of the Law, Speeches* 22 (1913).

A man may live greatly in the law as well as elsewhere; that there as well as elsewhere his thought may find its unity in an infinite perspective; that there as well as elsewhere he may wreak himself upon life, may drink the bitter cup of heroism, may wear his heart out after the unattainable.

OLIVER WENDELL HOLMES, *Profession of the Law, Speeches* 23 (1913).

The glory of lawyers, like that of men of science, is more corporate than individual.

OLIVER WENDELL HOLMES, Answer to Resolution of the Bar on Daniel S. Richardson, April 15, 1890, Speeches 47 (1913).

The highest reward that can come to a lawyer is the esteem of his professional brethren. That esteem is won in unique conditions and proceeds from an impartial judgment of professional rivals. It cannot be purchased. It cannot be artificially created. It cannot be gained by artifice or contrivance to attract public attention. It is not measured by pecuniary gains. It is an esteem which is born in sharp contests and thrives despite conflicting interests. It is an esteem commanded solely by integrity of character and by brains and skill in the honorable performance of professional duty. . . . In a world of imperfect humans, the faults of human clay are always manifest. The special temptations and tests of lawyers are obvious enough. But, considering trial and error, success and defeat, the bar slowly makes its estimate and the memory of the careers which it approves are at once its most precious heritage and an important safeguard of the interests of society so largely in the keeping of the profession of the law in its manifold services.

Chief Justice CHARLES EVANS HUGHES, *Remarks in Reference to the late George Wickersham,* 13 Proceedings Amer. Law Inst. 61 (1936).

The Bar is not a bed of roses, —it is either all bed and no roses, or all roses and no bed.

RUFUS ISAACS. See, Hewart, *Not Without Prejudice* 35: I remember Rufus Isaacs when he was working at the highest pressure saying that before he came to the Bar "he was told it was a bed of roses; but that was quite wrong—it is all bed and no roses or all roses and no bed."

The office of the lawyer . . . is too delicate, personal and confidential to be occupied by a corporation.

ROBERT H. JACKSON, *Functions of the Trust Co.,* 52 N.Y.S. Bar Rept. 144 (1929).

This vanishing country lawyer left his mark on his times, and he was worth knowing. He "read law" in the *Commentaries* of Blackstone and Kent and not by the case system. He resolved problems by what he called "first principles". He did not specialize, nor did he pick and choose clients. He rarely declined service to worthy ones because of inability to pay. Once enlisted for a client, he took his obligation seriously. He insisted on complete control of the litigation—he was no mere hired hand. But he gave every power and resource to the cause. He identified himself with the client's cause fully, sometimes too fully. He would fight the adverse party and fight his counsel, fight every hostile witness, and fight the court, fight public sentiment, fight any obstacle to his client's success. He never quit. . . . He moved for new trials, he appealed; and if he lost out in the end, he joined the client at the tavern in damning the judge—which is the last rite in closing an unsuccessful case, and I have officiated at many.

ROBERT H. JACKSON, *Tribute to Country Lawyers*, 30 A.B.A.J. 139 (1944).

He loved his profession, he had a real sense of dedication to the administration of justice, he held his head high as a lawyer, he rendered and exacted courtesy, honor and straightforwardness at the Bar. He respected the judicial office deeply, demanded the highest standards of competence and disinterestedness and dignity, despised all political use of or trifling with judicial power, and had an affectionate regard for every man who filled his exacting prescription of the just judge. The law to him was like a religion, and its practice was more than a means of support; it was a mission. He was not always popular in his community, but he was respected. Unpopular minorities and individuals often found in him their only mediator and advocate. He was too independent to court the populace—he thought of himself as a leader and lawgiver, not as a mouthpiece. . . . Often his name was in a generation or two, forgotten. It was from this brotherhood that America has drawn its statesmen and its judges. A free and self-governing Republic stands as a monument for the little known and unremembered as well as for the famous men of our profession.

ROBERT H. JACKSON, *Tribute to Country Lawyers*, 30 A.B.A.J. 139 (1944).

It too often is overlooked that the lawyer and the law office are indispensable parts of our administration of justice. Law-abiding people can go nowhere else to learn the ever changing and constantly multiplying rules by which they must behave and to obtain redress for their wrongs.

JACKSON, J., *Hickman v. Taylor,* 329 U.S. 495, 514 (1947).

Boswell: I mentioned that a gay friend had advised me against being a lawyer, because I should be excelled by plodding block-heads.

Johnson: Why, Sir, in the formulary and statutory part of law, a plodding block-head may excel; but in the ingenious and rational part of it a plodding block-head can never excel.

SAMUEL JOHNSON. Boswell, *Life of Johnson: 1766.*

Judges and lawyers took to wigs when other men in a frivolous moment took to them; unfortunately they retained the silliest adornment that human head has yet invented for itself when even physicians and bishops had recovered their wonted sobriety.

FREDERIC WM. MAITLAND, *From the Old Law Courts to the New,* 1 Eng. Illus. Mag. 6 (1883).

Craft is the vice, not the spirit of the profession. Trick is professional prostitution. Falsehood is professional apostasy. The strength of a lawyer is in thorough knowledge of legal truth, in thorough devotion to legal right. Truth and integrity can do more in the profession than the subtlest and wiliest devices. The power of integrity is the rule; the power of fraud is the exception. Emulation and zeal lead lawyers astray; but the general law of the profession is duty, not success. In it, as elsewhere in human life, the judgment of success is but the verdict of little minds. Professional duty, faithfully and well performed, is the lawyer's glory. This is equally true of the bench and of the bar.

JUDGE EDWARD G. RYAN, *Address, Univ. of Wisconsin Law School,* June, 1880.

The three proverbial roads to success at the bar—influence, a book, or a miracle.

Saying

In a profession, where unbounded trust is necessarily reposed, there is nothing surprising that fools should neglect it in their idleness, and tricksters abuse it in their knavery, but it is the more to the honour of those, and I will vouch for many, who unite integrity with skill and attention, and walk honourably upright where there are so many pitfalls and stumbling blocks for those of a different character. To such men their fellow citizens may safely entrust the care of protecting their patrimonial rights, and their country the more sacred charge of her laws and privileges.

SIR WALTER SCOTT, *The Antiquary*, ch. 43.

It is the pest of our profession that we seldom see the best side of human nature. People come to us with every selfish feeling newly pointed and grinded. . . . In civilized society, law is the chimney through which all that smoke discharges itself, that used to circulate through the whole house and put every one's eyes out; no wonder, therefore, that the vent itself should sometimes get a little sooty.

SIR WALTER SCOTT, *Guy Mannering*, ch. 39.

The law is the only profession which records its mistakes carefully, exactly as they occurred, and yet does not identify them as mistakes.

ELLIOTT DUNLAP SMITH, Conference on Teaching of Law in Liberal Arts Curriculum, November, 1954. See, 39 J. Am. Jud. Soc. 47.

To be wholly devoted to some intellectual exercise is to have succeeded in life; and perhaps only in law and the higher mathematics may this devotion be maintained, suffice to itself without reaction, and find continual rewards without excitement.

ROBERT L. STEVENSON, *Weir of Hermiston*, ch. 2.

Yes, my lords, I am amazed at his grace's speech. The noble duke cannot look before him, behind him, or on either side of him, without seeing some noble peer, who owes his seat in this house to his successful exertions in the profession to which I belong. Does he not feel that it is as honourable to owe it to these, as to being the accident of an accident?

LORD THURLOW, reply to Duke of Grafton during the inquiry into Lord Sandwich's administration of Greenwich Hospital. The Duke belittled the legal profession and Thurlow's recent admission into the peerage. See, Butler, *Reminiscences* 165 (1824).

Every person who enters into a learned profession undertakes to bring to the exercise of it a reasonable degree of care and skill. He does not undertake, if he is an attorney, that at all events you shall gain your case, nor does a surgeon undertake that he will perform a cure; nor does he undertake to use the highest possible degree of skill. There may be persons who have a higher education and greater advantages than he has, but he undertakes to bring a fair, reasonable, and competent degree of skill.

TINDAL, C.J., *Lanphier v. Phipos* (1838) 8 C. & P. 475, 479.

I cannot believe that a republic could subsist at the present time if the influence of lawyers in public business did not increase in proportion to the power of the people.

ALEXIS DE TOCQUEVILLE, *Democracy in America,* Pt. 1, ch. 16.

The more that we reflect upon all that occurs in the United States the more we shall be persuaded that the lawyers as a body form the most powerful, if not the only, counterpoise to the democratic element.

ALEXIS DE TOCQUEVILLE ibid.

The profession of the law is the only aristocratic element which can be amalgamated without violence with the natural elements of democracy, and which can be advantageously and permanently combined with them.

ALEXIS DE TOCQUEVILLE ibid.

As the lawyers constitute the only enlightened class which the people do not mistrust, they are naturally called upon to occupy most of the public stations. They fill the legislative assemblies, and they conduct the administration; they consequently exercise a powerful influence upon the formation of the law, and upon its execution.

ALEXIS DE TOCQUEVILLE ibid.

When every iniquity of the lawyers of the past has been admitted, we still find that there were abundant gentlemen of the long robe, haunted, even if they were not inspired and pervaded, by the spirit of righteousness. The illumination they shed may not always have been a beacon, but at any rate the wick never ceased altogether to glow, and down the centuries we see a succession of these unloved men boring away in their tedious frowsty courts, really struggling in that dim mediaeval light to import some semblance of justice, some thought for the common weal, into the limitless greed of robber barons, the unqualified imperatives of feudal chiefs and the grasping cunning of the baser sort.

H. G. WELLS, *The Work, Wealth and Happiness of Mankind* 353 (1931).

Profession (Overcrowded)

Never fear the want of business. A man who qualifies himself well for his calling never fails of employment in it.

THOMAS JEFFERSON, *Letter to Peter Carr, June 22, 1792.*

You must not indulge too sanguine hopes, should you be called to our bar. I was told, by a very sensible lawyer, that there are a great many chances against any man's success in the profession of the law; the candidates are so numerous, and those who get large practice so few. He said, it was by no means true that a man of good parts and application is sure of having business, though he, indeed, allowed that if such a man could but appear in a few causes, his merit would be known, and he would get forward; but that, the great risk was, that a man might pass half a life-time in the courts, and never have an opportunity of shewing his abilities.

SAMUEL JOHNSON. Boswell, *Life of Johnson*: *1777.*

Whereas the Number of Attorneys at Law that practice at the Barr in this Province are but few and that many persons Retain most of them on one side to the great prejudice and discouragement of others that have or may have suits at Law to the end therefore that Justice may be Equally administered and no Room left for Complaint be it Enacted by the Governour and Councill and Representatives Convened in Generall Assembly and by the Authority of the same that from and after the publication hereof that no person or persons That shall have any suit at Law in any of the Courts of Record Within this Province shall Retain more than two Attorneys at Law for the prosecution or management of any such Suit or process at Law that they shall have and if they Retain any more it shall be Lawful for the Justices of the bench where the Suit is Depending to order all such Attorneys as shall be Retained more than two as aforesaid to plead for the other side Without Returning the fee Received.

Laws of N.Y. 1695, c.49.

When one said that the number of Lawyers would marr the occupation, he answered, "No, for always the more Spaniels in the field, the more game."

Proverb. Camden, *Remains Concerning Britain: Wise Speeches* (quoting John Heywood) (1674).

Two attorneys can live in a town where one cannot.

Proverb. 4 Lean, *Collect.* 169 (1902).

There is always room at the top.

DANIEL WEBSTER—ascribed to. See, 190 N.&Q. 262, Latham, *Famous Sayings and Their Authors* 65.

Profits

Their argument was that "past and future profits" is merely "profits" writ large—for this reason, that time is exhaustively divided into past and future, and the present is merely a dividing line between the two. This is, of course, a profound and impressive truth, but there are times and places for everything, and I should hardly have thought a Tramway Act exactly the occasion which Parliament would choose for teaching business men metaphysics unawares—more especially as this statute applies to England as well as Scotland.

ROBERTSON, Lord Pres., *Edinburgh Street Tramways Co. v. Lord Provost,* 1894, 21 S.C. (4th ser.) 688, 704.

Progress

The center of gravity of legal development lies not in legislation, nor in juristic science, nor in judicial decision, but in society itself.

EUGEN EHRLICH, *Fundamental Principles of the Sociology of Law*: *Foreword* (1936, trans. by Moll).

Public opinion's always in advance of the Law.

JOHN GALSWORTHY, *Windows,* Act I.

[Law] like all human systems, will ever advance nearer to perfection, and ever fall short of it.

SIR WILLIAM JONES, *Isaeus*: *Preface.*

Social necessities and social opinions are always more or less in advance of Law. We may come indefinitely near to the closing of the gap between them, but it has a perpetual tendency to reopen. Law is stable; the societies we are speaking of are progressive. The greater or less happiness of a people depends on the degree of promptitude with which the gulf is narrowed.

SIR HENRY MAINE, *Ancient Law,* ch. 2.

Property

Property and law are born and must die together.

JEREMY BENTHAM, *Principles of the Civil Code,* 1 Works 309.

There are topics in Real Property
    both awkward and abstruse,
Like the shifting and the springing
    of that awful thing, the Use.

J.P.C., *Poetic Justice* 6 (1947).

Personal property has no locality.

LORD LOUGHBOROUGH, C.J., *Sill v. Worswick* (1791) 1 H. Bl. 665, 690.

Public Interest

It is to the interest of the public that the suppression of a prosecution should not be made matter of private bargain.

ERLE, C.J., *Clubb v. Hutson* (1865) 18 C.B. (N.S.) 414, 417.

For now the wharf and crane and other conveniences are affected with a publick interest, and they cease to be *juris privati* only; as if a man set out a street in new building on his own land, it is now no longer bare private interest, but it is affected with a publick interest.

SIR MATTHEW HALE, *De Portibus Maris* (in Hargrave, *Law Tracts* 77).

The notion that a business is clothed with a public interest and has been devoted to the public use is little more than a fiction intended to beautify what is disagreeable to the sufferers.

HOLMES, J., *Tyson & Bro. v. Banton,* 273 U.S. 418, 446 (1927).

Property does become clothed with a public interest when used in a manner to make it of public consequence, and affect the community at large.

WAITE, C.J., *Munn v. Illinois,* 94 U.S. 113, 126 (1876).

Public Policy

It is a very unruly horse, and when once you get astride it you never know where it will carry you. It may lead you from the sound law. It is never argued at all but when other points fail.

BURROUGH, J., *Richardson v. Mellish* (1824) 2 Bing. 229, 252.

Judges are more to be trusted as interpreters of the law than as expounders of what is called public policy.

CAVE, J., *Re Mirams* [1891] 1 Q.B. 594, 595.

That principle of the law which holds that no subject can lawfully do that which has a tendency to be injurious to the public, or against the public good.

LORD TRURO, *Egerton v. Brownlow* (1853) 4 H.L. Cas. 1, 196.

Public Welfare

The public good is in nothing more essentially interested than in the protection of every individual's private rights.

BLACKSTONE, *Commentaries*, bk 1, 139.

Public wrongs are but popular rights in embryo.

LORD DARLING, *Meditations in the Tea Room*, VII.

Sometime when the public good is pretended, a private benefit is intended.

COKE, 10 Rep. 142b.

Publicity

Two classes of people have poor public relations—mothers-in-law and attorneys-at-law.

ERLE STANLEY GARDNER (under pseud. A. A. Fair) *Some Women Won't Wait: Foreword* (paperback reissue).

Publicity is an evil substitute [for personal acquaintance] and the art of publicity is a black art; but it has come to stay, every year adds to its potency and to the finality of its judgments. The hand that rules the press, the radio, the screen and the far-spread magazine, rules the country; whether we like it or not, we must learn to accept it.

JUDGE LEARNED HAND, *Proceedings in Memory of Justice Brandeis*, 317 U.S. xv (1942).

Question (Law and Fact)

Every question of law arises out of a fact situation, and if there be no state of facts there can be no question of law.

DICKINSON, J., *United States v. Rodenbough*, 14 F. 2d 989, 990 (1926).

Question (Leading)

All interrogatories must, to some extent, make a suggestion to the witness. It would be perfectly nugatory to ask a witness, if he knew anything about something.

LORD LANGDALE, M.R., *Lincoln v. Wright* (1841) 4 Beav. 166, 171.

Quotations

I was told recently by a learned judge that I had in two or three instances attributed certain sayings or incidents to wrong personages. I think this by no means improbable, although I believe such instances to be very few. There is always a number of smart things straying about the world, like orphans, devoid of ostensible parentage, till some admirer takes pity upon them, and from ignorance or from mere whim affiliates them upon some well-known wit, who is not unlikely to have been their progenitor. On the Home Circuit, whenever we stumbled over one of these waifs, if it was of a respectable character, we in general ascribed it to Thesiger; if it was not sufficiently clothed to be presentable in decent society, we fathered it upon Serjeant Murphy; and if it savoured of conceit or self-complacency, Warren was sure to become the recipient.

ROBINSON, *Bench and Bar* 281 (4th ed. 1894).

Reading

A cursory and tumultuary reading doth ever make a confused memory, a troubled utterance, and an uncertain judgment.

COKE, 6 Rep.: *Preface.*

I had many an exciting day . . . reading the statutes and the dictionary and wondering how the characters would turn out.

MARK TWAIN, *Roughing It,* ch. 3 (Twain, while on the way to Nevada to become secretary to his brother the Governor of the territory relieved the tedium of the journey by reading the U.S. Rev. Statutes.)

Reason

No man (out of his own private reason) ought to be wiser than the law, which is the perfection of reason.

COKE, *First Institute 97b.*

Reason is the life of the law; nay, the common law itself is nothing else but reason.

COKE, *First Institute* 97b.

The reason of the law is the life of the law; for though a man can tell the law, yet, if he know not the reason thereof, he shall soon forget his superficial knowledge. But when he findeth the right reason of the law, and so bringeth it to his natural reason, that he comprehendeth it as his own, this will not only serve him for the understanding of that particular case, but of many others.

COKE, *First Institute* 183.

The reason of a resolution is more to be considered than the resolution itself.

HOLT, C.J., *Cage v. Acton* (1699) 12 Mod. 288, 294.

Neither rhyme nor reason.

Proverb. This brings to mind the story that Sir Thomas More when asked by an author his opinion of an impertinent book, desired him by all means to put it into verse and bring it to him again. This being done, Sir Thomas looking upon it said, Yea, now it is somewhat like; now it is rhyme; before, it was neither rhyme nor reason. Ray, *Proverbs* (1670).

The reason of a thing is not to be inquired after, till you are sure the thing itself be so. We commonly are at "What's the reason of it?" before we are sure of the thing. It was an excellent question of my Lady Cotton, when Sir Robert Cotton was magnifying of a shoe which was Moses' or Noah's, and wondering at the strange shape and fashion of it; "but Mr. Cotton," says she, "are you sure it is a shoe?"

JOHN SELDEN, *Table Talk*: *Reason.*

Reasonable Man

The man on the Clapham omnibus.

LORD BOWEN—attributed to. See, Collins, M.R., *McQuire v. Western Morning News Co.* [1903] 2 K.B. 100, 109.

No court has ever given, nor do we think ever can give, a definition of what constitutes a reasonable or an average man.

LORD GODDARD, C.J., *R. v. McCarthy* [1954] 2 Q.B. 105, 112.

The person concerned is sometimes described as "the man in the street" or "the man in the Clapham omnibus," or, as I recently read in an American author, "the man who takes the magazines at home, and in the evening pushes the lawn mower in his shirt sleeves."

GREER, L. J., *Hall v. Brooklands Auto Racing Club* [1933] 1 K.B., 205, 224.

He is one who invariably looks where he is going, and is careful to examine the immediate foreground before he executes a leap or bound; who neither star-gazes nor is lost in meditation when approaching trap-doors or the margin of a dock; who records in every case upon the counterfoils of cheques such ample details as are desirable, scrupulously substitutes the word 'Order' for the word 'Bearer', crosses the instrument 'a/c Payee only', and registers the package in which it is despatched; who never mounts a moving omnibus, and does not alight from any car while the train is in motion; who investigates exhaustively the *bona fides* of every mendicant before distributing alms, and will inform himself of the history and habits of a dog before administering a caress.

A. P. HERBERT, *Uncommon Law: Fardell v. Potts.*

Devoid, in short, of any human weakness, with not one single saving vice, *sans* prejudice, procrastination, ill-nature, avarice, and absence of mind, as careful for his own safety as he is for that of others, this excellent but odious character stands like a monument in our Courts of Justice, vainly appealing to his fellow-citizens to order their lives after his own example.

A. P. HERBERT, *Uncommon Law: Fardell v. Potts.*

Recreations

Recreations should not be used as professions, and trades, but to be used as medicines, to make men more able and fit for higher and greater affairs.

COKE, *Fourth Institute* 319.

Reform

He that will not apply new remedies must expect new evils; for time is the greatest innovator; and if time of course alter things to the worse, and wisdom and counsel shall not alter them to the better, what shall be the end?

BACON, *Essays: Of Innovations.*

It was the boast of Augustus . . . that he found Rome of brick, and left it of marble; a praise not unworthy a great prince, and to which the present reign also has its claims. But how much nobler will be the Sovereign's boast, when he shall have it to say, that he found law dear, and left it cheap; found it a sealed book—left it a living letter; found it the patrimony of the rich—left it the inheritance of the poor; found it the two-edged sword of craft and oppression—left it the staff of honesty and the shield of innocence.

HENRY BROUGHAM, *Present State of the Law,* Speech in House of Commons, February 7, 1828.

Lord Eldon, like the Spartan lawgiver, would have fain sworn his countrymen not to alter their laws after his death till they heard from him on the subject, and, in imitation of the Locrian penal law, would have soon ordained that every proposer of a new statute should come publicly with a halter round his neck, and adventure a hanging if he failed in his undertaking.

JOSEPH PARKES, *History of the Court of Chancery: Preface* (1828).

Judicial reform is no sport for the short-winded.

ARTHUR T. VANDERBILT (a frequent expression of his).

Remedy

Want of right and want of remedy are in one equipage.

COKE, 6 Rep. 58b.

It is a vain thing to imagine a right without a remedy; for want of right and want of remedy are reciprocal.

HOLT, C.J., *Ashby v. White* (1703) 2 Ld. Raym. 938, 953.

The categories of negligence are never closed.

LORD MACMILLAN, *Donoghue v. Stevenson* [1932] A.C. 562, 619.

Torts are infinitely various, not limited or confined, for there is nothing in nature but may be an instrument of mischief.

PRATT, C.J., *Chapman v. Pickersgill* (1762) 2 Wils. K.B., 145, 146.

Unkindness has no remedy at law.

Proverb. Ray, *Proverbs* (1678).

Reports and Reporting

Let this be the method of taking down judgments, and committing them to writing. Record the cases precisely, the judgments themselves word for word; add the reasons which the judges allege for their judgments; do not mix up the authority of cases brought forward as examples with the principal case; and omit the perorations of counsel, unless they contain something very remarkable.

BACON, *Advancement of Learning*, bk 8, Aph. 74.

Cases reported with too great prolixity would be drawn into a more compendious report, not in the nature of an abridgment, but tautologies and impertinences to be cut off; as for misprinting and insensible reporting, which many times confound the students, that will be *obiter* amended; but more principally if there be anything in the report, which is not well warranted by the record, that is also to be rectified.

BACON, *Proposition Touching the Compilation and Amendment of Laws* (1616).

Had it not been for Sir Edward Coke's Reports . . . the law by this time had been almost like a ship without ballast, for that the cases of modern experience are fled from those that are adjudged and ruled in former time.

BACON, ibid.

All the cases which are at this day clearly no law, but constantly ruled to the contrary, are to be left out; they do but fill the volumes and season the wits of students in a contrary sense of law.

BACON, ibid.

To give judgment privately, is to put an end to Reports. And to put an end to Reports is to put an end to the law of England.

BURKE, *Impeachment of Warren Hastings: Report on the Lords' Journals*, 1794.

When I was a nisi prius reporter, I had a drawer marked "Bad Law," into which I threw all the cases which seemed to me improperly ruled. I was flattered to hear Sir James Mansfield, C.J., say: "Whoever reads Campbell's Reports must be astonished to find how uniformly Lord Ellenborough's decisions were right." My rejected cases, which I kept as a curiosity—not maliciously—were all burnt in the great fire in the Temple when I was Attorney General.

LORD CAMPBELL, *Lives of the Lord Chancellors*: *Harcourt*, ch. 119.

The fellow taks doon ma' very words.

LORD ESKGROVE, objecting to a law reporter. Cockburn, *Memorials of His Time* 161 (1856).

And for that it is hard for a man to report any part or branch of any art or science justly and truly, which he professeth not, and impossible to make a just and true relation of anything that he understands not; I pray thee beware of chronicle law.

COKE, 3 Rep.: *Preface.*

When a man has a working knowledge of his business, he can spend his leisure better than in reading all the reported cases he has time for. They are apt to be only the small change of legal thought.

OLIVER WENDELL HOLMES, *Introduction* to *Continental Legal History Series*, v.1.

As to the multiplication of reports I don't bother much—I always say the last twenty years takes up most of the law into itself.

OLIVER WENDELL HOLMES, 2 *Holmes-Pollock Letters* 20.

This is an appeal from Bow County Court. In my view it is a disastrous example of the results of the misapplied industry of the compilers of law reports. A decided case is only worthy of report if it decides some principle of law and it is only deserving of citation in a later case if the same principle of law is involved. Unhappily very many cases are reported unnecessarily, and the practice has arisen, in a case involving no principle of law but purely a question of fact, of saying: "Here is a report of another case rather like this, so please decide it in the same way".

MACKINNON, L.J., *O'Grady v. M. Saper, Ltd.* [1940] 2 K.B. 469, 472.

Resemblance

With a pencil dipped in the most vivid colors, and guided by the hand of a master, a splendid portrait has been drawn exhibiting this vessel and her freighter as forming a single figure, composed of the most discordant materials, of peace and war. So exquisite was the skill of the artist, so dazzling the garb in which the figure was presented, that it required the exercise of that cold investigating faculty which ought always to belong to those who sit on this bench, to discover its only imperfection; its want of resemblance.

MARSHALL, C.J., *The Nereide,* 13 U.S. (9 Cranch) 388, 430 (1815).

Residence

A woman having a settlement
Married a man with none,
The question was, he being dead,
If that she had was gone?
Quoth Sir John Pratt, the settlement
Suspended did remain,
Living the husband; but him dead,
It doth revive again.
Chorus of Puisne Judges

Living the husband; but him dead,
It doth revive again.

See: *Shadwell v. St. John's Wapping* (1723) Burr. Sett. Cases 124.

A woman having a settlement,
Married a man with none;
He flies and leaves her destitute;
What then is to be done?
Quoth Ryder, the Chief Justice,
"In spite of Sir John Pratt,
You'll send her to the parish
In which she was a brat
Suspension of a settlement
Is not to be maintained;
That which she had by birth subsists
Until another's gained."
Chorus of Puisne Judges
That which she had by birth subsists
Until another's gained.

See: *R. v. Inhabitants of St. Botolph's* (1755) Burr. Sett. Cases 367.

In the following years he was a bird of passage of almost mechanical regularity.

LORD SUMNER, *Levene v. Inland Rev. Commrs.* [1928] A.C. 217, 226. On the question of residence for tax purposes.

Retirement

I am not to be paragraphed out of my place.

Chief Justice MELVILLE W. FULLER, to Holmes when newspapers were reporting his imminent retirement. Theodore Roosevelt was sending up trial balloons. See, 2 *Holmes-Pollock Letters* 161.

I come here in the closing busy hours of my judicial life, before I relapse into constitutional second childishness and mere oblivion.

CUTHBERT W. POUND, 7 N.Y. S. B. Bull. 43 (1935) (referring to compulsory retirement at age 70).

Reversal

The matter does not appear to me now as it appears to have appeared to me then.

BRAMWELL, B., *Andrews v. Styrap* (1872) 26 L.T. 704, 706.

In entering the order here appealed from vacating the probate court order allowing the mentioned fees, the circuit judge made it plain that he did so reluctantly, feeling that he was impelled by precedent to effect what he considered an unjust result. In his written opinion he said:

"The court fervently hopes the petitioners in this case will appeal his decision and that it will be promptly and definitely reversed by the Supreme Court in which event the court will join a host of others in dancing in the streets."

Let him prepare to dance. The order of the circuit court is reversed, with costs to defendants.

DETHMERS, C.J., *Detroit Edison Co. v. Janosz,* 350 Mich. 606, 614 (1957).

I feel myself bound to state that I must, when I decided that case, have seen it in a point of view, in which, after most laborious consideration, I cannot see it now.

LORD ELDON, L.C., *Ex parte Nolte* (1826) 2 Glynn & Jam. 295, 307.

We now think that we were then wrong and that the decision must be overruled for reasons we shall state.

L. HAND, J., *Metallizing Eng. Co. v. Kenyon,* 153 F.2d 516, 518 (1946).

Upon this case being re-argued and re-considered, I am thoroughly convinced that my former decree was wrong.

LORD HARDWICKE, L.C., *Walmesley v. Booth* (1741) 2 Atk. 25, 27.

I am entitled to say of that opinion what any discriminating reader must think of it—that it was as foggy as the statute the Attorney General was asked to interpret. It left the difficult borderline questions posed by the Secretary of War unanswered, covering its lack of precision with generalities which, however, gave off overtones of assurance. . . . It would be charitable to assume that neither the nominal addressee nor the nominal author of the opinion read it. That, I do not doubt, explains Mr. Stimson's acceptance of an answer so inadequate to his questions. But no such confession and avoidance can excuse the then Attorney General.

JACKSON, J., *McGrath v. Kristensen,* 340 U.S. 162, 176 (1950). On the decision in this case, Jackson voted with the majority of the court contrary to an opinion he had rendered when Attorney General.

Since I have endured in the present case the refined but well-merited torture of listening to almost the whole of my somewhat prolix judgment in the previous case read to me viva voce, I will say at once that I have found very little therein which has been of any assistance to me in this case.

LANGTON, J., *The Torni* [1932] P. 27, 33.

River

A river is more than an amenity, it is a treasure. It offers a necessity of life that must be rationed among those who have power over it.

HOLMES, J., *New Jersey v. New York,* 283 U.S. 336, 342 (1931).

Roman Law

The grand destinies of Rome are not yet accomplished; she reigns throughout the world by her reason, after having ceased to reign by her authority.

HENRI D'AGUESSEAU—attributed to.

Only in a sense was it true that our Common Law was not based on the Roman law, for we had used the Roman law as the Turks used the remains of the splendid temples of antiquity. We had pulled out the stones and used them in constructing buildings which we called our own.

SIR GEORGE JESSEL, *Speech in House of Commons on the Bankruptcy Bill,* 1869, Hansard, 3rd ser. cxcv, 143.

English lawyers seem from the outset to treat the Roman law much as our church treats the Apocrypha; it is instructive but not authoritative.

FREDERIC WM. MAITLAND, *Bracton's Notebook: Introduction* 6 (1887).

Salvage

As the boat appears to have saved him quite as much as he the boat that account is in equilibrio.

LOWELL, J., *Price v. Sears,* 19 Fed. Cas. (No. 11,416) 1321, 1322 (1877).

Self Confidence

I have never swum, but I have no doubt I could if I tried.

HENRY BROUGHAM. Lord Grey and Brougham were crossing a ford when the tide rendered it not too safe. Grey turned and asked Brougham if he could swim. See, Trevelyan, *Lord Grey of the Reform Bill* (1920) 191.

Shelley's Case

The rule in Shelley's Case, the Don Quixote of the law, which, like the last Knight errant of chivalry, has long survived every cause that gave it birth and now wanders aimlessly through the reports, still vigorous, but equally useless and dangerous.

DOUGLAS, J., *Stamper v. Stamper,* 121 N.C. 251, 254 (1897).

That was putting the case in a nutshell. But it is one thing to put a case like Shelley's in a nutshell and another thing to keep it there.

LORD MACNAGHTEN, *Van Grutten v. Foxwell* [1897] A.C. 658, 671.

Sheriff

The whole history of English justice and police might be brought under this rubric, "The Decline and Fall of the Sheriff."

FREDERIC WM. MAITLAND, *Justice and Police* 69 (1885).

Ship

A ship is the most living of inanimate things.

OLIVER WENDELL HOLMES, *Common Law* 26 (1881).

Silence

He has occasional flashes of silence, that make his conversation perfectly delightful.

SYDNEY SMITH, referring to Thomas Macaulay. See, 1 Holland, *Memoir of Smith* 320.

Slavery

A slave is not a mere chattel. He bears the impress of his Maker, and is amenable to the laws of God and man; and he is destined to an endless existence.

McLEAN, J., *Scott v. Sandford*, 60 U.S. (19 How.) 393, 550 (1857).

The state of slavery is of such a nature, that it is incapable of being introduced on any reasons, moral or political, but only by positive law, which preserves its force long after the reasons, occasion, and time itself from whence it was created, is erased from memory. It is so odious, that nothing can be suffered to support it, but positive law. Whatever inconveniences, therefore, may follow from the decision, I cannot say this case is allowed or approved by the law of England; and therefore the black must be discharged.

LORD MANSFIELD, C.J., *Sommersett Case* (1772) 20 How. St. Tr. 1, 82.

The air of England has long been too pure for a slave, and every man is free who breathes it. Every man who comes into England is entitled to the protection of English law, whatever oppression he may heretofore have suffered, and whatever may be the colour of his skin: "*Quamvis ille niger quamvis tu candidus esses.*" Let the negro be discharged.

Ascribed to Lord Mansfield by Campbell in his *Lives of the Chief Justices*, ch. 34 but not found in the reports. Hargrave, *arguendo* used the expression that England was "too pure an air for a slave to breathe in" and gave as his source, 2 Rushworth, *Hist. Coll.* 468. See, *Sommersett Case*, 20 How. St. Tr. 1, 51.

Socialism

The notion that with socialized property we should have women free and a piano for everybody seems to me an empty humbug.

OLIVER WENDELL HOLMES, *Ideals and Doubts*, 10 Ill. L.R. 1, 3 (1915).

Sovereignty

The King, moreover, is not only incapable of doing wrong, but even of thinking wrong; he can never mean to do an improper thing; in him is no folly or weakness.

BLACKSTONE, *Commentaries*, bk 1, 246.

The King himself ought not to be subject to any man, but he ought to be subject to God and the law, since law makes the King. Therefore let the King render to the law what the law has rendered to the King, viz. dominion and power for there is no King where will rules and not the law.

BRACTON, *De Legibus et Consuetudinibus Angliae*, f. 5b.

The King hath no prerogative but that which the law of the land allows him.

COKE, *Case of Proclamations* (1611) 12 Rep. 74, 76.

The King can never be poor when his subjects are rich.

COKE, *Third Institute* 194.

It is a favorite maxim of the Civil Law that whatsoever pleases the Prince has the effect of law. The laws of England do not sanction any such maxim, since the King of that land rules his people not only regally but also politically, and so he is bound by oath at his coronation to the observance of his law.

SIR JOHN FORTESCUE, *De Laudibus Legum Angliae,* ch. 34.

I wish the state of society was so far improved, and the science of government advanced to such a degree of perfection, as that the whole nation could in the peaceable course of law, be compelled to do justice, and be sued by individual citizens.

JAY, C.J., *Chisholm v. Georgia,* 2 Dall. (U.S.) 419, 478 (1793).

The prince is not above the laws, but the laws above the prince. *Non est princeps super leges, sed leges super principem.*

PLINY, *Panegyricus* 65.

Willy, Willy, Harry, Ste,
Harry, Dick, John, Harry 3;
One, two, three Neds, Richard 2,
Henry 4, 5, 6. Then who?
Edward 4, 5, Dick the Bad,
Harrys twain and Ned the Lad;
Mary, Bessie, James the Vain,
Charlie, Charlie, James again;
Will and Mary, Anna Gloria,
Georges four, Will, Victoria.

Popular catch, for memorizing the order of English sovereigns.

When I forget my King, may my God forget me.

LORD THURLOW, Speech, House of Lords, December 15, 1788, at the time of the incapacity of George III. 2 Stanhope, *Life of Pitt* 10.

The will of the Emperor has the force of law, because by the passage of the *lex regia* the people transfers to him and vests in him all its own power and authority.

ULPIAN, *Digest,* (Justinian) i, IV, 1.

Speed

The cases are remanded to the District Courts to take such proceedings and enter such orders and decrees consistent with this opinion as are necessary and proper to admit to public schools on a racially nondiscriminatory basis with all deliberate speed the parties to these cases.

WARREN, C.J., *Brown v. Bd. of Education,* 349 U.S. 294, 301 (1955).

"But with unhurrying chase,
And unperturbed pace,
Deliberate speed, majestic instancy."

There is no good reason to think that the United States Supreme Court was quoting from Francis Thompson's *The Hound of Heaven,* when in May 1955 Chief Justice Warren used the words "deliberate speed" in its opinion on the enforcement of its decrees in desegregation cases. But Thompson clearly anticipated, and very precisely described how the Court expects us to go about it.

CHARLES CURTIS, *Commonplace Book* 111 (1957).

A question like the present should be disposed of without undue delay. But a State cannot be expected to move with the celerity of a private business man; it is enough if it proceeds, in the language of the English Chancery, with all deliberate speed.

HOLMES, J., *Virginia v. West Virginia,* 222 U.S. 17, 19 (1911).

Stare Decisis

If it be that previous decisions must be rescinded, at least let them be interred with honour.

BACON, *Advancement of Learning,* bk 8, Aph. 95.

Stare decisis is ordinarily a wise rule of action. But it is not a universal, inexorable command.

BRANDEIS, J., *Washington v. Dawson & Co.,* 264 U.S. 219, 238 (1924).

The doctrine of *stare decisis* does not command that we err again when we have occasion to pass upon a different statute.

BRANDEIS, J., *Di Santo v. Pennsylvania,* 273 U.S. 34, 42 (1927).

We are not here compelled by Erie R. Co. v. Tompkins, 304 U.S. 64 . . . to play the role of ventriloquist's dummy to the courts of some particular state.

FRANK, J., *Richardson v. Comm'r Int. Rev.,* 126 F. 2d 562, 567 (1942).

This Court, unlike the House of Lords, has from the beginning rejected a doctrine of disability at self-correction.

FRANKFURTER, J., *Helvering v. Hallock,* 309 U.S. 106, 121 (1940).

What is that occasional interference with what is perhaps abstract justice as compared with the inconvenience—the disastrous inconvenience—of having each question subject to being reargued and the dealings of mankind rendered doubtful by reason of different decisions, so that in truth and in fact there would be no real final Court of Appeal?

LORD HALSBURY, L.C., *London St. Tramways v. London Co. Council* [1898] A.C. 375, 380. This case finally established the rule that the House of Lords was bound by its own decisions.

A decision of this House upon a question of law is conclusive, and that nothing but an Act of Parliament can set right that which is alleged to be wrong in a judgment of this House.

LORD HALSBURY, L.C., *London St. Tramways Co. v. London Co. Council* [1898] A.C. 375, 381.

I had supposed that our judicial responsibility is for the regularity of the law, not for the regularity of pedigrees.

JACKSON, J., *Williams v. North Carolina,* 317 U.S. 287, 324 (1942). Case involved status of divorced parties.

To bring adjudications of this tribunal into the same class as a restricted railroad ticket, good for this day and train only. I have no assurance, in view of current decisions, that the opinion announced today may not shortly be repudiated and overruled by justices who deem they have new light on the subject.

ROBERTS, J., *Smith v. Allwright,* 321 U.S. 649, 669 (1944).

The law becomes not a chart to govern conduct, but a game of chance; instead of settling rights and liabilities it unsettles them. . . . Respect for tribunals must fall when the bar and the public come to understand that nothing that has been said in prior adjudication has force in a current controversy.

ROBERTS, J., *Mahnich v. Southern S.S. Co.,* 321 U.S. 96, 112 (1944).

State

What constitutes a State?
Not high-rais'd battlements, or labour'd mound,
Thick wall, or moated gate;
Not cities proud, with spires and turrets crown'd;
Not bays and broad-arm'd ports,
Where, laughing at the storm, rich navies ride;
. . .
No:—Men, high-minded Men,

. . .
Men who their duties know,
But know their rights, and knowing, dare maintain;
Prevent the long-aim'd blow,
And crush the tyrant while they rend the chain.
These constitute a state,
And sov'reign Law, that state's collected will,
O'er thrones and globes elate
Sits empress, crowning good, repressing ill.

SIR WILLIAM JONES, *Ode in Imitation of Alcaeus.*

Statute of Frauds

That unfortunate statute, the misguided application of which has been the cause of so many frauds.

BACON, V.C., *Morgan v. Worthington* (1878) 38 L.T. 443, 445.

Statute of Uses

A law whereupon the inheritances of this realm are tossed at this day, as upon a sea, in such sort that it is hard to say which bark will sink and which will get to the haven.

BACON, *Reading Upon the Statute of Uses.*

A statute made upon great consideration, introduced in a solemn and pompous manner, by this strict construction, has had no other effect than to add at most, three words to a conveyance.

LORD HARDWICKE, L.C., *Hopkins v. Hopkins* (1738) 1 Atk. 581, 591.

Then there is that marvellous monument of legislative futility, the Statute of Uses, the statute through which not mere coaches and four, but whole judicial processions with javelin-men and trumpeters have passed and re-passed in triumph. It has been said of this ambitious statute that its sole effect has been to "add three words to a conveyance."

FREDERIC WM. MAITLAND, *Law of Real Property,* 112 Westminster Rev. 351 (1879); also in 1 Coll. Pap. 191.

Suicide

For, he said, Sir James Hales was dead, and how came he to his death? It may be answered by drowning; and who drowned him? Sir James Hales; and when did he drown him? In his life-time. So that Sir James Hales being alive caused Sir James Hales to die; and the act of the living man was the death of the dead man.

BROWN (ANTHONY), J., *Hales v. Petit* (1562) 1 Plowd. 253, 262. (The Court held that the goods of Sir James Hales were forfeit to the Crown "as punishment upon the living man for the act done in his life time, which was the cause of his death afterwards".)

First Clown: Here lies the water; good. Here stands the man; good. If the man go to this water and drown himself, it is, will he, nill he, he goes,—mark you that? But if the water comes to him, and drown him, he drowns not himself; argal, he that is not guilty of his own death shortens not his own life.
Second Clown: But is this law?
First Clown: Ay, marry, is't; crowner's quest law.

SHAKESPEARE, *Hamlet,* V, 1.

Surety

Almost all who sign as surety have occasion to remember the proverb of Solomon: "He that is surety for a stranger shall smart for it, and he that hateth suretyship is sure." But they are nevertheless held liable upon their contracts, otherwise there would be no smarting, and the proverb would fail.

APPLETON, C.J., *Mayo v. Hutchinson,* 57 Me. 546, 547 (1870).

It would be as difficult for me to conceive of a surety's liability continuing after the principal obligation was discharged, as of a shadow's remaining after the substance was removed.

RANSOM, C.J., *Farmers & Mech. Bk. v. Kingsley,* 2 Doug. (Mich.) 379, 403. (1846).

Talk

That barbers talk cannot be disputed. Some talk more, some less, some humorously, some not, but talk they do. It is traditional and hereditary with them.

PETTE, J., *Vann v. Ionta,* 157 Misc. (N.Y.) 461, 465 (1935).

Taxation

"It was as true," said Mr. Barkis, "as turnips is. It was as true," said Mr. Barkis, nodding his nightcap, which was his only means of emphasis, "as taxes is. And nothing's truer than them."

CHARLES DICKENS, *David Copperfield,* ch. 21.

They combed his mane, they pared his nails, cut off his tail, set him on end, sent him to school, and made him pay taxes.

RALPH WALDO EMERSON, *Inspiration.*

The words of such an act as the Income Tax . . . merely dance before my eyes in a meaningless procession: cross-reference to cross-reference, exception upon exception—couched in abstract terms that offer no handle to seize hold of—leave in my mind only a confused sense of some vitally important, but successfully concealed, purport, which it is my duty to extract, but which is within my power, if at all, only after the most inordinate expenditure of time. I know that these monsters are the result of fabulous industry and ingenuity, plugging up this hole and casting out that net, against all possible evasion; yet at times I cannot help recalling a saying of William

James about certain passages of Hegel: that they were no doubt, written with a passion of rationality; but that one cannot help wondering whether to the reader they have any significance save that the words are strung together with syntactical correctness.

LEARNED HAND, *Thomas Walter Swan,* 57 Yale L.J. 167, 169 (1947).

Taxes are what we pay for civilized society.

HOLMES, J., *Compania Gen. De Tabacos v. Coll. Int. Rev.,* 275 U.S. 87, 100 (1927).

The power to tax is not the power to destroy while this Court sits.

HOLMES, J., *Panhandle Oil Co. v. Mississippi ex rel Knox,* 277 U.S. 218, 223 (1928).

This petition brings up for solution one of those difficult jigsaw tax law puzzles all too common in the present deplorable crazy quilt patchwork state of the Internal Revenue laws. Of this one we think it may be truly said, "This kind cometh not out save by fasting and by prayer."

HUTCHESON, J., *Houston Textile Co. v. Comm'r.,* 173 F.2d 464 (1949).

Excise: A hateful tax levied upon commodities and adjudged not by the common judges of property, but wretches hired by those to whom excise is paid.

SAMUEL JOHNSON, *Dictionary.*

Income tax, if I may be pardoned for saying so, is a tax on income.

LORD MACNAGHTEN, *London Co. Council v. Atty. Gen.* [1901] A.C. 26, 35.

No country ever takes notice of the revenue laws of another.

LORD MANSFIELD, C.J., *Holman v. Johnson* (1775) 1 Cowp. 341, 343.

If taxation and representation were to go hand in hand, then, this country had an undoubted right to tax America, because she was represented in the British parliament: she was represented by the members for the county of Kent, of which the thirteen provinces were a part or parcel; for in their charters they were to hold of the manor of Greenwich in Kent, of which manor they were by charter to be parcel.

SIR JAMES MARRIOTT, *Speech in House of Commons (1782)* 22 Parl. Hist. 1184. Reporter stated that this opinion raised a very loud laugh.

The power to tax involves the power to destroy.

MARSHALL, C.J., *McCulloch v. Maryland,* 17 U.S. (4. Wheat.) 316, 431 (1819).

Names were made to matter more than mathematics or economics.

THOMAS REED POWELL, *More Ado About Gross Receipts Taxes,* 60 Harv. L.R. 501, 503 (1947).

Taxes are the life-blood of government.

ROBERTS, J., *Bull v. United States,* 295 U.S. 247, 259 (1935).

Thought

Most men think dramatically, not quantitatively.

OLIVER WENDELL HOLMES, *Law and the Court, Speeches* 99 (1913).

The secret isolated joy of the thinker, who knows that, a hundred years after he is dead and forgotten, men who never heard of him will be moving to the measure of his thought.

OLIVER WENDELL HOLMES, *Profession of the Law, Speeches* 24 (1913).

Time

Whence it is, that in our law, the goodness of a custom depends upon its having been used time out of mind; or, in the solemnity of our legal phrase, time whereof the memory of man runneth not to the contrary.

BLACKSTONE, *Commentaries: Introduction 67.*

Time hath his revolution, there must be a period and an end of all temporal things, *finis rerum,* an end of names and dignities, and whatsoever is terrene, and why not of De Vere? For where is Bohun? where's Mowbray? where's Mortimer? etc. Nay, which is more and most of all, where is Plantagenet? they are entombed in the urns and sepulchres of mortality. And yet let the name and dignity of De Vere stand so long as it pleaseth God.

CREW, C.J., *Oxford Peerage Case* (1625) W. Jones 101, 102.

Time has been on Marshall's side, and that the theory for which Hamilton argued, and he decided, and Webster spoke, and Grant fought, and Lincoln died, is now our corner-stone.

HOLMES, C.J., on motion that the court adjourn on February 4, 1901, the one hundredth anniversary of the day Marshall took his seat as Chief Justice, 178 Mass. 627.

Title

And the English poet saith,
"For true it is, that neither fraud nor might
Can make a title where there wanteth right."

COKE, 8 Rep. 153.

Cursed be he that removeth his neighbor's landmarks.

Deuteronomy 27:17.

If Time destroys the evidence of title, the laws have wisely and humanely made length of possession a substitute for that which has been destroyed. He comes with his scythe in one hand to mow down the muniments of our rights; but, in his other hand the law-giver has placed an hour-glass, by which he metes out incessantly those portions of duration, which render needless the evidence that he has swept away.

WM. C. PLUNKET, *arguendo,* in Irish Court of Chancery on behalf of Trinity College. See, Brougham, *Statesmen of Time of George III: Lord Chief Justice Bushe.*

Tort

Thoughts much too deep for tears subdue the Court
When I assumpsit bring, and godlike waive a tort.

J. L. ADOLPHUS, *The Circuiteers.* See, 1 L.Q.R. 233 (1885).

Treason

After this kind of reasoning they will not be guilty, till they have success; and if they have success enough, it will be too late to question them.

TREBY, C.J., *Trial of Captain Vaughan* (1696) 13 How. St. Tr. 485, 533. The indictment was for adhering to and giving aid and comfort to the enemy.

Treaty

They never enter into any alliance with any other state. They think leagues are useless things, and reckon that, if the common ties of human nature do not knit men together, the faith of promises will have no great effect upon them: and they are the more confirmed in this by that which they see among nations round about them, who are no strict observers of leagues and treaties.

SIR THOMAS MORE, *Utopia*, bk 2.

Trespass

By the laws of England, every invasion of private property, be it ever so minute, is a trespass. No man can set his foot upon my ground without my licence, but he is liable to an action, though the damage be nothing.

LORD CAMDEN, C.J., *Entick v. Carrington* (1765) 19 How. St. Tr. 1029, 1066.

Trial

But the Judge said he never had summed up before;
So the Snark undertook it instead,
And summed it so well that it came to far more
Than the Witnesses ever had said!

LEWIS CARROLL, *The Hunting of the Snark: The Barrister's Dream.*

Gracious lady, we implore,
Go away and sin no more,
And if that effort be too great,
Go away at any rate.

Popular ballad at the time of the trial of Queen Caroline for adultery, 1821. George IV's harsh treatment of his consort aroused much sympathy for the Queen. In her defense, however, Lord Denman made use of an unfortunate quotation: "If no one come forward to condemn thee, neither will I condemn thee. Go, and sin no more."

A jury trial is a fight and not an afternoon tea.

RIDDELL, J., *Dale v. Toronto R. W. Co.* (1915) 34 Ont. L.R. 104, 108.

Tears have always been considered legitimate arguments before a jury, and while the question has never arisen out of any such behavior in this Court, we know of no rule or jurisdiction in the Court below to check them. It would appear to be one of the natural rights of counsel, which no Court or constitution could take away. It is certainly, if no more, a matter of the highest personal privilege. Indeed, if counsel has them at command, it may be seriously questioned whether it is not his professional duty to shed them whenever proper occasion arises, and the trial Judge would not feel constrained to interfere unless they were indulged in to such excess as to impede or delay the business of the Court.

WILKES, J., *Ferguson v. Moore,* 98 Tenn. 342, 351 (1897).

Trusts

A trust is altogether the same that a use was before 27 Hen. 8, and they have the same parents, fraud and fear; and the same nurse, a court of conscience.

ROBERT ATKYNS, arguendo, *Attorney General v. Sands* (1669) Hard. 488, 491.

Trusts are children of equity; and in a court of equity they are at home—under the family roof-tree, and around the hearth of their ancestor.

BLECKLEY, J., *Kupferman v. McGhee*, 63 Ga. 250, 256 (1879).

A constructive trust is the formula through which the conscience of equity finds expression.

CARDOZO, J., *Beatty v. Guggenheim Exploration Co.*, 225 N.Y. 380, 386 (1919).

A trustee is held to something stricter than the morals of the market place. Not honesty alone, but the punctilio of an honor the most sensitive, is then the standard of behavior.

CARDOZO, C.J., *Meinhard v. Salmon*, 249 N.Y. 458, 464 (1928).

My old master, the late Lord Justice Selwyn, used to say, "The main duty of a trustee is to commit *judicious* breaches of trust."

LINDLEY, M.R., *Perrins v. Bellamy* [1899] 1 Ch. 797, 798. In a later case Lord Lindley remarked that the words "main duty" are a mistake. They ought to be "great use". See: *National Trustees Co. of Australasia v. General Finance Co.* [1905] A.C. 373, 376.

Truth

What is truth? said jesting Pilate; and would not stay for an answer.

BACON, *Essays*: *Of Truth*.

The half truths of one generation tend at times to perpetuate themselves in the law as the whole truths of another, when constant repetition brings it about that qualifications, taken once for granted, are disregarded or forgotten.

CARDOZO, C.J., *Allegheny College v. National Chautauqua Co. Bank,* 246 N.Y. 369, 373 (1927).

Truth, the mother of justice.

COKE, *Second Institute* 524.

If the respondent is, as we must take him to be, sincere, there are many ways open to him of telling the public that he is not a surgeon other than the way of telling the public that he is a surgeon.

LORD HEWART, C.J., *Jutson v. Barrow* [1936] 1 K.B. 236, 245. The respondent's argument was that the placing of the word "manipulative" before the word surgeon was intended to show that he was not registered as a surgeon under the Medical Act.

I used to say, when I was young, that truth was the majority vote of that nation that could lick all others.

OLIVER WENDELL HOLMES, *Natural Law,* 32 Harv. L.R. 40 (1918).

When men have realized that time has upset many fighting faiths, they may come to believe even more than they believe the very foundations of their own conduct that the ultimate good desired is better reached by free trade in ideas—that the best test of truth is the power of the thought to get itself accepted in the competition of the market, and that truth is the only ground upon which their wishes safely can be carried out.

HOLMES, J., *Abrams v. United States* 250 U.S. 616, 630 (1919).

Truth, like all other good things, may be loved unwisely—may be pursued too keenly—may cost too much.

KNIGHT-BRUCE, V.C., *Pearse v. Pearse* (1846) 1 De Gex & Sm. 12, 28.

Ingenuity is one thing, and simple testimony another and "plain truth", I take it, "needs no flowers of speech."

LORD MANSFIELD, C.J., *Wilkes v. Wood* (1763) 19 How. St. Tr. 1153, 1176 n. (referring to Pope, *Imitations of Horace,* I, 6: "Plain truth, dear Murray, needs no flow'rs of speech.")

There is an idiom in truth, which falsehood never can imitate.

NAPIER, L.C., *Low v. Holmes* (1858) Drury Cases, Temp. Napier, 290, 323.

U. S. Supreme Court

It is a mistake to suppose that the Supreme Court is either honored or helped by being spoken of as beyond criticism. On the contrary, the life and character of its justices should be the object of constant watchfulness by all, and its judgments subject to the freest criticism. The time is past in the history of the world when any living man or body of men can be set on a pedestal and decorated with a halo. True, many criticisms may be, like their authors, devoid of good taste, but better all sorts of criticism than no criticism at all. The moving waters are full of life and health; only in the still waters is stagnation and death.

DAVID JOSIAH BREWER, *Lincoln's Day Address,* 1898.

No matther whether th' constitution follows th' flag or not, th' supreme coort follows th' iliction returns.

FINLEY PETER DUNNE, *Mr. Dooley's Opinions: The Supreme Court's Decisions.*

The United States Supreme Court has wittily been called the "court of ultimate conjecture."

JEROME FRANK, *Law and the Modern Mind* 46n. (1930).

It sat almost as a continuous constitutional convention which, without submitting its proposals to any ratification or rejection, could amend the basic law.

ROBERT H. JACKSON, *Struggle for Judicial Supremacy* x (1941).

We are not final because we are infallible, but we are infallible only because we are final.

JACKSON, J., *Brown v. Allen,* 344 U.S. 443, 540 (1953).

The judiciary of the United States is the subtle corps of sappers and miners constantly working under ground to undermine the foundations of our confederated fabric.

THOMAS JEFFERSON, *Letter to Thomas Ritchie, December 25, 1820.*

There is no danger I apprehend so much as the consolidation of our government by the noiseless, and therefore unalarming, instrumentality of the supreme court.

THOMAS JEFFERSON, *Letter to Judge William Johnson, March 4, 1823.*

I do not forget the position assumed by some that constitutional questions are to be decided by the Supreme Court, nor do I deny that such decisions must be binding in any case upon the parties to a suit as to the object of that suit, while they are also entitled to very high respect and consideration in all parallel cases by all other departments of the Government. And while it is obviously possible that such decision may be erroneous in any given case, still the evil effect following it, being limited to that particular case, with the chance that it may be overruled and never become a precedent for other cases, can better be borne than could the evils of a different practice.

ABRAHAM LINCOLN, *First Inaugural Address, March 4, 1861.*

At the same time, the candid citizen must confess that if the policy of the Government, upon vital questions affecting the whole people is to be irrevocably fixed by decisions of the Supreme Court, the instant they are made in ordinary litigation between parties in personal actions the people will have ceased to be their own rulers, having to that extent practically resigned their Government into the hands of that eminent tribunal. Nor is there in this view any assault upon the court or the judges. It is a duty from which they may not shrink to decide cases properly brought before them, and it is no fault of theirs if others seek to turn their decisions to political purposes.

ABRAHAM LINCOLN, *First Inaugural Address, March 4, 1861.*

When there are grave doubts about the "constitutionality" of a statute, the Supreme Court has always been ready to remove them, but unfortunately it has only too often removed these doubts by holding the statute unconstitutional. It is in the advantageous position of being able not only to declare constitutional acts unconstitutional, but unconstitutional acts constitutional.

WILLIAM SEAGLE, *The Quest for Law* 314 (1941).

The Supreme Court is placed at the head of all known tribunals, both by the nature of its rights and the class of justiciable parties which it controls.

ALEXIS DE TOCQUEVILLE, *Democracy in America,* Pt. 1, ch. 8.

Validity

A statute valid as to one set of facts may be invalid as to another. A statute valid when enacted may become invalid by change in the conditions to which it is applied.

BRANDEIS, J., *Nashville, C. & St. L.Ry. v. Walters,* 294 U.S. 405, 415 (1935).

Not what has been done under a statute, but what may reasonably be done under it, is the test of its validity.

CARDOZO, C.J., *Matter of Richardson,* 247 N.Y. 401, 420 (1928).

Verbosity

O judge not a book by its cover
Or else you'll for sure come to grief,
For the lengthiest things you'll discover
Are contained in what's known as a Brief.

J.P.C., 116 Just. P. 640 (1952).

He can compress the most words into the smallest ideas of any man I ever met.

ABRAHAM LINCOLN. Hill, *Lincoln, the Lawyer* 218.

War Crimes

Civilisation asks whether law is so laggard as to be utterly helpless to deal with crimes of this magnitude by criminals of this order of importance. It does not expect that you can make war impossible. It does expect that your juridical action will put the forces of International Law, its precepts, its prohibitions and most of all, its sanctions, on the side of peace, so that men and women of good will in all countries, may have "leave to live by no man's leave underneath the law."

ROBERT H. JACKSON, *Opening for the Prosecution, Trial of German Major War Criminals,* Proceedings of the International Military Tribunal at Nuremberg, Nov. 21, 1945.

We must never forget that the record on which we judge these defendants today is the record on which history will judge us tomorrow. To pass these defendants a poisoned chalice is to put it to our own lips as well. We must summon such detachment and intellectual integrity to our task that this trial will commend itself to posterity as fulfilling humanity's aspirations to do justice.

ROBERT H. JACKSON, ibid.

"The warrant of no man excuseth the doing of an illegal act." Political loyalty, military obedience are excellent things, but they neither require nor do they justify the commission of patently wicked acts. There comes a point where a man must refuse to answer to his leader if he is also to answer to his conscience.

SIR HARTLEY SHAWCROSS, Chief Prosecutor for Gt. Britain, *Opening Speech at the trial of the Major War Criminals, Nuremberg, Dec. 4, 1945.* Proceedings of International Military Tribunal (Lond. 1946, pub. by auth. of Atty. Gen.) Pt. 2, 85.

Warranties

Warranties are favoured in law, being part of a man's assurance; but estoppels are odious.

COKE, *First Institute* 365b.

Webster, Daniel

Daniel Webster struck me much like a steam-engine in trowsers.

SYDNEY SMITH—1 Holland, *Memoir of Smith* 238.

Will

I anticipate with satisfaction that henceforth the group of ghosts of dissatisfied testators who, according to a late Chancery judge, wait on the other bank of the Styx, to receive the judicial personages who have misconstrued their wills, may be considerably diminished.

LORD ATKIN, *Perrin v. Morgan* [1943] I All E.R. 187, 194.

The nonsense of one man cannot be a guide for that of another.

BULLER, J., *Smith v. Coffin* (1795) 2 H. Bl. 444, 450.

Few men pinched with the messengers of death have a disposing memory.

COKE, 10 Rep.: *Preface.*

The only authentic evidence, in spite of Sir Oliver Lodge, which we have of the survival of life after death is the ability of the judges to read the intention of the testator long after he has been buried.

FREDERICK E. CRANE, *Address,* 3 N.Y.S. Bar Bull. 168 (1931).

This is what the lawyer who drew the will has caused Miss Watson to say is her intention.

CRANE, J., *Matter of Watson,* 262 N.Y. 284, 299 (1933).

When a testator has executed a will in solemn form you must assume that he did not intend to make it a solemn farce, —that he did not intend to die intestate when he has gone through the form of making a will.

LORD ESHER, M.R., *Re Harrison* (1885) 30 Ch.D. 390, 393.

Ye lawyers who live upon litigants' fees,
And who need a good many to live at your ease,
Grave or gay, wise or witty, whate'er your degree,
Plain stuff or Queen's Counsel, take counsel of me.
When a festive occasion your spirit unbends,
You should never forget the Profession's best friends;
So we'll send round the wine and bright bumper fill,
To the jolly testator who makes his own will.

LORD NEAVES, *Jolly Testator Who Makes His Own Will.*

Testators are good; but a feeling more tender
Springs up when I think of the feminine gender;
The testatrix for me, who, like Telemarque's mother
Unweaves at one time what she wove at another.
She bequeaths, she repeats, she recalls a donation,
And she ends by revoking her own revocation,
Still scribbling or scratching some new codicil,
Oh! success to the woman who makes her own will.

ibid.

'Tisn't easy to say 'mid her varying vapours
What scraps should be deemed testamentary papers;
'Tisn't easy from these her intentions to find,
When perhaps she herself never knew her own mind.
Every step that we take there arises fresh trouble—
Is the legacy lapsed? is it single or double?
No customer brings so much grist to the mill
As the wealthy old woman who makes her own will.

ibid.

You had better pay toll when you take to the road
Than attempt by a bye-way to reach your abode;
You had better employ a conveyancer's hand
Than encounter the risk that your will shouldn't stand.
From the broad beaten track where the traveller strays
He may land in a bog or be lost in a maze:
And the Law, when defied, will revenge itself still
On the man and the woman who make their own will.

ibid.

In some instances homemade pies are superior. Wills never.

PAGE, SURR. J., *Matter of Douglas*, 195 Misc. (N.Y.) 661, 662 (1949).

The will is to be read in the light of what has happened, not so much for the purpose of determining its validity, as for the purpose of seeing clearly by such light what is possible in the way of separating the good from the bad. In thus construing the will the court does not perform a radical operation to remove a malignant growth, where either the disease or the operation will take the life out of the testamentary document. The irritation of invalidity has produced, not a cancer, but, at worst, an epidermal callosity which may be harmlessly removed.

POUND, J., *Matter of Trevor*, 239 N.Y. 6, 18 (1924).

He may make a will upon his nail for any thing he has to give.

Proverb. Fuller, *Proverbs* (1732).

Has the testator been what is called, and very properly called, his own conveyancer? Has he left it to the Court to make out from general expressions what his intention is, or has he so defined that intention that you have nothing to do but to take the limitations he has given you, and to convert them into legal estates?

LORD ST. LEONARDS, *Egerton v. Earl of Brownlow* (1853) 4 H.L. Cas. 1, 210.

Men should not sin in their graves.

STRANGE, M.R., *Thomas v. Britnell* (1751) 2 Ves. Sr. 313, 314.

Wills

I, CHARLES LOUNSBURY, being of sound and disposing mind and memory . . . do now make and publish this my last will and testament. . . . ITEM: And first, I give to good fathers and mothers, but in trust for their children, nevertheless, all good little words of praise and all quaint pet names, and I charge said parents to use them justly but generously as the needs of their children shall require.

WILLISTON FISH, *A Last Will,* 42 Harper's Weekly 867 (Sept. 3, 1898). This will, a fictional creation, has been frequently quoted and reprinted, often with considerable variation from the original. It has sometimes been called, for no reason, the "insane man's" will. See, Josephine Fish Peabody, *Williston Fish and "A Last Will",* 52 C. & C. No. 3 (1947).

ITEM: I leave to children exclusively, but only for the life of their childhood, all and every, the dandelions of the fields and the daisies thereof, with the right to play among them freely, according to the custom of children, warning them at the same time against the thistles. And I devise to children the yellow shores of creeks and the golden sands beneath the waters thereof, with the dragon-flies that skim the surface of said waters, and the odors of the willows that dip into said waters, and the white clouds that float high over the giant trees.

And I leave to children the long, long days to be merry in, in a thousand ways, and the Night and the Moon and the train of the Milky Way to wonder at, but subject, nevertheless, to the rights hereinafter given to lovers; and I give to each child the right to choose a star that shall be his, and I direct that the child's father shall tell him the name of it, in order that the child shall always remember the name of that star after he has learned and forgotten astronomy.

ibid.

ITEM: I devise to boys jointly all the useful idle fields and commons where ball may be played, and all snow-clad hills where one may coast, and all streams and ponds where one may skate, to have and to hold the same for the period of their boyhood. And all meadows, with the clover blooms and butterflies thereof; and all woods, with their appurtenances of squirrels and whirring birds and echoes and strange noises; and all distant places which may be visited, together with the adventures there found, I do give to said boys to be theirs. And I give to said boys each his own place at the fireside at night, with all pictures that may be seen in the burning wood or coal, to enjoy without let or hindrance and without any incumbrance of cares.

ibid.

ITEM: To lovers I devise their imaginary world, with whatever they may need, as the stars of the sky, the red, red roses by the wall, the snow of the hawthorn, the sweet strains of music, or aught else they may desire to figure to each other the lastingness and beauty of their love.

ibid.

ITEM: To young men jointly, being joined in a brave, mad crowd, I devise and bequeath all boisterous, inspiring sports of rivalry. I give to them the disdain of weakness and undaunted confidence in their own strength. Though they are rude and rough, I leave to them alone the power of making lasting friendships and of possessing companions; and to them exclusively I give all merry songs and brave choruses to sing, with smooth voices to troll them forth.

ibid.

ITEM: And to those who are no longer children or youths or lovers I leave Memory, and I leave to them the volumes of the poems of Burns and Shakespeare, and of other poets, if there are others, to the end that they may live the old days over again freely and fully, without tithe or diminution; and to those who are no longer children or youths or lovers I leave, too, the knowledge of what a rare, rare world it is.

ibid.

To my loving, kind sister I give and bequeath,
For her tender regard, when this world I shall leave,
If she choose to accept it, my rump-bone may take,
And tip it with silver, a whistle to make.

WILLIAM RUFFELL, *Will.* Ruffell, a resident of Suffolk, England gave copies to friends but original was not found after his death. See, 12 N. & Q. (1st ser.) 81.

Wire-Tapping

The makers of our Constitution undertook to secure conditions favorable to the pursuit of happiness. They recognized the significance of man's spiritual nature, of his feelings and of his intellect. They knew that only a part of the pain, pleasure and satisfactions of life are to be found in material things. They sought to protect Americans in their beliefs, their thoughts, their emotions and their sensations. They conferred, as against the Government, the right to be let alone—the most comprehensive of rights and the right most valued by civilized men.

BRANDEIS, J., *Olmstead v. United States,* 277 U.S. 438, 478 (1928).

Dirty business.

HOLMES, J., *Olmstead v. United States,* 277 U.S. 438, 470 (1928).

Witnesses

I have always told a jury that if a fact is fully proved by two witnesses, it is as good as if proved by a hundred.

BULLER, J., *Calliland v. Vaughan* (1798) 1 Bos. & Pul. 210, 212.

For witnesses, like watches, go
Just as they're set, too fast or slow.

SAMUEL BUTLER, *Hudibras,* Pt. II, Canto II, 1.361.

By the mouth of two or three witnesses shall he die that is to be slain. Let no man be put to death, when only one beareth witness against him.

Deuteronomy 17:6 (There is a Roman maxim: *Testis unus testis nullus*—one witness is no witness).

Name, Jo. Nothing else that he knows on. . . . Knows a broom's a broom and knows it's wicked to tell a lie. Don't recollect who told him about the broom, or about the lie, but knows both. Can't exactly say what'll be done to him arter he's dead if he tells a lie to the gentlemen here, but believes it'll be something wery bad to punish him, and serve him right—and so, he'll tell the truth.

"This won't do, gentlemen!" says the coroner, with a melancholy shake of the head. . . . "You have heard the boy; 'can't exactly say' won't do, you know. We can't take that in a Court of Justice, gentlemen. It's terrible depravity. Put the boy aside."

CHARLES DICKENS, *Bleak House,* ch. 11.

A cloud of witnesses.

Hebrews 12:1.

A faithful witness will not lie but a deceitful witness uttereth a lie.

Proverbs 14:5.

Witnesses are liars, damned liars, and experts.

Saying.

Woman

Nature has given women so much power that the law has very wisely given them little.

SAMUEL JOHNSON, *Letter August 18, 1763, to Dr. Taylor.* See 5 Notes & Queries (6th ser.) 342.

Discussions are habitually necessary in courts of justice, which are unfit for female ears. The habitual presence of women at these would tend to relax the public sense of decency and propriety. If, as counsel threatened, these things are to come, we will take no voluntary part in bringing them about.

RYAN, C.J., *Matter of the motion to admit Miss Lavinia Goodell to the Bar,* 39 Wis. 232, 246 (1875).

When women go to Law, the Devil is full of Business.

JOHN WEBSTER, *The Devil's Law-Case: sub title* (1619).

Word

The meaning of words varies according to the circumstances of and concerning which they are used.

BLACKBURN, J., *Allgood v. Blake* (1873) L.R. 8 Ex. 160, 162.

The logic of words should yield to the logic of realities.

BRANDEIS, J., *Di Santo v. Pennsylvania,* 273 U.S. 34, 43 (1927).

The search is for the just word, the happy phrase, that will give expression to the thought, but somehow the thought itself is transfigured by the phrase when found.

BENJAMIN N. CARDOZO, *Growth of the Law* 89 (1924).

Words in themselves may be harmless, while accent and manner may make them deadly.

DENT, Pres., *State v. Kerns,* 47 W. Va. 266, 269 (1899).

Words are chameleons, which reflect the color of their environment.

L. HAND, J., *Commissioner v. National Carbide Co.*, 167 F.2d 304, 306 (1948).

A word generally has several meanings, even in the dictionary. You have to consider the sentence in which it stands to decide which of those meanings it bears in the particular case, and very likely will see that it there has a shade of significance more refined than any given in the word-book.

OLIVER WENDELL HOLMES, *Theory of Legal Interpretation*, 12 Harv. L.R. 417 (1899).

It is not the first use but the tiresome repetition of inadequate catch words which I am observing—phrases which originally were contributions, but which, by their very felicity, delay further analysis for fifty years.

OLIVER WENDELL HOLMES, *Law in Science—Science in Law*, 12 Harv. L.R. 443, 455 (1899).

It is one of the misfortunes of the law that ideas become encysted in phrases and thereafter for a long time cease to provoke further analysis.

HOLMES, J., *Hyde v. United States* 225 U.S. 347, 391 (1912).

A word is not a crystal, transparent and unchanged, it is the skin of a living thought and may vary greatly in color and content according to the circumstances and the time in which it is used.

HOLMES, J., *Towne v. Eisner*, 245 U.S. 418, 425 (1918).

I have seldom found much good result from hypercritical severity, in examining the distinct force of words. Language is essentially defective in precision; more so, than those are aware of, who are not in the habit of subjecting it to philological analysis.

JOHNSON, J., *Martin v. Hunter*, 14 U.S. (1 Wheat.) 304, 374 (1816).

Most of the disputes in the world arise from words.

LORD MANSFIELD, C.J., *Morgan v. Jones* (1773) Lofft 160, 176.

As men, whose intentions require no concealment, generally employ the words which most directly and aptly express the ideas they intend to convey, the enlightened patriots who framed our constitution, and the people who adopted it, must be understood to have employed words in their natural sense, and to have intended what they said.

MARSHALL, C.J., *Gibbons v. Ogden*, 22 U.S. (9 Wheat.) 1, 188 (1824).

For words, which are no other than the verberation of the air, do not constitute the statute, but are only the image of it, and the life of the statute rests in the minds of the expositors of the words, that is, the makers of the statutes.

SERJ. SAUNDERS, arguendo, *Partridge v. Strange* (1552) 1 Plowd. 77, 82.

Syllables govern the world.

JOHN SELDEN, *Table-Talk*: *Power, State.*

That lawyer's Paradise where all words have a fixed, precisely ascertained meaning.

JAMES BRADLEY THAYER, *Preliminary Treatise on Evidence* 428 (1898).

Writings

Little fragments of my fleece that I have left upon the hedges of life.

OLIVER WENDELL HOLMES, *Collected Legal Papers*: *Preface* (1920).

Youth

Young men are fitter to invent than to judge; fitter for execution than for counsel; and fitter for new projects than for settled business.

BACON, *Essays: Of Youth and Age.*

A man has but one youth, and considering the consequence of employing that well, he has reason to think himself very rich; for that gone, all the wealth in the world will not purchase another.

ROGER NORTH, *On the Study of the Laws* 5.

INDEX OF AUTHORS

Index of Authors

INDEX

Index

D

J

K